BV4012.2 .B36 1998
Benner, David G.
Care of souls :
revisioning Christian
nurture and counsel

PORTLAND CENTER LIBRARY
GEORGE FOX UNIVERSITY
PORTLAND, OR. 97223

Also by David G. Benner

Baker Encyclopedia of Psychology (editor)

Psychotherapy in Christian Perspective (editor)

Psychotherapy and the Spiritual Quest

Christian Counseling and Psychotherapy

Psychology and Religion (editor)

Counseling and the Human Predicament: A Study of Sin, Guilt, and Forgiveness (coauthor)

Healing Emotional Wounds

Christian Perspectives on Human Development (coauthor)

Strategic Pastoral Counseling: A Short-Term Structured Model

Understanding and Facilitating Forgiveness (coauthor)

Choosing the Gift of Forgiveness: How to Overcome Hurts and Brokenness (coauthor)

Money Madness and Financial Freedom: The Psychology of Money Meanings and Management

Free at Last: Breaking the Bondage of Guilt and Emotional Wounds

Baker Encyclopedia of Psychology and Counseling, 2d ed. (coeditor)

PORTLAND CENTER LIBRARY
GEORGE FOX UNIVERSITY
PORTLAND, OR. 97223

Care of Souls

Revisioning Christian Nurture and Counsel

David G. Benner

paternoster

 Baker Books

A Division of Baker Book House Co
Grand Rapids, Michigan 49516

PORTLAND CENTER LIBRARY
GEORGE FOX UNIVERSITY
PORTLAND, OR. 97223

© 1998 by David G. Benner

Published by Baker Books
a division of Baker Book House Company
P.O. Box 6287, Grand Rapids, MI 49516-6287

and

Paternoster Press
P.O. Box 300, Carlisle, Cumbria, CA3 0QS
United Kingdom

Printed in the United States of America

All rights reserved. No part of this publication may be reproduced, stored in a retrieval system, or transmitted in any form or by any means—for example, electronic, photocopy, recording—without the prior written permission of the publisher. The only exception is brief quotations in printed reviews.

Library of Congress Cataloging-in-Publication Data

Benner, David G.
    Care of souls : revisioning Christian nurture and counsel / David G. Benner.
      p. cm.
    Includes bibliographical references and index.
    ISBN 0-8010-9063-6 (pbk.)
      1. Pastoral counseling. 2. Psychotherapy—Religious aspects—Christianity.
    I. Title.
    BV4012.2.B36 1998
    253.5—dc21   98-35618

British Library Cataloging-in-Publication Data is available from the British Library.

U.K. ISBN 0-85364-960-X

Unless otherwise indicated, Scripture quotations are from the Revised Standard Version of the Bible, copyright 1946, 1952, 1971 by the Division of Christian Education of the National Council of the Churches of Christ in the USA. Used by permission.

Scripture quotations identified JB are from THE JERUSALEM BIBLE, copyright © 1966 by Darton, Longman & Todd, Ltd. and Doubleday, a division of Bantam Doubleday Dell Publishing Group, Inc. Reprinted by permission.

Scripture quotations identified KJV are from the King James Version of the Bible.

Scripture quotations identified NKJV are from the New King James Version. Copyright © 1979, 1980, 1982 by Thomas Nelson, Inc. Used by permission. All rights reserved.

For current information about all releases from Baker Book House, visit our web site:
http://www.bakerbooks.com

To

Margaret Millicent Benner
1920–1996

a master builder of souls

Contents

Acknowledgments

This book represents the development of thoughts begun in my now out-of-print *Psychotherapy and the Spiritual Quest* (1988) and subsequently extended in lectures in North America, Europe, South Africa, and Southeast Asia. Chapters 4 and 6 are based on material previously published in that earlier book. Others began as lectures for the Institute of Clinical Theology, Atlanta, Georgia (chapter 1), Charles University, Prague, Czech Republic (chapter 2), the Institute for Christian Spirituality, Cape Town, South Africa (chapter 5), Wesley Counselling Centre, Singapore (chapter 7), Rhodes University, Port Elizabeth, South Africa (chapter 8), and the Clinical Theology Association, Oxford, United Kingdom (chapter 10). Gratitude impels me to acknowledge the many people who interacted with me in these contexts and whose input has been so formative in this book. The richness of hundreds of hours of dialogue can never be reflected on paper, but more than any of my previous books, this one reflects the contribution of a large number of people, and my name should not stand alone on its title page.

Several people deserve special mention for sharing themselves with me in ways that have greatly influenced this book and my life. My deepest appreciation to Paul and Valmai Welsh, Judy Bassingwaite, Peter and Pat Van de Kastelle, Brenda Joscelyne, Peter Woods, Trevor and Debbie Hudson, Jaro Krivohlavy, Henry Madibo, George Malik, Merran Welsh, Bob and JoAnn Harvey, Gary Moon, Julie and Danny Ng, Tom and Trish Cunningham, Philip and Emilyn Wong, J. Harold Ellens, and Harold Rhoades— all fellow soul shepherds. Also, my deepest thanks again to my wife, Juliet, for her soul companionship of so many years. This book would not have been possible, and my life would be less rich, without these people.

Introduction

The Rediscovery of Soul and the Recovery of Its Care

Until the beginning of the twentieth century, the concept of the soul was a mainstay in the understanding of persons that was advanced by theologians and philosophers and accepted by most people who took the time to reflect on the matter. All this changed quite rapidly in the early twentieth century. Suddenly, the soul became unfashionable. The reasons for this are complex, and a careful exploration of them lies beyond the scope and focus of this book. However, two are particularly noteworthy: the reaction of theologians against the prevailing Platonic view of soul and the rise of modern psychology.

Plato's view of the soul had been singularly influential among both philosophers and theologians for two millennia. Corrupting the earlier Hebraic understanding of the nature of persons, the Platonic view emphasized an immortal soul that was imprisoned in a mortal body and yearned for release at death. The rediscovery by theologians of the more holistic Old Testament view of persons led to the discrediting of the Platonic soul and a rejection of the body-soul dualism associated with it. Tainted by its Platonic associations, the concept of soul receded to a back burner in the theological kitchen.[1]

Any conception of soul whatsoever was anathema to modern psychology. This was quite paradoxical since the word *psychology* literally means "the science of the soul." However, under the overriding influence of philosophical positivism, the science of the soul was about to become the science without a soul as psychologists avoided anything unobservable, taking behavior as their focus of study.[2] Seeking to align itself with science and distance itself from religion, modern psychology viewed the soul as unnecessary baggage from its past and sought to avoid it at all costs. Quickly, it became equally irrelevant to most other people in an increasingly materialistic, secular, and psychological culture.

What a surprise, therefore, when suddenly in the last decade the concept of the soul once again made a reappearance. Led by Thomas Moore's best-seller, *Care of the Soul,*[3] publishers quickly recognized a new market and followed with a spate of other titles on the subject. Even more surprising is the fact that this renewed interest in the soul and its care occurs within a context of renewed interest in spirituality. Interest in souls has been accompanied by interest in angels, channeling, meditation, and Gregorian chant. The soul that was rediscovered was, therefore, not some ethereal, immortal, Platonic essence of being, but a very vital, embodied, spiritual core of personality.

The significance of this reemergence of the soul and the corresponding interest in spirituality is hard to overestimate. On the one hand, it seems to represent a reaction against materialism. Whatever else the soul is, it is unseen and nonmaterial. As such, it simply was not supposed to exist in a culture that gave primacy to the pursuit of things that could be seen, felt, and put into bank accounts.

On the other hand, the spirituality that has been associated with the rise of interest in the soul in the past decade is also a reaction against religion, particularly Christianity. For many of those who are interested in the recovery of the spiritual, the last place they would look to find guidance in this quest would be the church. The rise of spirituality appears to be a response not only to the bankruptcy of materialism but also to the perceived irrelevance of the traditional religions of the West.

Sensing this, Christians have often viewed these developments with suspicion and animosity. Dismissively calling the spiritualities "New Age" and pouncing on the obvious points of divergence from historic Christian visions of the spiritual life, we have often failed to appreciate the spiritual hunger that is reflected in those who embrace the non-Christian spiritualities of the late twentieth century. We have also failed to understand the shift in dominant worldview that is associated with the current demise of modernity. As noted by many observers of this shift, the West is no longer simply post-Christian; it is now also postmodern. The recovery of the soul and the rise of interest in the spiritual both form a fundamental part of this development.

Without minimizing the important challenges these developments represent to Christianity, the two groups of people who form the primary audiences of this book—pastors and Christian mental health professionals—should also recognize the tremendously important opportunities they present. The soul is the meeting point of the psychological and the spiritual. This means that soul care that draws on both the best insights of modern therapeutic psychology as well as the historic Christian approaches to the care and cure of persons will never again be able to accept the artificial distinction of the psychological and spiritual. A proper understanding of the soul reunites the psychological and the spiritual and directs the activities of those who care for the souls of others in such a way that their care touches the deepest levels of people's inner lives.

For Christian clergy this holds the possibility of reversing their marginalization from the affairs of the soul. The acceptance of the distinction between the psychological and spiritual aspects of persons that was suggested by the rise of modern therapeutic psychology resulted in the church being judged to be relevant only to the spiritual part of persons. With the interior world now fragmented and God thought to be primarily interested in religious matters, the church largely abandoned efforts to chart or offer guidance regarding matters of the inner life in its totality. This ultimately lead to the displacement of clergy by psychotherapists as curates of the soul. If clergy are to be restored to their rightful place of responsibility for the care and cure of souls, it is essential that the psychospiritual nature of the soul be clearly understood.

Christian mental health professionals may be in even greater need of recovering an understanding of the soul and its care. Typically offering a form of care that draws its energy and direction solely from modern psychotherapeutic visions of healing, Christian mental health professionals have often been left groping for ways to integrate their personal Christian faith into their practice. One of the flaws of this integration metaphor is that it assumes two things that are basically separate can, by creativity and effort, be connected. This misses the point that they are already connected. The soul is the meeting point of the psychological and the spiritual. Its care must, by necessity, include both spiritual and psychological aspects. Christian mental health professionals who dare to embrace the paradigm shift that is involved in repositioning counseling and psychotherapy as soul care are offered the possibility of a care and cure of souls that is more vital, spiritual, and distinctively Christian.

For both Christian clergy and mental health professionals, the reemergence of the soul and recovery of interest in its care offers the possibility for a more holistic Christian ministry. Christian soul care that succeeds in reunifying the psychological and spiritual aspects of persons holds the promise of relevance and potency that has often been lacking in the ministrations of both Christian clergy and mental health professionals.

A proper understanding of the soul also holds the promise of revitalizing Christian spirituality. Another consequence of the acceptance of the artificial distinction between the psychological and spiritual aspects of persons has been a practice of Christian spirituality that emphasized knowing God but failed to emphasize knowing self. Tragically, this has often lead to a spirituality that is neither grounded nor vitally integrated within the fabric of total personhood. Not only does such a spirituality fail to transform us in the depths of our being, it also leads to all the dangers associated with a lack of integrity. A spirituality that fails to involve the totality of our being is inevitably a spirituality that furthers our fragmentation. On the other hand, an understanding of Christian spirituality that affirms the interdependence of the deep knowing of God and self is a spirituality that integrates us in our depths and makes us both whole and holy.

The key to these possibilities is the recovery of the rich tradition of historic Christian soul care, enriched by the best insights of modern therapeutic psychology. Even if it were possible to reverse history, it is never desirable. Vital Christian soul care is not to be found by attempting to recover the past. The Christian life is to be redemptive, not regressive. The challenge is to recover the good from the past and then allow this good to be informed by the best insights of the present.

Churches seeking relevance to the lives of men and women living on one side or the other of the shadow of the third millennium desperately need to understand the dynamics of the soul and its care. Clinical mental health professionals who have assumed so much of the responsibility for this care in recent decades need to understand how the psychological concerns people bring to them mask underlying spiritual concerns. Beyond this, all who seek to help others grow as humans and as Christians need to better understand what is involved in such growth. Parents, teachers, friends, as well as counselors, pastors, and spiritual guides all need maps of the terrain we traverse when we walk with others on their journey as humans who seek to follow Christ. This is what we shall seek to describe.

Before doing so, it is important to recognize that the nature of the soul defies precise cartography. If maps of the soul eliminate mystery, they also eliminate the soul. We will need to be prepared, therefore, for definitions that may seem vague and boundaries that appear hazy. As we shall discover, spirit and mystery are closely connected. While not everything that is mysterious is spiritual, the genuinely spiritual always retains an element of mystery. Maps of the soul should not, therefore, be expected to eliminate the mystery that is inevitably a part of the psychospiritual nature of persons.

Our journey toward an understanding of the soul and its care will begin with an exploration of the history of Christian soul care, identifying the major elements of a Christian understanding of the soul and the essential components of its care. We will then explore the reasons for the twentieth-century decline of religious and rise of therapeutic soul care, noting some of the gains and losses associated with this development. This will lead us to an examination of the relationship between the psychological and spiritual aspects of persons and the way in which both are involved in the distinctive form of spirituality associated with Christ following. An exploration of the psychospiritual focus of Christian soul care will then conclude this first section of the book.

Part 2 of the book moves from theory to practice, beginning with an exploration of dialogue as the core of soul care. Here we will reflect on the lessons to be learned from both therapeutic and pastoral dialogue, identifying the ideals and challenges of this demanding form of interpersonal engagement. We will then examine the role of the unconscious in Christian spirituality and growth toward wholeness, paying particular attention to ways of working with dreams that aid such growth. This will be followed by a consideration of the various forms of Christian soul care and the ways in which each can best support the other. We will then conclude with an examination of the practical challenges involved in both giving and receiving soul care.

The organizing theme of what follows is the relationships between the psychological and spiritual. We will discover this relationship in the history of Christian soul care as well as at the very heart of Christian spirituality. Following this lead, we will find the psychological and spiritual to be inextricably interconnected in the unconscious, in our dreams and symptoms, and in health and pathology. This, in turn, will lead to what we will call the psychospiritual focus of soul care dialogue.

The goal of our journey will be to make a contribution to the recovery of distinctively Christian soul care by developing an understanding of such care that can be of practical help to those involved in providing it to others. As we shall see, this includes a much larger group of people than pastors and mental health professionals. Parents, educators, friends, those involved in Christian ministry of any sort, health care professionals, lay counselors, and all who seek to provide Christian nurture, care, or healing of persons are in the business of offering soul care. All these and more can benefit from an understanding of what is involved in soul care, and all have crucial roles to play in its recovery as an essential component of the church's ministry. It is to this end that this book is written.

Part 1

Understanding Soul Care

1

What Is Soul Care?

While the notion of caring for souls may have a somewhat quaint sound to the modern ear, the activity it describes has long had a central place in Christianity, and before that, in Judaism. The English phrase, "care of souls," has its origins in the Latin *cura animarum*. While *cura* is most commonly translated as *care*, it actually contains the idea of both care and cure. *Care* refers to actions that are designed to support the well-being of something or someone. *Cure* refers to actions that are designed to restore well-being that has been lost. The Christian church has historically embraced both meanings of *cura* and has understood soul care to involve nurture and support as well as healing and restoration.

Understanding the concept of *cura* is relatively easy compared to understanding the concept of *animarum*. Philosophers have debated the nature of the soul for millennia and are still far from a consensus. Theologians also have found a definition of *soul* elusive because of the great variety of ways in which the original Hebrew and Greek words have been translated in Scripture.

Soul is the most common translation of the Hebrew word *nepesh* and the Greek word *psyche*. The biblical meanings of these concepts are extremely rich. In the Old Testament, for example, the meanings of *nepesh* range from life, the inner person (particularly thoughts, feelings, and passions), to the whole person, including the body. The soul is understood as that which distinguishes humans from animals and living from dead. It is also the source of emotions, the will, and moral actions. Similarly, in the New Testament, *psyche* carries such meaning as the totality of a person, physical life, mind, and heart. Here, soul is also presented as the religious center of life and as the seat of desire, emotions, and identity.

Many biblical scholars suggest that the best single word for both *nepesh* and *psyche* is either *person* or *self*. The great advantage of such an understanding is that both words carry the connotation of wholeness. Self is not a part of a person but their totality. Similarly, personhood is not some part of us; it points to the totality of our being. George Eldon Ladd argues that "recent scholarship has recognized that such terms as body, soul, and spirit are not different separable faculties of man but different ways of seeing the whole person."[1] This understanding is echoed by the vast majority of contemporary biblical scholars.

In such a view, we do not have a soul, we are soul. Similarly, we do not have a spirit, we are spirit. Nor do we have a body, we are body. Humans are a living and vital whole. Unified and whole does not mean that the component parts cannot have an independent existence.[2] The Bible suggests that body and soul are separated at death and remain so until the resurrection of the body. However, this separation is temporary and is an artificial state of humanity. In eternity, we will once again be embodied souls and inspirited bodies. This is the normal state of human persons.

As a working definition, let us understand *soul* as referring to the whole person, including the body, but with particular focus on the inner world of thinking, feeling, and willing. Care of souls can thus be understood as the care of persons in their totality, with particular attention to their inner lives.[3] This can never be accomplished by ignoring a person's physical existence or the external world of behavior. Properly understood, soul care nurtures the inner life and guides the expression of this inner life through the body into external behavior. This is what it means to speak of the care of souls as the care of persons in their totality. Bodily care may include care of the inner person but does not, unfortunately, always do so. However, soul care cannot neglect concern for the whole person—body, soul, and spirit.

Caring for souls is caring for people in ways that not only acknowledge them as persons but also engage and address them in the deepest and most profoundly human aspects of their lives. This is the reason for the priority of the spiritual and psychological aspects of the person's inner world in soul care. It is these aspects of our life that mark us most distinctively as human. Genuine soul care, however, is never exclusively focused on any one aspect of a person's being (spiritual, psychological, or physiological) to the exclusion of all others. If care is to be worthy of being called soul care, it must not address parts nor focus on problems but engage two or more people with each other to the end of the nurture and growth of the whole person.

In summary, therefore, we can define soul care as the support and restoration of the well-being of persons in their depth and totality, with particular concern for their inner life. Using language we will develop more fully later, the goal of such care can be described as fostering the psychospiritual growth and health of this inner person.

Soul Care in Ancient Greece

In his book *The Therapy of the Word in Classical Antiquity*, Pedro Lain Entralgo traces the Western origins of soul care to the ancient Greek rhetoricians of the fifth century B.C.[4] While this was probably not, in fact, the earliest occurrence of organized soul care, it is a significant one because it was the ancient Greeks who first differentiated care of bodies from care of souls. Plato noted that the task of the physician of the body was to heal through physical means, whereas the task of the physician of the soul was to heal through verbal ones. He viewed rhetoric as the charm of carefully chosen words, and in describing their healing powers for maladies of the soul, he even recognized the crucial value of catharsis in soul cure. While his distinction between the care of bodies and souls had the undesirable effect of distancing each from the other, his identification of dialogue as the primary mode of soul care was to have a significant impact on the subsequent development of soul care.

None of the ancient Greek rhetoricians, however, surpassed Socrates in his clarity of vision and fervor of activity as a physician of souls. Socrates called himself a healer of the soul, and it is from the Greek *iatros tes psuches* we derive the English word *psychiatrist*. In the *Apology* Socrates testifies that having survived the dangers of war in his youth, he was set apart by God to the life of philosophy. But this was no ivory tower academic profession. In describing his life, he states that "[I] spend all my time going about trying to persuade you, young and old, to make your first and chief concern not for your bodies nor for your possessions, but for the highest welfare of your souls."[5] By means of the studied use of words to persuade, challenge, and guide, Socrates understood his task as leading people through a state of perplexity toward the ultimate goal of perfection. He also introduced us to an extremely rich understanding of the therapeutic potential of soul care dialogue, articulated by him almost twenty-five hundred years before Freud was to be credited with the development of his so-called "talking cure."

Apart from the Greek and early Roman civilizations, most civilizations in history have, until the present, made soul care a religious specialization. Indeed, the history of soul care reveals the presence of such a function from ancient Semitic cultures right up to the present. Each culture and each religion has understood and implemented this care in slightly different ways. However, in each case it has involved what could be described as "the sustaining and curative treatment of persons in those matters that reach beyond the requirements of the animal life."[6]

Soul Care in Judaism

The roots of Christian soul care actually predate Greek civilization by many centuries, lying in ancient Israel. Jewish soul care operated within an explicitly moral framework and was closely connected to instruction in the law. Four classes of holy men—priests, scribes, prophets, and wise men—cared for souls by interpreting and applying the Torah to life.[7]

The soul care responsibilities of priests primarily involved the expiation of guilt when the covenant law was broken. Although typically pictured as principally involved in making offerings on behalf of those who broke the law, they were also extensively involved in the exposition of the law. Scribes, and later Pharisees, specialized in applying the law to everyday life. With lifestyles close to that of the average citizen, they offered advice from the Torah for the problems of living encountered by ordinary people. Although prophets did not become involved in the guidance of individuals, the focus of their soul care was the entire nation. They too worked explicitly out of the moral context provided by the law. While the prophets worked upon people's emotions to arouse repentance, wise men relied more upon argument and reasoned admonition. Wise men counseled their fellows on principles of the good life, often drawing not only on the Torah but also on ancient wisdom from Egypt, Mesopotamia, and possibly Greece.[8] Rabbis later replaced the wise men as spiritual guides.

One of the most powerful biblical images for one who cares for the souls of others is the Old Testament image of the shepherd. Shepherds lead their sheep to places of nourishment and safety, protect them from danger, and are regularly called upon for great personal sacrifice. They are characterized by compassion, courage, and a mixture of tenderness and toughness. The prophet Ezekiel presents the soul shepherd as one who leads and guides the sheep, arranges for their food, ensures their safety, heals the sick, binds up the broken, and seeks out and finds the lost (Ezek. 34:2–16). When the soul shepherds appointed by God did not adequately carry out these responsibilities, God himself was described as feeding his flock (Ezek. 34:15), carrying the young lambs in his bosom (Isa. 40:11), and gently leading people to places of rest and nourishment (Ps. 23:2). This imagery is carried over into the New Testament in which Christ is presented as the Good Shepherd who is the guide and protector of his sheep and who lays down his life for them.

Jesus as the Model Soul Shepherd

In the history of soul care, Jesus occupies a unique place. At one level he could be understood to be a moral teacher, very much in the tradition of the priests, scribes, prophets, and wise men of Judaism. He undoubtedly saw what he was doing as continuous with what they had done for centuries before him. Critical as he was of the scribes and Pharisees, he often functioned in a similar manner to them. Frequently called "rabbi," he claimed to have come to fulfill the law, not abrogate it. Wherever he went he proclaimed the ethical demands of the will of God and called individuals and communities to repentance and an understanding of the importance of working toward the coming of his kingdom on earth.

Jesus was much more than a moral teacher, however. His concern was not just for God's law; more fundamentally it was for God's people. As presented in the Gospels, his primary method of soul care was dialogue. Jesus strove to lead people toward repentance and a conversion that would flow out of the heart and into every sphere of life. His was a message of salvation, of new and abundant life. He proclaimed this message through word and deed to all whom he encountered. While verbal instruction was certainly present, his frequently indirect and even paradoxical methods of teaching suggested that he not simply sought cognitive assent to his teaching but a total reorientation of life.

Jesus' approach to soul care was based upon his conviction of the immense worth of persons. The importance of the conversion of even one individual is the theme of his parables in Luke 15. Here we are presented with the great happiness associated with redemption: the joy of the shepherd on the recovery of the one lost sheep, the gladness of the woman who found her one lost coin, and finally, the rejoicing of the angels in heaven over the repentance of one sinner. The importance of the soul is also emphasized in Jesus' teaching regarding the offense against the soul of a new convert. He asserts that it is better to be weighted with a millstone and dropped into the sea than to cause a young convert to sin (Mark 9:42).

McNeill suggests that Jesus presents us with two great gifts that are the object of our deepest strivings: spiritual renewal and spiritual repose.[9] Spiritual renewal is offered in the new birth—a concept at the very heart of Jesus' teaching. Here we are provided with the possibility of a new beginning that is so radical and complete as to be best expressed in the analogy of birth. The gift of spiritual repose is described as rest for the souls of those who labor and are heavy laden (Matt. 11:28–30). Toil is not abolished; rather, Jesus offers to replace a heavy yoke with a light one and to provide restored strength for the task.

An extremely instructive task is to read through the Gospels with the purpose of identifying characteristics of Jesus as the model soul shepherd. Such an exercise will show that in his dealings with people, Jesus:

- met them where they were
- was compassionate
- acted out of an explicit moral context but was never condemning
- spoke with authority
- invited choice
- asked probing questions
- affirmed faith responses
- was scandalously inclusive
- set limits and took care of himself
- dealt with each person uniquely and individually
- related in a manner that affirmed people's value
- was never coercive or manipulative
- spoke in ordinary language
- didn't minimize the costs of discipleship
- dealt at the level of motivation, not just behavior
- preferred dialogue over monologue
- respected, but wasn't limited by, cultural norms
- demonstrated a holistic respect for the close relationship of body and soul

- never allowed his own needs to get in the way of meeting the needs of others
- challenged people to never settle for less than God's best for them
- gave in proportion to receptivity and spiritual hunger
- invited engagement, not passive receptivity
- gave what people needed, not what they asked for
- identified embedded spiritual issues
- allowed people to ignore or reject his help
- gave himself, not just advice
- accepted the trust people placed in him

Soul Care in Christianity

Two components have always been central to soul care in Christianity: the response to the need of a remedy for sin and assistance in spiritual growth. It is interesting to note that these two components are closely related to the two meanings of the Latin phrase *cura animarum* discussed earlier. The *cure* of souls can be thought of as the response to our need for a remedy for sin, while the *care* of souls is the response to our need for assistance in spiritual growth. Christian soul care has historically attempted to combine both of these.

Although sin has been understood in different ways in each of the major Christian traditions, its remedy in soul care has usually centered around confession and repentance. Roman Catholics have focused principally on specific sins, beginning with their recollection and moving toward their enumeration in the confessional. When Luther published his criticisms of Roman Catholic soul care in 1520, he acknowledged some value in the enumeration and contemplation of specific sins but placed more emphasis on acknowledgment of one's sinfulness as a condition of heart.[10] Puritans, Lutheran Pietists, and Calvinist Revivalists continued this emphasis and additionally emphasized the *feeling* of repentance as well as the *experience* of forgiveness and rebirth. This more experiential approach to dealing with sin has been a dominant element in many Protestant denominations since that time.

The second element of Christian soul care has been to aid the individual's spiritual development. This has often been viewed as movement through a series of stages between depravity and holiness. While discussion of stages of spiritual development is often associated with Roman Catholic theology, in fact such a developmental perspective on the spiritual life has had an important place within Protestantism as well. Its pinnacle is perhaps seen in the Puritan theologians. In the sixteenth century, William Perkins detailed ten stages of spiritual growth, and other Puritans continued these efforts of spiritual morphology. However, regardless of the particular theory of spiritual development employed, Christian soul care has usually sought to move people toward spiritual maturity by aiding their progress through some set of stages of the spiritual life.

The Christian church has, since the time of Christ, made the care of souls one of its primary functions. We see this as early as the first century, where letters of spiritual guidance, quite comparable to the letters employed by Luther and the other Reformers as their primary tools of soul care, are preserved for us in the New Testament. They reflect the desire of the early Christians to guide the spiritual development of others who seek to follow Christ.

The first sign of soul care on any sizable scale appears to be among the Desert Fathers in Egypt, Syria, and Palestine in the fourth and fifth centuries. Disciples would seek out these holy men for aid in increasing personal holiness. Their task was to father their spiritual children through prayer, concern, and guidance. The Desert Fathers emphasized the dangers of traveling the spiritual road without a guide. But their leadership was not authoritarian; spiritual fathers were to teach first by example and only secondly by word. Two great representatives of this tradition of desert spirituality were Evagrius Ponticus (345–399) and John Cassian (360–435).

The Eastern Orthodox tradition also esteemed the role of the spiritual guide. The seventh-century guide St. Dorotheos states in his *Directions on Spiritual Training* that "no men are more unfortunate or nearer perdition than those who have no teachers on the way to God."[11] This sentiment is echoed by St. Simeon in the eleventh century who held that it is impossible for anyone to learn by himself what he called "the art of virtue," and so he urged those seeking spiritual growth to find a spiritual guide. It is interesting to note that this idea of teaching virtue is very similar to the view of soul care held by the Greek rhetoricians and philosophers. In fact, one of the earliest articulations of the view that soul healing requires the involvement of another person is found in the writings of the Roman philosopher Cicero (106–43 B.C.), who stated that the soul that is sick cannot heal itself except by following the instruction of others who are wise.

By the fifteenth century, Christian soul care had spread to Russia, where the spiritual guide was the *startsy* (Russian for "old man"). The *startsy* took as his role model Christ as the Good Shepherd. The primary function of the shepherd was seen to be the willingness to suffer for and along with the sheep. Consequently, the *startsy* had to be one who had the ability to love others and to make the suffering of others his own. This notion of vicarious suffering on the part of the soul shepherd has tremendous implications for those who offer soul care. Soul shepherds cannot remain safely aloof from the suffering of those to whom they offer care. Rather, they must incarnate themselves and, entering into the inner world of those with whom they engage, must often vicariously experience and absorb their suffering.[12]

While the earliest spiritual guides tended to be clergy and often were monks, over time more and more of those filling this office in the pre-Reformation church of the West were laity. In the Celtic church in Great Britain, several of the most famous spiritual guides were women. Similarly, in the thirteenth century the Dominicans involved nuns in the task of spiritual guidance. The qualifications remained the same; guides were to be persons of insight and discernment who had made progress in their own spiritual pilgrimage and who could lovingly lead others toward spiritual growth.

The practice of spiritual guidance has not received much attention in Protestant traditions. This is probably due to Protestants' suspicion of acts that seem to undermine the place of Christ as the only mediator between persons and God. This de-emphasis was, however, not intended by the early Reformers. Luther was personally involved in a ministry of spiritual direction with a number of individuals, and his *Letters of Spiritual Counsel* remains a classic in spiritual literature.[13] Zwingli, while recommending confession to God alone, suggested that it was appropriate to consult a wise Christian counselor for assistance in the spiritual life. Calvin also served as a spiritual guide to a number of people. While he stressed that the individual Christian's subservience should only be to God, he saw an important role for the spiritual guide.

Developments in seventeenth-century Pietism and Puritanism also make clear that the reformation did not abolish the role of the spiritual guide. Philipp Jakob Spener, known as the father of Pietism, conducted such a far-flung correspondence of spiritual counsel that he came to be called "the spiritual counselor of Germany." Similarly, the writings of Puritans such as William Perkins, Immanuel Bourne, and Richard Baxter all clearly illustrate the important place that spiritual guidance had in Puritanism. Anglicanism has also retained a lively interest in soul care. A number of recent books on spiritual guidance, including Kenneth Leech's *Soul Friend* and Tilden Edwards's *Spiritual Friend,* arise from within this tradition.[14]

The Christian Understanding of Soul Care

Reviewing the long history of the Christian care of souls, William Clebsch and Charles Jaekle suggest that Christian soul care has involved four elements, each coming into ascendancy over the others in certain periods of church history. These four elements are healing, sustaining, reconciling, and guiding.[15]

Healing involves efforts to help others overcome some impairment and move toward wholeness. These initiatives of cure can involve physical healing as well as spiritual healing, but the focus is always the total person, whole and holy. *Sustaining* refers to acts of caring designed to help a hurting person endure and transcend a circumstance in which restoration or recuperation is either impossible or improbable. *Reconciling* refers to efforts to reestablish broken relationships. The presence of this component of care demonstrates the communal, not simply individual, nature of Christian soul care. Finally, *guiding* refers to helping people make wise choices and thereby grow in spiritual maturity.

Across history, Christian soul shepherds have heard confessions, given encouragement and counsel, offered consolation, taken actions to protect the community from external and internal threats, preached sermons, written books and letters, visited people, developed and run hospitals, organized schools and offered education, and undertaken social and political involvements. All these and many more actions have been undertaken to the end of "the elimination and relief of sin and sorrow and the presentation of all people perfect in Christ to God."[16] This suggests that the overarching goal of Christian soul care may be thought of as character formation—the formation of the character of Christ within his people.

If we understand the concept of discipline broadly enough, this too may be a way of understanding the master goal of Christian soul care. Discipline is not primarily punishment but help directed toward "deeply implanting within the character of a people the basic norms, patterns, and sensibilities that govern the culture of the group."[17] Discipline can, therefore, be thought of as individual and corporate experiences designed to help Christians develop the character of Christ and thereby become whole and holy. Understood as such, discipline has been very much at the core of Christian soul care for most of its history.

What can we conclude from what we have reviewed thus far? What does it mean to care for the souls of people from a Christian perspective? While we are still far from being ready to answer this question in any final form, we can at this point draw together a few tentative conclusions:

1. *Christian soul care is something we do for each other, not to ourselves.* While we do have a responsibility to care for ourselves and for that care to address the deepest recesses of our inner life, it confuses the understanding of the ancient responsibilities of *cura animarum* to describe this as soul care. The history of Christian soul care makes

abundantly clear that the care of souls is a Christian act of neighbor-love. When Jesus taught that we should love our neighbor as ourselves, he was making a point about care of others, not self-care. The principle of self-care is implicit within it but is not its essence. Careful attention to one's inner life is an indispensable prerequisite of caring for the souls of others, and for this reason, we will look closely at what this involves in chapter 11. However, this is not what the church has referred to when it has called Christians to the care of souls. When we make it so, we trivialize a concept that lies at the core of the mission of the Christian church.

2. *Christian soul care operates within a moral context.* Not only should Christian soul care be associated with love, forgiveness, and grace, it should also provide an opportunity for moral inquiry into how life should be lived. This does not make soul care the same as moral instruction and certainly does not make it synonymous with moral persuasion. However, those who seek to offer Christian soul care should understand that such care must include opportunity for moral reflection. Morality is a deep part of all of human life. Therefore, moral considerations belong at the very heart of care for others that is intended to be life-enhancing. How to introduce such a moral component to soul care without becoming moralistic is a major challenge and one to which we shall return in chapter 7.

3. *Christian soul care is concerned about community not just individuals.* Discipline, a component of Christian soul care, is designed to help Christians develop the character of Christ, individually and collectively. Preparation for taking up one's responsibilities within community and living out one's life within this context is part of the goal of Christian soul care. Christian soul care addresses individuals as a part of a network of relationships. The individual is of supreme importance; however, the individual is only capable of being fully and uniquely a self in relationship. Christian soul care takes this social and communal framework seriously.

4. *Christian soul care is normally provided through the medium of dialogue within the context of a relationship.* As such, Christian soul care

PORTLAND CENTER LIBRARY

is not something we do to people. Rather, it is something we do with them. When such dialogue follows the pattern of Jesus it is, among other things, never coercive or manipulative and is highly individualized. The challenges of engaging in such dialogue are also something to which we shall return in chapter 7.

5. *Christian soul care does not focus on some narrow spiritual aspect of personality but addresses the whole person.* While it gives priority to the nurture of the rich interconnecting psychospiritual tapestry of feeling, thinking, and willing that makes up the inner life, it is also vitally concerned for the expression of this inner life in external behavior.

6. *Finally, Christian soul care is much too important to be restricted to the clergy or any other single group of people.* As we shall see later, the spectrum of contemporary Christian soul care involves parents, educators, friends, clergy, spiritual directors, counselors and psychotherapists, and a broad range of others. Ultimately, all Christians are called to the task of caring for the souls of others.

2

The Rise of Therapeutic Soul Care

As presented in the first chapter, *cura animarum* is a religiously based form of care of persons that has been particularly associated with Christianity but that has roots going back to Judaism. While this is true, it is only part of the story; it only brings us to the beginning of the twentieth century and the first developments of therapeutic soul care. The rise of therapeutic psychology in this last century has had a profound impact on soul care and must, therefore, be critically examined. Before doing so, however, we should first consider the precursors to this shift—earlier developments that were occurring within Christian soul care itself that paved the way for the rise of therapeutic soul care.

From Care of Souls to Cure of Minds

While the shift from the care of souls to the cure of minds is principally associated with the rise of modern psychology in the early twentieth century, earlier changes in both Catholic and Protestant soul care served to pave the way for this development. After the Council of Trent (1545–1563), the Catholic practice of soul care experienced a severe narrowing of focus, becoming principally concerned with decisions about religious vocations. Soul curates increasingly took as their primary role the guardianship of orthodoxy, and the major preoccupation became the avoidance of heresy and dubious forms of mysticism.

Protestants were altering their understanding and practice of the care of souls in even more radical ways. This was primarily associated with their emphasis on the priesthood of all believers and the central place of the Bible in personal salvation and spiritual growth. The understanding of care of souls that increasingly came to be accepted as the Protestant method is illustrated in the writings of Martin Bucer, whose book, *On The True Cure of Souls*, appeared in 1538. Basing his understanding of *cura animarum* on Ezekiel 34:16, Bucer argued that the duty of all Christians to each other was "to draw to Christ those who are alienated; to lead back those who have been drawn away; to secure amendment of life in those who fall into sin; to strengthen weak and sickly Christians; to preserve Christians who are whole and strong, and urge them forward in all good."[1] Protestants frequently described these activities as shepherding in order to distinguish them from soul care practiced by Roman Catholics, this being associated in their minds with discipline and authority. In supposed contrast, the shepherd was to be gentle, sensitive, and tender. The office of the spiritual shepherd was to be one of love and concern not one of authority.

Seventeenth-century Quakers initiated a form of mutual admonition and guidance that was, in practice, group soul care. This came to replace personal and individualized soul care for other Protestant groups as well. Wesley only rarely spoke or wrote of the care or cure of souls, and when he did he referred to preaching. Once again this reflects the central place of the Word in Protestant understandings of soul care. The stress in Wesleyan and later Holiness churches was on the direct action of God in the life of the individual, and consistent with this, spiritual guidance was de-emphasized.

Several prominent Catholic writers also questioned the necessity of relationships of spiritual guidance. The Jesuit James Walsh argued that spiritual direction "becomes useful and necessary only when the individual who is living the life of the Christian community to its fullest extent possible becomes aware of God's special call to perfection."[2] In this view spiritual guidance is only for the spiritual elite, not for everyone. Of even more importance, however, was his opinion that it should only be practiced by soul care specialists. Such people should not merely possess the personal characteristics long associated with the office but should also receive specialized training.

Associated with this professionalization of soul care was also the rise of pastoral counseling. In his *History of Pastoral Care in America*, E. Brooks Holifield states that the transformation of the cure of souls into pastoral counseling began in America in 1905 among a group of Episcopalians at the Emmanuel Church in Boston.[3] The rector of Emmanuel Church, Elwood Worcester, and his associate, Samuel McComb, asked whether the care of souls would continue to be guided by tradition or by the science of psychotherapy. Their recommendation was clearly that it was time for the church to embrace science. What came to be known as the Emmanuel Movement soon attracted support from Congregationalists, Presbyterians, and some Baptists, and within three years the group had its own journal—*Psychotherapy*. Holifield called this the beginning of the movement from saving souls to supporting self-realization.

Holifield argues that pastoral counseling was an important force in the development of America's therapeutic culture. In fact, he suggests that the reason America may have been so ripe for psychotherapy as a new method of soul care was that its early history was heavily influenced by Pietism. Historically, Pietism and Puritan variations of Pietism have involved a subjective psychological focus on interior experiences. This spiritual introspection, what Holifield calls a "preoccupation with inwardness, rebirth, conversion, [and] revival,"[4] was basic to American consciousness. It was, therefore, only a small step to translate introspective spiritual piety into secular psychological piety, and the evolution of pastoral counseling and psychotherapy in the early twentieth century was a major force in this movement.

Great Britain also saw the beginning of interest in psychotherapy as a new technology for the cure of souls within this same period. The Guild of Pastoral Psychology, of which Carl Jung was president, and the Institute of Religion and Medicine were both committed to building bridges between psychology and theology. Subsequent to this, the Clinical Theology Association, under the leadership of psychiatrist Frank Lake, came into being as an organization providing training in pastoral counseling in Great Britain.

Unquestionably, the most significant force in the movement of soul care from religion to psychology was the seventeenth- and eighteenth-century growth of science and the subsequent nineteenth-century decline of religion. Historian of psychotherapy Jan Ehrenwald describes the demise of religious soul cure as occurring "when magic has been eroded by critical reason, and religion, emptied of its meaning, has become a formalized institution, a repository of magic rituals and observances."[5] He goes on to argue that psychotherapy arose as a stopgap effort to fill the spiritual void left by the demise of religion. Its challenge was "to meet unmet metaphysical needs . . . without recourse to mythical ideologies or magic ritual."[6]

The great hope of science was that it would provide new solutions to old problems without the trappings of religion. With faces toward the future, modern persons strode ahead with the confidence that myth and ritual were forever left behind in the pre-scientific era. What happened, however, was the replacement of old myths with new myths. Myth, not to be confused with non-truth, is response to mystery. Thus, the hope to eliminate myth through science was naive, and the new scientific responses to the mysteries of the human soul were as much myth as the older religious responses.

Jacob Needleman observes that "modern psychiatry arose out of the vision that man must change himself and not depend for help upon an imaginary God. Over half a century ago, mainly through the insights of Freud and through the energies of those he influenced, the human psyche was wrested from the faltering hands of organized religion and was situated in the world of nature as a subject for scientific study."[7] Removed from its floundering basis in religion, the care of souls now rested securely in the hands of modern science. The care of sinful souls was recast as the cure of sick minds, and psychotherapists replaced clerics as the culturally sanctioned soul curates.[8]

Therapeutic Culture and Pastoral Counseling

Born in the midst of this emerging ascendancy of therapeutic culture, pastoral counseling was profoundly influenced by these developments. Its history has been marked by continuous tension between the pastoral and the psychological perspectives, and since the achievement of its mature form in the 1940s and 1950s, it has often borne more resemblance to modern psychotherapy than to the historic procedures associated with spiritual guidance.

While the authority and meaning of pastoral counseling was grounded in the pastoral office, the new psychological sciences offered fresh language and powerful techniques that have been quite seductive. In spite of the fact that the major authors in pastoral counseling have repeatedly called for the primacy of theology and the pastoral tradition in shaping pastoral counseling, the actual practice of pastoral counseling has often merely mimicked current psychological fads. Thus, North American pastoral care has gone through phases during which it was dominated by Rogerian client-centered therapy, Freudian psychoanalysis, the growth and group therapies of the human potential movement, and the interpersonal therapies having their origins in the work of Harry Stack Sullivan, family systems therapy, and object relations theory. Noting this lamentable fact, Thomas Oden describes the role of the pastoral counselor as that of "trying to ferret out what is currently happening or is likely to happen next in the sphere of emergent psychologies and adapting it as deftly as possibly to the work of ministry."[9] Unfortunately, however, this adaptation has often been uncritical and consequently, the distinctiveness of pastoral counseling has often been compromised.

The syncretistic incorporation of models and technologies that are more clinical than pastoral have often undermined the uniqueness of pastoral ministry. It has also encouraged pastoral counselors to function as poorly trained, generic psychotherapists and preachers as prophets of self-actualization rather than proclaimers of the gospel. Tragically, it has also often led clergy to abandon the distinctives of their historic soul care role.

Parishioners who are increasingly influenced by the psychological society in which they live and out of which their views of themselves and relationships are formed also contribute to the ascendancy of therapeutic soul care within the church. Clergy easily feel that relevance in preaching demands a psychological perspective in sermons and that professionalism in pastoral care demands an adoption of the norms of the clinical therapeutics. Thus sermons and pastoral dialogue increasingly include psychological constructs and values such as self-love, self-knowledge, and self-actualization. Therapeutic culture has dominated not just society but the church as well, and much has been lost as a result.

It is clear, however, that therapeutic soul care has a great deal to offer a religious soul, care which seeks revitalization. Christianity appears to have been faltering in its response to the needs of men and women in the late nineteenth century, and the rise of therapeutic psychology offers it great resources. But, as we have noted, the recent history of soul care suggests both advances as well as corruptions and compromises in the distinctively Christian nurture of the life of persons. This makes the task of the recovery of authentic Christian soul care challenging. Not as simple as a naive attempt to restore and limit ourselves to first-century Christian understandings and practices, a genuine restoration must critically sift through more recent accretions and separate the wheat from the chaff. This will be an ongoing part of what follows.

However, while therapeutic psychology has much to offer Christian soul care, it is not the great hope of the church, nor is its basic message the same as the gospel. If the message and methods of the church are essentially psychological, then the church has lost its reason for existence. I do not happen to think this is the case. The church must, therefore, be careful not to trade its soul for a mess of psychological pottage. Sometimes it appears to have done just this.

Curiously, while Christian soul care was being influenced by its new rival, therapeutic soul care, the latter was being discovered to be more religious than scientific. Psychology, the science of the soul, may have indeed become the science without a soul, but therapeutic psychology was much less successful than its academic counterpart (experimental psychology) in distancing itself from religion.

The Religious Nature of Therapeutic Soul Care

One of psychotherapy's harshest critics, and of such critics the one who has been most clear in identifying its religious nature, is psychiatrist Thomas Szasz. In his book, *The Myth of Psychotherapy,* Szasz argues that psychotherapy is little more than repackaging of religious soul care. He notes that "contrition, confession, prayer, faith, inner resolution, and countless other elements are expropriated and renamed as psychotherapy."[10] Furthermore, he argues that not only does psychotherapy adopt important elements of religious soul care and present them as its own discoveries, it then sets itself up as the enemy of religious soul care. He states, "Psychiatry is not merely indifferent to religion, it is implacably hostile to it. Herein lies one of the supreme ironies of modern psychotherapy: it is not merely a religion that pretends to be a science, it is actually a false religion that seeks to destroy true religion."[11]

Support for the assertion that psychotherapy is an alternate religious system comes from several other sources. Consider, for example, the rise of humanistic psychology in the 1960s and 1970s. Thomas Oden describes encounter groups and other intensive group experiences as a demythologized, secular, Judeo-Christian religion.[12] He bases this assertion on the similarities of encounter groups to both Christian Pietism and Jewish Hasidism of the eighteenth and nineteenth centuries. The major similarities noted by Oden are an emphasis on intense emotional experience (usually occurring within a small group), a zealous pursuit of honesty, a focus on here-and-now experience, the goal of interpersonal intimacy, and frequent, long, and intense meetings. A similar thesis is also developed by Paul Vitz in his book *Psychology as Religion.*[13] Vitz argues that popular psychology, particularly what he calls "selfism," is a major American religion. Furthermore, he asserts that while this new religion has its roots in Christianity, it is deeply anti-Christian in most of its basic tenets.

According to psychologist of religion Lucy Bregman, pop psychology is a nontraditional psychological religion that is viewed by many as enabling the rediscovery of "the essential inner core of what religion is all about, while shedding the already withered externals."[14] Interestingly, she notes that while such inner-experience religiousness sees itself as a replacement for the failing religions of the West, in actuality it represents even more the failure of psychology as a science to answer religious questions. Pop psychology, therefore, may be the answer to the failure of scientific psychology to adequately replace religion.

Psychotherapeutic soul care is not what it pretends to be. Writing in the *Journal of Operational Psychiatry*, psychiatrist E. Mansell Pattison argues that psychotherapy is a "supernaturalistic system that parades itself as a naturalistic system."[15] Denying its religious heritage, it is, however, unable to escape from it. This is the Freudian dynamic of the return of the repressed: That which is denied or repressed is not eliminated; it is merely displaced from consciousness. However, as Freud pointed out, such repressed unconscious contents seldom remain unconscious; they press for expression and consciousness. In the case of psychotherapy, its religious roots and essential spiritual nature cannot be forever concealed. One historian of psychotherapy notes that "it is becoming increasingly clear that the needs psychotherapy is called upon to meet transcend the naturalistic frame of reference to which it has been confined."[16] This is in large part responsible for the crisis facing contemporary psychotherapy; it is a crisis of identity of a science without a soul.

The great paradox of therapeutic psychology is that instead of replacing religion, in many ways it has come to serve as the functional religion of secularized Western society. Despite its packaging as a social science, psychotherapy is much more similar to religion than science—more a matter of spiritual guidance for problems in living than an empirically derived technical treatment of mental disorders. Writing in the seventies when the cult of self-worship was at its peak in North America, American psychologist Paul Vitz argued that psychotherapists had become the priests in the new religion of selfism—a religion with Christian roots but dangerously anti-Christian basic direction.[17]

This is not to argue that psychotherapy meets all the criteria of a formal religion. Instead, the argument is that rather than viewing it as a value-free, technical therapeutic, it should be understood as a functional religion. Phillip Rieff was one of the first people to note this.[18] He described the tremendous culture-shaping force of therapeutic psychology, noting that it provides much more than a technology for treating mental illness. He argued that the rise of modern therapeutic psychology is responsible for the transformation of the dominant character type of Western persons. According to Rieff, Christian culture, reeling and on the ropes since the French Revolution, has now been replaced by psychological culture. In this new cultural milieu, psychotherapy plays many of the social and personal roles once served by religion.

Is this relationship between psychotherapy and religion intrinsic or merely an artifact of the currently dominant psychotherapies? Perry London describes several factors that make psychotherapy intrinsically a moral and religious enterprise.[19] The first is that psychotherapy patients do not separate moral and psychological phenomena in the way that psychotherapists often do. A question such as, "Is it okay to feel angry?" is not merely a psychological question; it is also very much a moral one. The reason it is a moral question is that it is a question of how one should live one's life. Questions of whether or not to have an abortion or have an affair or leave one's spouse are moral questions, not because abortion, sex, and divorce are moral topics but because they concern matters of how life should be lived. In the same way, therefore, questions of how to handle one's emotions, how to understand an interpersonal conflict, or how to deal with a terminal illness are all moral questions not merely psychological ones, because they deal with how one ought to live one's life.

The concerns patients bring to psychotherapists routinely push therapists beyond what consensually validated scientific research has established. This fact was noted by Jung, who stated that "patients force the psychotherapist into the role of the priest and expect and demand that he shall free them from distress. That is why we psychotherapists must occupy ourselves with problems which strictly speaking belong to the theologian."[20]

A second factor that makes psychotherapy intrinsically religious is that psychotherapists are human beings whose own personal values very much participate in their work with their patients. It is impossible for therapists not to have and act on personal values. Psychotherapy is obviously an intensely value-laden process, and the values of both patient and therapist shape the dialogue. It is as impossible for therapists to leave their value judgments outside the consulting room door as it is for patients to leave theirs, and what a strange and potentially dangerous thing it would be if it were! It seems amazing that we ever believed that would be desirable, even if it were possible.

Several additional similarities between psychotherapy and religion also serve to make psychotherapy intrinsically religious. Psychotherapy and religion stand in close relationship to each other as the two major sources of modern individual identity formation.[21] Both provide concepts and technologies for the ordering of the interior life and can, therefore, be thought of as strategies of personal salvation. Both psychotherapy and religion can also be thought of as serving the function of establishing a deep structure for understanding life—an understanding that is acquired and lived out through the enactment of myths and ritual.[22] Furthermore, both religion and psychotherapy attempt to answer questions of ultimacy and human obligation. That is, both serve to provide religious direction to life by proposing matters of ultimate importance and indicating at least the contours of an ethical system for making decisions about how to live one's life. In this regard, they serve as what Rieff called a positive culture, that is, they provide images of the nature of the world, the purpose of life, and basic principles by which life would be lived.[23] Finally, both religion and psychotherapy serve to elevate self-esteem and enhance social integration. Both, therefore, serve vitally important individual and social purposes.

It seems clear that the modern therapeutic psychologies have filled the space left by the decline of institutional religion and operate not just as treatment technologies but as a functional religion. It is important, therefore, to critically evaluate psychotherapies in this light, not simply in terms of their clinical efficacy but also in terms of their religious horizons. These religious horizons can best be discerned in the values of the therapy, most particularly in the assumptions of necessities for healthy functioning. Statements of psychological needs often serve as the Trojan horse that brings moral judgments into psychotherapeutic theory and practice. It is important, therefore, to examine this language of needs carefully as it often serves to insulate choices from moral scrutiny and cloak moral judgments in psychological packaging.

Thus, for example, we may be told that in order to be whole, humans need a relationship with the unconscious self, or sexual gratification, or an absence of external moral codes, or awareness of their body, or to express their feelings. Such statements naively translate what may be a good into a supreme good. By means of this process, psychology moves from being a descriptive science to a prescriptive social institution. Psychology now begins to generate its own set of moral imperatives, ones that must compete with the moral codes of the traditional religions. Because psychology is neither properly equipped for nor sufficiently self-conscious about its role as a religion, however, it does not provide a framework either for answering how these goods relate to other goods or for a harmonization and ordering of its moral imperatives.

Don Browning suggests that this blurring of boundaries between psychological needs and their moral patterning is the major reason why therapeutic psychology, while launched as a social science, has not remained in the limited sphere of a science. Instead of merely describing the world it investigates, therapeutic psychology has also played an intentional role in shaping it, particularly our self-understanding and ways of relating to each other. Browning suggests that contemporary psychotherapies are religious systems "in so far as they attempt to answer our insecurities, give us generalized images of the world, and form the attitudes we should take toward the value of life, the nature of death, and the grounds for morality."[24] His argument is that this movement from the objective activities of science to the moral activities of religion is inevitable given the subject matter. This does not make psychotherapy illegitimate, but it does demand

that we be self-conscious and critical about these moral imperatives that form an imbedded part of any psychotherapy. We must
recognize that they are an extrapolation from the data of science.
They are not, simply and strictly speaking, the products of science.

Soul Care in a Therapeutic Culture

We ended chapter 1 on the threshold of the twentieth century
with soul care still firmly within the domain of religion. Although
the winds of change were beginning to stir in the Christian practice of this ancient tradition, particularly in the de-emphasis and
restricted focus on soul care seen in Protestantism, no significant
rival for the care of souls had as yet appeared.

As we have noted in this chapter, all this changed quite rapidly
in the twentieth century. Therapeutic psychology offered a revi-
talized vision of the care of souls that promised to remove such
care from the faltering hands of religion and place it within those
of science. Although there were pockets of resistance, the church
largely embraced these developments, clamoring to get aboard
the bandwagon that it hoped would rescue it from marginalization. Pastoral counselors and other religious soul curates who
managed to find a place for themselves within this therapeutic
culture did, in fact, seem to find new and more vital ways of offering their care, and large numbers of new soul care professionals
entered the field through the ever burgeoning training programs
of the various mental health professions.

How could anyone question that this was anything other than
progress? But, in fact, the rise of therapeutic soul care has resulted
in both great gains as well as great losses for soul care. These gains
and losses become clear when we first remind ourselves of the
distinctives of therapeutic soul care. The most prominent of these
are professionalism, individualism, psychological reductionism,
and the elimination of a moral framework. Each of these has had
an immense impact on soul care.

As already noted, the rise of professionalism preceded the dramatic shift toward therapeutic soul care witnessed in the first

decades of this century. However, the rapid consolidation of public confidence in the new cadre of professional clinical soul curates meant that amateurism in soul care quickly came to be viewed as involving the provision of substandard care, not simply an absence of formal training or remuneration. While the professionalization of soul care has resulted in gains such as the development of an organized body of literature, training and credentialing initiatives, and a great expansion of the number of people available to provide soul care, it has also resulted in such costs as a de-emphasis on personal qualifications at the expense of technical ones and the provision of an easy way for soul curates to hide behind a role and not engage in an I-Thou encounter with those they seek to serve. It has also led to an inferiority complex on the part of those not certified by the clinical therapeutic professions; such people easily judge themselves to be less than adequately qualified for care that has been increasingly cast as a psychological rather than spiritual enterprise.

The culture of individualism that is associated with therapeutic soul care has had an even greater impact. While not true of all forms of psychotherapy, the bulk of psychotherapeutic soul care treats individuals as if they exist apart from family or other defining communal relationships. The myth that lies at the basis of this is that we are, and contain, individual selves that are only secondarily and superficially attached to other selves. Psychotherapeutic soul care takes these individual, autonomous selves as its focus, setting as its goal the liberation and fulfillment of the individual. This has led to the dominance of therapeutic metaphors of self-actualization, freedom, and growth over historic soul care metaphors of self-denial, discipline, and service. It has also resulted in what can be described as ethical egoism. This is the notion that the pursuit of self-actualization should be the supreme ethical principal of life since such a pursuit serves as a trustworthy guide to right behaviors.[25] Thus, the good of the individual is assumed to lead to the good of the wider community—an assumption that many ethicists would argue is somewhat naive.

Paradoxically, the tendency of therapeutic soul care to reduce psychospiritual phenomena to psychological ones may be the feature of such care that has, on balance, had the most positive impact for soul care. While it has often been associated with an arrogant dismissal of anything genuinely spiritual, it has also had the result of providing a great deal of help in understanding the psychological substrate of religious and spiritual experiences. Given that psychological and spiritual aspects of human functioning are inextricably connected, the understanding of the psychological foundations of spiritual experience cannot but help us understand these spiritual experiences and needs. Our relationship with God is mediated by the same psychological processes and mechanisms as those that mediate relationships with other people. Consequently, the illumination of those processes and mechanisms has the potential to provide great help in understanding and facilitating a person's spiritual response. This, among other reasons, is why I argue that for all the problems associated with the rise of therapeutic soul care, we should not attempt to reverse history but to redeem its contributions.

The elimination of a moral framework from therapeutic soul care has been associated with the mistaken view that psychotherapy is better understood as a technical treatment of illness or disorder than as a personal and religiously directed relationship offering guidance in living. Understood as a technical treatment of disorder, therapeutic soul care seeks to operate within a climate of ethical neutrality—something that is obviously impossible for a human to do. Associated with this effort has been the ethic of therapeutic nondirectiveness—something that is equally impossible and questionable. These naive attempts to avoid dealing with the moral dimension of life have had the consequence of making the therapeutic soul care encounter somewhat artificial and often less than useful. While the various psychotherapies do, in fact, contain implicit moral frameworks and ethical ideals, these are seldom made explicit. Consequently, they typically operate beyond conscious scrutiny and in so doing are of potentially even greater impact.

Under the influence of the modern psychotherapies, soul care has changed irrevocably. Until the beginning of the twentieth century, no one seriously doubted that it was, in essence, a deeply personal encounter of two people. The interaction took the primary form of dialogue—something not done by one person to another, but something shared by one person with another. Under the influence of the therapeutic culture, dialogue was transformed into the technical skills of listening and talking. However, once dialogue is made a technical skill, the interaction is less an I-Thou encounter than an I-It procedure. Therapeutic soul curates may have an advanced level of skill in such things as attending, reflection of feelings, and identification of discrepancies in communication, but these may be at the expense of genuine dialogue. They may be highly adept at listening while simultaneously processing what is heard, but this may be at the expense of deep engagement. And they may excel at objective analysis of what is communicated, but this may be at the expense of significant personal encounter.

It is not just the process of soul care that has changed; the qualifications of those who provide such care have also changed significantly. Prior to the ascendancy of therapeutic soul care, personal qualifications prevailed over technical ones. The primary qualification was spiritual maturity. Within therapeutic culture, those who guide others in the matters of the soul are those with advanced education, specialized technical training, a demonstrated grasp of the foundational theoretical concepts and models, and suitable professional credentialing. The condition of their own soul matters little beyond screening that seeks to weed out those with the most malignant psychopathology.

Counterbalancing these losses, however, are several significant gains that have also been associated with the rise of therapeutic soul care. Chief among these is the development of clinical tools and conceptual maps that offer a great deal of help for the exploration, healing, and nurture of the soul. The clinical tools associated with therapeutic soul care have the potential to greatly aid such things as the resolution of deep-seated emotional wounds, movement through impediments to forgiveness, the enhancement of the capacity for intimacy, the fostering of self-knowledge, and the increased capacity of freedom from inner compulsion. All these are appropriate components of the care of souls, and those who are able to draw on the resources of therapeutic psychology will be greatly aided in their work. Of even more value than these tools, however, are the conceptual maps that have been developed for the understanding of the inner life of persons. Depth psychology offers great help in understanding the psychospiritual dynamics of the soul. The importance of these conceptual maps to soul guides who wish to be informed by psychology, even if not dominated by its culture, is hard to overestimate.

What is discovered when we consult the best available maps of the inner world is that this world is not neatly divided into spiritual and psychological compartments. Nor is the inner world well separated from the outer. Body, soul, and spirit intertwine in a complex fashion in humans. The relationship between these aspects of persons reveals boundaries that are highly permeable and parts that are only intelligible in the light of the whole.

3

The Boundaries of the Soul

As we noted at the conclusion of the last chapter, not only is the inner world of persons not neatly divided into psychological and spiritual parts, neither is the relationship between our bodies and the psychospiritual inner world as neat as we might think. This suggests that we need to consider the way in which these aspects of persons relate to each other. Or put another way, it suggests the importance of examining the boundaries of the soul.

We should note at the outset of such a discussion that the long history of debate on these matters within philosophy, theology, and psychology makes abundantly clear that there are no simple answers to the questions we ask. Furthermore, the technical and esoteric nature of these debates means that much of what has been written on these questions is of limited usefulness to the person whose interest is in soul care rather than the debates themselves.

However, in spite of this, there clearly is a consensus by theologians, psychologists, and medical scientists on the issue of the nature of persons and the interactions of what we think of as our parts. The understanding of the nature of persons that best fits the theological, psychological, and medical data is that humans are a somatopsychospiritual whole. The implication of this is that the care of souls is nothing less than the care and nurture of the well-being of whole persons.

Theological Foundations for the Unity of Personhood

Until recently there has not been a consensus among theologians as to the picture of personhood presented in Scripture. Discussions of biblical anthropology have usually taken the form of arguments over the number of basic parts of persons—dichotomists arguing for two (body and soul), and trichotomists arguing for three (body, soul, and spirit). But increasingly the suggestion is being made in theological circles that to ask how many parts there are to persons is to ask the wrong question of Scripture.

To search for parts of persons is to be confronted with many more than three. Even if we confine ourselves to Pauline psychology, we are forced to consider conscience, heart, flesh, mind, old man, new man, inner man, outer man, and many other concepts—all contenders for inclusion as basic parts of personality. However, to view these terms as describing parts of persons is to seriously misunderstand biblical psychology. Body, soul, and spirit are not independent faculties of persons but different ways of seeing and describing the whole person. The biblical emphasis in discussions of the nature of persons is first and foremost on their essential unity of being.

This is nowhere more clear than in the Old Testament. The very possibility of analytically breaking a person down into component parts was completely alien to the ancient Hebrew mentality, which was not concerned with details but rather with grasping the totality. This means that to read into the Hebrew descriptions of persons an analytic attempt to describe parts is to seriously misunderstand both the intent and psychology of the Old Testament writers. The basis of Old Testament psychology is that persons in their totality stand in relation to God and can only be understood in the light of this relationship.

Glen Whitlock expands on this idea in a paper entitled "The Structure of Personality in Hebrew Psychology." He asserts that the fundamental belief of the Hebrews in relation to psychology was the essential and irreducible unity of personality. Parts always point to the whole and are understandable in the context of the whole. Thus, he states:

> It is not the body nor the mind which acts but it is the total person. It is the total "I" who confronts God. It is the total "I" which is responsible to God. . . . To the Hebrew, evil resides in the total person. It is the whole man who sins. . . . In the Hebrew concept of repentance the person repents not for the separate acts which he has committed, but for being the kind of person (the totality of his person) in which sinful acts could originate and be committed.[1]

Hebrew psychology was, therefore, clearly a holistic psychology. Parts were never seen as ultimate realities but only as conceptualizations having no independent existence. They were not seen as contrasting elements but rather as different aspects of one vital and integral wholeness of personality.

When we turn to the New Testament, we encounter a broad range of anthropological terms that again we must understand not as parts or components of persons but as characteristics of the whole person. G. C. Berkouwer summarizes this understanding as follows: "No part of man is emphasized as independent of other parts; not because the various parts are unimportant but because the Word of God is concerned precisely with the whole man in relation to God." He goes on: "It appears clearly, then, that Scripture never pictures man as a dualistic or pluralistic being, but that in all its varied expressions, the whole man comes to the fore."[2]

In summary, it seems clear that the scriptural view of persons is a holistic one. The basic teaching on human personality presented in both Old and New Testaments is that of the unity of our being. While unified and whole does not mean that the component parts cannot have an independent existence, it does mean that the normal state of human persons is as embodied souls and inspirited bodies. "Human individuality is of one piece, it is not composed of separate or independent parts. This assertion is essential to the theology of the whole Bible."[3]

Humans are not a composite of a number of parts; we do not have a spirit or have a body—we are embodied spirits. Thus, while it is appropriate to speak of attributes or characteristics of a person (such as spirituality or embodiedness), these must always be understood in the light of the more primary wholeness of personality. Kenneth Leech states the matter as follows: "The Christian gospel is concerned with the human person, with his loves and his fears. So there can be no easy division of that person into 'spiritual' and 'psychological' any more than we can divide him into 'body' and 'soul.' It is the whole person that breathes, experiences, and worships God."[4]

Humans are ultimately only understandable in the light of this primary and irreducible wholeness. It makes no sense, therefore, to break persons apart in order to attempt to understand them. This should not only serve as a critique of reductionistic methods of psychology but should also indicate the absurdity of attempting differential diagnosis of psychological and spiritual problems. Soul (*psyche*) and spirit (*pneuma*), terms used interchangeably in Scripture, present us with two perspectives on the inner nature of persons. *Spirit* denotes life as having its origin in God, and *soul* denotes life as constituted in humans. Both, however, describe the immaterial inner core of human personality—a core that I am describing as our psychospirituality.

Arnold DeGraaff adds an interesting footnote to these conclusions by pointing out that the impetus to the current theological emphasis on the unity of personhood has not come primarily from a study of Scripture but from the growing psychological and medical consensus about the same fact.[5] Let us, therefore, briefly consider some of these findings and conclusions.

Psychological Contributions to the Understanding of the Unity of Persons

Out of a desire to avoid what was judged to be the unscientific and unverifiable generalizations regarding human nature generated by philosophy and theology, the dominant perspective adopted by academic psychologists has been reductionistic and atomistic. No longer would the focus be on such speculative entities as the soul, spirit, or will. The methods of science required that the focus of study be observable behaviors, and this new methodology quickly came to dictate what was studied and what was not. The reductionistic nature of such a perspective is well illustrated in the following statement of John Watson, founder of behavioral psychology:

> Human beings do not want to class themselves with other animals. They are willing to admit that they are animals but "something else, in addition." It is this "something else" that causes the trouble. In this "something else" is bound up everything that is classed as religion, the life hereafter, morals. . . . The raw fact is that you, as a psychologist, if you are to remain scientific, must describe the behavior of man in no other terms than those you would use in describing the behavior of an ox.[6]

Not surprisingly, by adopting such a perspective, humans have often been stripped of all that made them distinctively human as relevance of psychological research was sacrificed on the altar of methodological rigor. This was a primary criticism of each of the later more holistic and humanistic schools of psychology that arose in reaction to the limitations of behaviorism. Reviewing the movement of psychology from earlier molecular approaches to the study of persons to the more recent holistic approaches, Calvin Hall and Gardner Lindzey conclude that today nearly all psychologists subscribe to a holistic viewpoint. They go on to state:

> Who is there in psychology today who is not a proponent of the main tenets of organismic theory that the whole is something greater than the sum of its parts, that what happens to a part happens to the whole, and that there are no separate compartments within the organism? . . . Who believes there are isolated events, insulated processes, detached functions? Very few, if any, psychologists subscribe any longer to an atomistic viewpoint.[7]

While atomism has largely been replaced by a more holistic perspective in psychology, until recently, spiritual aspects of personhood have generally been ignored or assumed to be reducible to psychological ones. Freud is a good example of such a reduction of spiritual and religious phenomena to psychological processes. Over the course of his writings, he equated religion to a variety of psychopathological states, comparing it to psychosis (paranoia), neurosis (obsessive compulsive disorder), and infantile neurotic states. He also dubbed it a manifestation of the Oedipus complex, a mass delusion, a neurotic relic, and "blissful hallucinatory confusion." He explained spirits and demons as projections of emotional impulses, God as the displacement of oedipal ambivalence and as a cosmic projection of the father-complex, and mysticism as a regressive reactivation of the infant's lack of ego boundaries. This is but a brief sample of Freud's opinions on religion. It does, however, demonstrate not only the reductionistic nature of his views but also his persistent psychopathological bias.[8]

Carl Jung illustrates a much less reductionistic and psychopathological approach to the understanding of the place of spirituality in personality. Jung's clinical experience convinced him of the deep interconnection of spiritual and psychological aspects of persons and of the crucial role spiritual considerations played in psychological healing. It was he, for example, who asserted that among his patients over thirty-five years of age, there had not been a single one whose problem was not fundamentally that of finding a religious outlook on life. He went on: "It is safe to say that every one of them fell ill because he had lost that which the living religions of all ages have given to their followers, and none of them have been really healed who did not regain this religious outlook."[9]

Thomas Moore also found his clinical experience as a psychotherapist pointing to the inextricable interrelationship of the spiritual and psychological aspects of personhood. Describing the soul as that which integrates the worlds of the material and the spiritual, he asserts that spirituality has a fundamental and important place in soul care. Moore argues that a spiritual life of some sort is absolutely essential for psychological health, but he then also notes that an unhealthy spirituality produces an unhealthy state of psychological functioning.[10]

My own experience also supports the argument Moore makes about the impact of one's spiritual functioning on one's psychological well-being. Religious practices and spiritual commitments have a unique capacity either to heal or poison one's soul. Religious faith has the potential to integrate and transform all parts of the psychic structure and at its best operates in a manner that is deeply restorative, recuperative, and maturing. But this potential is not always realized. Religious faith can also become entangled with pathological dynamics and be more a part of the problem than the solution. When this occurs, the person would probably be better off without religion. Whatever its promised advantages in a life hereafter, its contribution to life in the present is clearly negative.

At its best, a life grounded in a healthy spirituality is integrated and directed in a way that is quite impossible without such a reference point. At its worst, however, a life that is associated with a set of religious practices and commitments that are legalistic and devoid of grace is usually characterized by obsessiveness, rigidity, and an absence of love and vitality. As noted by Gordon Allport many years ago, religion has a singular capacity to integrate human personality. However, when religious and spiritual aspects of functioning are themselves unhealthy, they also have a unique and dangerous ability to erode psychological health and undermine well-being.

Human personality is of a single, seamless fabric, and personhood is unified in a deep and basic way. When examined without reductionistic or materialistic biases, the inner life of persons is clearly seen to reflect the deep intertwining of psychological and spiritual needs and processes. In fact, so close are these to each other that any attempt to separate the psychological from the spiritual results in a loss of the fundamental unity of the soul. Furthermore, only by accepting this basic underlying unity is it possible to move toward greater degrees of integration of the disparate aspects of personhood. Compartmentalization creates disunity; to define some sphere of personhood as independent of and unrelated to another or to the whole is to introduce a breach into the radical unity that characterizes human persons.

57

Nowhere is this seen more clearly than with patients diagnosed with multiple personality disorder. Even in people with what appears to be a totally fragmented personality, there exists a deeper, more fundamental, single, unified self. In such people the fragmentation can manifest itself in the presence of dozens of different altered personalities, each with unique self-concepts and self-presentations, values, moods, aesthetic tastes, sexual orientations, and patterns of physiological responses. However, underlying their obvious and very real differences is a coordinated self-system that makes it possible to discern a unity of selfhood. Treatment is seriously hampered by accepting the veracity of the patient's experience of being a multiplicity of persons inhabiting a single body. Only by helping the patient understand and experience the deeper unity of personality that exists can significant progress toward integration of personality be made.[11]

Medical Contributions to the Understanding of the Unity of Persons

Perhaps the most basic compartmentalization into which we have been seduced has been that of the distinction between the body and the mind. This distinction has its roots in Plato—roots that were reinforced by Descartes and that subsequently came to form an almost unquestioned part of how we viewed ourselves and others. However, recent research in the field of psychoneuroimmunology (PNI) has made clear just how misleading and artificial such a distinction is.

The term *psychoneuroimmunology* was first coined in 1981 to describe the study of the effects of stress on the functioning of the immune system.[12] Although the term is somewhat daunting, it is an attempt to study the interaction of the mind and emotions (psycho), the brain and the central nervous system (neuro), and the body's cellular defenses against disease (immunology).[13] PNI researchers investigate the complex network of interactions between these elements and what has been discovered has been the single most important factor in reshaping traditional ideas of mind and body in modern times. Despite the mixed and some-times conflicting findings, there is an increasingly compelling body of scientific evidence suggesting an inextricable interaction between mind and body at the root of both health and disease. Before reviewing this evidence, it may be helpful to briefly describe the fundamental components of the PNI system.

At the core of the PNI system is the relationship between two more basic body systems, the central nervous system (the brain and the spinal cord) and the immune system. Both are a complex and communicative network of components that interact among themselves and with the external environment. The primary pur-pose of the immune system is to maintain health by fighting against such foreign invaders as bacteria, fungi, viruses, toxic chemicals, and cancer. It also acts as a regulatory mechanism pre-venting the body's component parts from turning against each other, identifying and then killing mutant cells that might develop into cancer. It does this primarily by means of two types of white blood cells: B cells (bone marrow derived), which produce chem-icals that neutralize poisons made by disease organisms while helping the body mobilize its own defenses, and T cells (thymic derived), which seek and destroy cancer cells and other invading bacteria and viruses. Both these types of cells interact continu-ously with another branch of the immune system that produces messenger substances that influence other immune cells.

The mind-body connection in the PNI system is primarily seen in the manner in which the immune system works in tandem with the central nervous system (primarily the brain) and the environment (particularly the psychosocial environment of stres-sors, supports, satisfactions, anxieties, and emotions). There is considerable evidence that emotions, attitudes, and negative stress can all adversely affect the functioning of the immune system. Numerous studies have also demonstrated a suppression of the immune system following bereavement—an effect seen at two months after the bereavement but not at two weeks. Anxiety, depression, and repressed emotions have been demonstrated to play a particularly important role in suppressing immune system functioning. Specific diseases that have been shown to be strongly correlated with such psychosocial factors are rheumatoid arthritis (which is associated with anger, suppressed emotions, nervousness, reserve, perfectionism, and restlessness), cardiovascular disease (which is highly associated with repressed hostility and being a hot reactor to environmental stimulation), and cancer (which is associated with nonassertiveness, the inability to express emotions, and hopelessness or depression).[14]

While a good deal of research has gone into attempts to better understand specific disease vulnerabilities, the most promising results have been associated with what is called immunosuppression proneness. A common core of characteristics are shared by those who are most at risk for all major diseases. Such people are generally quiet, introverted, reliable, conscientious, restricted in the expression of their emotions (especially anger), conforming, self-sacrificing, sensitive to criticism, emotionally distant, overactive, stubborn, rigid, and controlling. They also deny their dependence on others and make great effort to maintain postures of independence. Stress has also been repeatedly shown to be a significant cause of immunosuppression proneness.

It remains unclear just how such lifestyle and personality variables as these work to suppress the immune system. However, it is becoming abundantly clear that mental and emotional states can contribute to both the development of disease as well as to the maintenance and creation of health. Studies done at Harvard University, for example, have shown that merely watching a film of Mother Teresa's work caring for the sick and poor in Calcutta increased the strength of the immune system. Even more remarkable was the fact that this finding occurred regardless of whether those watching the film approved of her work. Evidence also suggests that such things as laughter, relaxation, positive visualization, feelings of peace and contentment, and a positive attitude toward oneself all contribute toward health. Other research has pointed to the health-producing effects of living in loving relationships, of positive religious experiences (sense of forgiveness, worship, etc.), and of the possession of a sense of life-coherence, that is, a feeling that something ties all of us together and that the parts of one's life are connected. People who have this sense that life has personal meaning form the 75 percent of the population who gets 25 percent of the major illnesses. Those without such meaning form the other 25 percent of the population who gets 75 percent of the major illnesses.[15]

This is supported by a major study conducted at Johns Hopkins University. A follow-up at midlife of a large group of medical students found that those who were the healthiest in their forties had the most positive relations with their parents as children, strong self-esteem, an optimistic outlook on life, relatively low levels of depression, and a marked ability to cope with stress. In contrast, those with the most serious illnesses in the fifth decade of their lives reported less satisfactory relationships with their parents and others and lower overall levels of happiness. As a group, these individuals were between three and four times as likely to develop cancer.[16]

Oncologist Dr. Bernie Siegel, in his book *Love, Medicine and Miracles,* argues that unconditional love is the most powerful stimulant for the immune system. Quite simply, love heals. He reports that presence of emotional support increases the survival time of cancer patients by a factor of about 2 to 2.5. Those who do the best have emotional support from others, overcome their fear and hate, and come to see something good in their illness.

Siegel also argues that spirituality is essential to healing. He goes on to state that "spirituality means the ability to find peace and happiness in an imperfect world and to feel that one's own personality is imperfect but acceptable. From this peaceful state of mind come both creativity and the ability to give love unselfishly. Acceptance, faith, forgiveness, peace, and love are the traits that define spirituality for me. These characteristics always appear in those who achieve unexpected healing of serious illness."[17]

It is now abundantly clear that psychological variables (emotional states, attitudes, and cognitions) can change brain chemistry and subsequently produce body changes. Conversely, the process can also work the opposite way; physiological changes in the body (for example, trauma or tissue damage) can also change brain chemistry and subsequently modify emotions, thinking, and other psychological variables. Mind and body are so closely interconnected that it is no longer appropriate to view health or illness merely as body states. It is the whole person who falls ill, not a body or some organ of the body. Similarly, it is the whole person who experiences health. These new understandings of health and illness give unequivocal evidence of the close interaction of mind and body and support the fundamental somatopsychospiritual unity of personhood argued for in this chapter.

The Care of Somatopsychospiritual Persons

When we examine the boundaries of the soul, we discover that the soul encompasses all of our personhood. No part of self exists outside its orb. Our spirituality emerges out of our minds and bodies and has no independent existence apart from them. In fact, forms of spirituality that are not sufficiently grounded in bodily existence and tied to the normal mechanisms and processes that make up the rest of our psychological life are dangerous as they represent a dissociative state. Such states are pathological because of their disconnectedness.

We do not have a part of personality that relates to God or yearns to be in such a relationship. The totality of our being yearns for and responds to such a relationship. Furthermore, our relationship with God is mediated by the same psychological processes and mechanisms as those involved in relationships with other people. The spiritual quest is, at one level, a psychological quest, and every psychological quest can be understood to be in some way reflective of our basic spiritual quest. Psychological and spiritual aspects of human functioning are inextricably interconnected, and any segregation of spirituality and psychology is, therefore, both artificial and destructive to the true understanding of either.

Efforts to separate the spiritual, psychological, and physical aspects of persons inevitably result in a trivialization of each. When spirituality is equated with "that part of us that relates to God," suddenly we are in a position of relating to God with only a part of our being. It is then only a short step to God being seen as more interested in certain parts of us than others. The dividing line between the sacred and the secular then cuts right through the fabric of personality. In the resulting fragmentation, persons become a collection of assorted parts, some of more value than others. As noted above, when the spiritual is separated from the physical, the result is a spirituality that lacks groundedness—an ethereal experience that has no connection to the rest of one's life.

Such an artificial separation also results in a serious trivialization of the psychological aspects of persons. The domain of psychology is everything else that is left over after we take out the spiritual. Such parts of personhood are not even of sufficient importance to be involved in our relationship with God, who is credited with having created us. Psychological aspects of persons become secondary mechanisms in human personality. The real stuff of personality is spiritual. The psychological sphere is somehow inferior to and independent of the real or deepest self—our spiritual self.

Similarly, when the psychological is separated from the physical, the result is a naive and potentially dangerous psychology. Psychological health and pathology must be understood as involving both spiritual and physical components, and a disembodied psyche is as dangerous as a disembodied spirituality.

Nowhere is the impoverishment of persons more clear, however, than when they are reduced to their physical existence. So-called health care that focuses only on bodies as carriers of disease is not really oriented toward health in the sense of wholeness and well-being but rather quite simply to disease eradication. The care of persons who are inextricably somatopsychospiritual wholes requires that we view and relate to them as such. This does not mean that one or another aspect of personhood cannot be our primary focus. It does mean, however, that soul care that is worthy of its name should always nurture and care for the person's inner psychospiritual life while attending to the ways in which this life is lived out and influenced by physical and external realities.

4

Psychology and Spirituality

In the last chapter we discovered that the boundaries of the soul are difficult to delineate. New understandings of the mind-body connection give strong evidence of the imprecision of current maps of this boundary. The difficulty in distinguishing between spiritual and psychological dynamics of the inner life should, therefore, be of no surprise.

An understanding of the relationship between spiritual and psychological aspects of persons is vitally important for anyone who desires to provide soul care. Psychospiritual dynamics form the major threads of the interwoven fabric that constitutes the inner life of a person. An examination of these dynamics will, therefore, occupy this and the next two chapters. In the present chapter we will reflect on the relationship between psychology and religion and then examine a number of psychological understandings of spirituality. In chapter 5, the focus will be on a Christian understanding of spirituality, while in chapter 6 we will examine the intertwining of psychological and spiritual issues as they emerge within soul care dialogue.

Psychology and Religion

Before turning to psychology's attempts to understand spirituality, it might be profitable to reflect briefly on the mutual suspicion, misunderstanding, and animosity that has characterized the relationship between psychology and religion over the past century. When examined carefully, most of the tensions can be seen to have resulted from a failure to understand and respect each other's unique perspectives. Consider, for example, the failure to understand or accept the validity of the differing levels of explanation that are typically utilized by psychology and religion. It is quite possible to describe persons, or any phenomenon, from a number of different vantage points, none of which should preclude the truth or usefulness of the others. While such explanations may not be easily reconciled, they are not necessarily in conflict.

To illustrate this, think for a moment of an electronic sign. A scientist giving an explanation of such a sign might exhaustively describe its workings in terms of the electrochemical processes that are involved and yet completely exclude any reference to the sign's message. An artist might explain the sign in terms of its design principle, and completely ignore the electrochemical and hermeneutical levels of explanation. Finally, a literary critic might think both of these explanations completely miss the point of the sign, that is, its message. Such a person might expound the text contained on the sign with absolutely no reference to the other two levels of analysis.

Do these levels of explanation conflict with each other? They only conflict if one is offered as the *only* level of analysis and as a complete and comprehensive explanation in itself. Such an explanation could be described as being reductionistic. Reductionistic explanations are those that assert that only one level of explanation represents truth and that all others are, at best, unnecessary or, at worst, illusory. Merely offering an explanation at a more basic level of analysis is not necessarily to offer a reductionistic explanation. In the illustration of the electronic sign, the scientist's explanation only becomes reductionistic if he or she asserts that this is all there is to the sign, arguing that its supposed message or meaning is explained away by the electro-chemical explanation.

Rather than viewing the simplest or most basic explanation of any phenomenon as making redundant all higher levels of analysis and their respective explanations, the various levels of explanation should be viewed as complementary to each other. Thus, the basic level of analysis of any phenomenon is to consider it within the framework of the laws of physics. However, in order to truly understand the phenomenon, higher levels of analysis will also be necessary. In terms of ultimate meaning, the most abstract or general level of analysis is usually the most significant.

Psychology has rightly been criticized as often being reductionistic in its understandings of higher level phenomena such as religion. If, for example, a psychologist suggests that a religious experience is nothing more than a complex set of neurophysiological events or a regressive reactivation of feelings of infantile omnipotence, he or she is engaging in reductionistic thinking. Either or both of these levels of explanation may be valid, but they do not negate the value of other levels of explanation.

On the other hand, theologians have often behaved in what appears to be an antireductionistic manner but which is, in reality, equally reductionistic. They have resisted analysis at lower levels of explanation, preferring high-level abstractions. Thus, the same religious experience may be described in terms of an encounter with the numinous, an apprehension of the transcendent, or a surrender to the Ground of Being. While these descriptions may be quite valid in themselves, if they are offered as the only way to understand the religious experience, then such an explanation is equally reductionistic to that offered by the psychologist. Both psychology and theology have been guilty of reductionistic thinking, and this has produced a good deal of the tension that exists between the fields of psychology and religion.

The failure to understand each other's perspectives has often resulted in misunderstandings, particularly around the use of common language. Thus, for example, concepts such as guilt, forgiveness, faith, evil, and even God are employed in both religious and psychological literature. However, they are packed with quite different meanings—meanings that are often so different that misunderstandings occur when it is assumed that the two groups are talking about the same thing.

Consider, for example, the concept of God. When theologians speak of God, they have historically referred to an entity who is assumed to have an existence independent of the experience of the person making the statement. The theological assertion that "God is love" has usually been understood as an assertion about the character of God, not merely a description of the experience of a particular individual or a group of individuals. Such faith assertions are, however, beyond the realm of psychology. Psychology does not have access to data that gives it the right to make any assertions about either the existence or nonexistence of God. Although psychologists have often lost sight of this fact, as psychologists they must remain agnostics regarding the existence of God. As humans they are free to adopt whatever faith posture they choose, whether atheism, deism, theism, or something else. However, as psychologists they do not possess the competence to make these determinations. Such judgments are not within the domain of psychology.

Psychology can do no more than describe human experience and behavior. Psychology's discussion of God may, therefore, strike the theologian as being too naturalistic. This is, however, the only god that can be known by the psychologist as psychologist. Thus, for example, when Jung describes God as a part of the self, he should not be understood as making a theological assertion but rather a psychological one. The only thing he is capable of describing is this interiorized god, a god which, from the perspective of the theologian, will be necessarily lacking in transcendence. Jung's religious discussions should, therefore, be understood as descriptions of the human experience of God, not descriptions of God, and his insight should be understood to be the fact that we encounter God at the core of our being, not somewhere outside of the self, in the periphery of personality or in the external world.

This distinction between theological and psychological language has not always been clear. Psychologists have on occasion spoken as theologians, making unjustifiable jumps from their domain of competence to opinions regarding something about which they have no particular expertise, and perhaps the same has occurred in the opposite direction. Freud is, of course, a particularly clear example of this sort of blurring of boundaries. The fact that people's ideas about God are shaped in the context of their experience with their parents says nothing about the actual existence of a God. Nor does the fact that humans seem to display a universal yearning for a divine being. This is the gap between psychological analysis and theological discourse. All that psychologists as psychologists can affirm or negate lies within the realm of psychological reality, whether this be the experience of people, ideas, gods, or fictional beings.

Properly understood, psychology and religion are recognized to stand in close relation to each other because of their shared interest in solutions to the human predicament. However, while similar, they are obviously not the same. These differences should not be posited in terms of differences of subject matter or even goals. Psychology and religion do not deal with different kinds of reality or even with totally different domains of human experience. Each grapples with real aspects of human experience and seeks to make sense of the data it considers. The difference between them should not be sought at this level.

According to Paul Tillich, the difference should be discerned in the perspectives each brings to the common reality they explore.[1] Psychology, according to Tillich, seeks to understand the structure of being while theology seeks to understand its meaning. These perspectives are both different and, at the same time, inextricably interconnected. Psychology can never deduce either meaning or morality from its scientific and descriptive activities, and yet it also cannot operate outside of considerations of either. Similarly, theology is not well equipped to render personality dynamics intelligible, and yet it offers a perspective on life that only becomes meaningful when it is imbedded in the core of a person's psychospiritual functioning. Each needs the other. There is ample work to be done by both and unique opportunities for even greater accomplishments if psychologists and theologians can begin to learn to work together with respect, cooperation, and an absence of imperialism.

Toward a Psychology of Spirituality

In his discussion of the relationship between psychology and spirituality, Robert Doran noted two extreme positions that must be avoided if any useful understanding is to be achieved. The first of these is the reduction of spirituality to psychology, wherein spiritual experience is supposedly completely explained by basic psychological constructs and processes. The second equally fatal error, in Doran's view, is to divorce spirituality from psychology so completely that spirituality becomes a separate realm of human activity that is not integrated with either psychological reality or the rest of life.[2]

Unfortunately, the bulk of psychological writings on spirituality have fallen into one or the other of these traps. Psychologists have offered numerous dismissals of religious and spiritual experience, and religionists have countered with so-called psychologies of the spiritual life that leave it no more than a dissociated state that is disconnected from the rest of psychic reality.

For fleeting moments, even Freud himself seemed aware of this danger. For example, he acknowledged at one point that his theories did not exhaust the explanation of religious phenomena but merely added a new facet to them.[3] Later he also stated that merely because something is an illusion, that is, derived from human wishes, does not mean it is necessarily false.[4] Even a Freudian explanation of religious or spiritual experience may, therefore, assist us in understanding the psychological substrate of such experience. However, it certainly does not explain the experience away or tell us anything about its essence, meaning, or value.

What we seem to need, therefore, is a view of spirituality that situates such experience within the overall framework of psychospiritual functions and processes of personality. In pursuit of such an understanding, we will briefly review the contributions of theorists working within four systems of psychology that have been sympathetic to human spirituality: analytical psychology (Carl Jung), we-psychology (Fritz Kunkel), existential psychology (Søren Kierkegaard, John Finch, and Adrian van Kaam), and contemplative psychology (Gerald May and William McNamara).

Analytical Psychology

The work of Carl Jung (1875–1961) is perhaps the best beginning point in a review of psychological perspectives on spirituality because no theorist in psychology is more closely connected with spirituality than Jung. In contrast to Freud, who was antagonistic toward religion, Jung was sympathetic toward it and developed a psychology that places religious and spiritual needs at the very center of the psyche. While Freud viewed religion as an illusory crutch, Jung understood it to be a natural part of the human condition and an indispensable foundation to health and wholeness.

The central concept in Jung's view of spirituality is that of individuation. Individuation refers to the lifelong process of becoming whole through the synthesis of conscious and unconscious aspects of personality. In more technical terms, Jung viewed this as the establishment of a relationship between the ego (which is the center of consciousness) and the self (which is the innermost center, extending beyond consciousness to include the unconscious). Jung viewed individuation as a religious process, describing it as the submission of the ego-will to God's will. Spiritual growth was thus viewed as the movement away from the ego as the center of personality toward the self as that center.

The self in Jungian psychology is a somewhat mystical concept. Verda Heisler suggests that the Jungian self "extends from the psyche of the individual into the far reaches of the universe as a container of the divine creative force which is unfolded in the development of man but which also far transcends not only the human individual but also the human race."[5] The self, according to Jung, is the true center of our personality; the ego should only be a way station toward integration. The problem is that people tend to get stuck in ego-centeredness. However, the wholeness that is the goal of the spiritual quest cannot be obtained apart from movement to the self as center.

More concretely, what this entails is the process of integrating the various complementary and conflicting elements of personality into the self. Of particular importance in this process is the integration of the shadow. The shadow consists of those psychic qualities that, because of their incompatibility with conscious values and goals, have been denied a place in consciousness or in the self. These unconscious aspects of personality must be integrated within the rest of personality if we are to become the authentic and whole persons we should be.

Individuation, thus viewed, is transcendence beyond the limited, selective, and even deceptive functioning of ego-centeredness. This road to salvation is attained through increased consciousness, that is, through increasing knowledge of ourselves. Jung felt that when we become aware of the opposites inherent in our nature, we then not only know ourselves but also God. According to Jung, the God image does not coincide with the unconscious as a whole but with a special component of it—the archetype of the self. Spiritual growth is thus the discovery of this God-image within the self and the integration of it into the rest of personality.

Jung's contributions to the psychology of spirituality are many. First and foremost would be his understanding of the naturalness of spirituality to human experience. In contrast to Freud, Jung believed it is not the presence of spirituality that is pathological but rather its absence. Jung's psychology of religious experience allowed him to remove religion from the realm of neuroses and place it firmly within the realm of creative expressions of the deepest aspects of the self. In so doing, he restored the religious function to psychic life. Also important is Jung's insight regarding the fact that God is encountered within the core of the self, not somewhere in the farther reaches of the cosmos. This is ultimately the reason that religion is so natural to humans. Because Jung was not a theologian, he was in no position to address the question of whether a transcendent God also exists outside of and beyond the self. As a psychologist, however, he correctly noted that God can be discovered within the deepest recesses of the self and that this discovery holds unique potential as a point of integration of the rest of personality.

Because God resides within the unconscious, Jung correctly realized that spirituality must involve the language of the unconscious (symbols), not merely the language of the conscious (words). Furthermore, his discovery of the important role of symbols in the integration of the psyche is also a major contribution to our understanding of the place of symbol and liturgy in religious life. Spirituality and psychology are here deeply interconnected.

Jung's teaching that spiritual and psychological health both depend on an open relationship between conscious and unconscious forces in personality is also a major contribution to spirituality. Perhaps more than any other depth psychologist, Jung has shown the way toward the creation of an attitude of friendship and cooperation between the conscious and unconscious aspects of personality. Furthermore, his recognition of the importance of the individual's transcendence of incomplete conceptions of the self as a step in spiritual growth is also helpful. His discussion of psychological types is also very valuable as a means of understanding the unique ways in which different individuals will experience and express their relationship to God. Finally, his criterion for the discernment of true and false spirituality is also a most valuable contribution to a psychology of spirituality. It was his suggestion that the integration of a person's inner and outer worlds is the major way in which true and false spirituality, as well as mysticism and psychoses, may be distinguished from each other. Such a distinction has important implications for spiritual development.

As a psychologist, Jung probably deserves high marks. His contributions to the psychological understanding of spirituality are significant. However, while it may seem strange to evaluate him also as a theologian, it is quite appropriate. Jung often wrote as a theologian and even more frequently is read as one. His "Answer to Job" is one particularly good example of his theological writing in that it represents his effort to develop a psychotheology of evil.[6] In this essay, Jung analyzes the character of God, exploring God's conflict over and limitations around the management of evil. So extensive is such theologizing in his writings that at least one theologian has suggested that Jung is better thought of as a moral philosopher or theologian than as a psychologist.[7]

As a theologian, Jung's marks would probably have to be much lower, at least if the reference point is Christian theology. When

73

evaluated in the light of historic Christianity, the major limitation of Jung's view of spirituality appears to be his failure to adequately represent God's transcendence or to provide for our self-transcendence. Jung's God is completely interiorized, leading to a self that is deified.

In contrast to this totally immanent God who inhabits the collective unconscious, the God of Christianity is both immanent and transcendent. Christian salvation, therefore, allows for our transcendence beyond and above ourselves. In fact, as we shall see later, Christian spirituality has always viewed such self-transcendence as essential to spiritual growth. While Jung attempts to build self-transcendence into his model, in actuality he hovers much closer to self-fulfillment in his concerns.

In his analysis of the relationship between Jungian psychology and Christian spirituality, Robert Doran concludes that the major limitation of Jung's contribution to Christian spirituality is that "the innermost region of our interiority is . . . no longer ourselves, but the place of grace, where the gift of God's love is poured forth into our hearts by the Holy Spirit who has been given to us."[8] Jung interprets this innermost center not in terms of grace but of nature. Doran argues that this equation of God and self makes prayer into talking to one's self, thus destroying the self-transcendent experience of genuine Christian spirituality.

When the Jungian vision of the individuation of personality becomes the end of the spiritual quest, what Jung offers must be seen as an alternative to Christian spirituality. While a personality centered in self is undoubtedly healthier and closer to wholeness than one centered in ego, it still falls far short of Christian salvation. In Christian salvation the self is grounded and centered in Jesus Christ and is, thereby, renewed into the image in which it was originally created. We then have more than integration of personality; what we have is the indwelling of a new spirit within us, the Holy Spirit, and the outworking of his life within ours. Jungian psychology appears, therefore, to make significant contributions to an understanding of spirituality in general. It makes, however, a poor substitute for genuine Christian spirituality.

We-Psychology

Although his work is much less well known than Jung's, Fritz Kunkel (1889–1956) built on the ideas of Jung and appears to have avoided the major limitations encountered in the Jungian vision of spirituality. Kunkel was a disciple and colleague of Alfred Adler and a correspondent of Jung. He sought to develop an explicitly religious psychology based on a synthesis of Freud, Adler, and Jung. His starting point was the question of why it is so difficult to move beyond egocentricity. Jung emphasized knowledge as the vehicle for movement beyond self-centeredness, but Kunkel felt more than this was necessary. He set as his objective the understanding of the development and operation of egocentricity as the major obstacle to surrender to God.

Kunkel roots egocentricity in early childhood, viewing it as a natural adjustment to the child's egocentric environment. He describes it as "a normal reaction to an abnormal situation . . . the absence of the right kind of love."[9] Because parental love is always egocentric to some degree, it is therefore inevitably incomplete. As a result, the child always sustains narcissistic injuries of one sort or another, and the child's defense against these is egocentricity. This is a revolt against what Kunkel describes as the innate "we-feeling," which, in his view, is the capacity of the young child to experience others as a part of the self. In this regard, Kunkel notes that the self is not synonymous with one's own self; rather it should be viewed as always including the "we-experience"—the experience of interpersonal connectedness. A return to the we-feelings of the preegocentric child is, in Kunkel's view, our hope for growth and wholeness. This gives rise to the name for his system of psychology: we-psychology. In contrast to other approaches to psychology, Kunkel argued for this broader ego-transcendent self as the route to genuine connectedness with others and God.

While this broader view of self may have been implicit in Jung, he de-emphasized the importance of others in both the emergence of the self and its continued functioning. However, others are indispensable for self in Kunkel's thought. In fact, the sterility of egocentric life is precisely because we are cut off from the creativity and energy that comes from our relationships to others at our deepest center. Relationships with others may, in fact, be present for the egocentric person. However, until egocentricity is rooted out of the very core of our personality, we will not experience the deep connectedness with others that Kunkel calls the we-experience.

The inevitable breach of the infant's original connectedness with the mother leads to egocentricity. In essence this involves the substitution of a sham center, the ego, for our real center, the self. Because the ego (me) is much more constricted than the self (me in relationships), the result is alienation. The ego subsequently becomes more and more brittle as it is called upon to do a job it was never intended or equipped to do. The ego thus becomes a shell around our personality—a shell we build to protect us from further hurt. However, this leaves us stripped of the resources we need to live, and ultimately egocentricity brings us to a crisis. Kunkel viewed this crisis as our only hope for movement beyond egocentricity:

> In any form the crisis simply leads to the realization growing out of uncomfortable experiences that there is a need for a readjustment of one's thinking and behavior. The individual comes to feel that he must do something different. Old ways of behaving are no longer satisfactory, so new ones must be adopted. A turning point has been reached. There may be a total collapse of the whole Ego-pattern or merely a minor modification of some one of its elements. . . . The egocentric form of psychic life breaks down because it proves to be erroneous in its content and too rigid in its form. The attempts of the individual to save his Ego only lead him nearer to the crisis.[10]

Kunkel suggests that this is the meaning of Christ's paradoxical teaching that he who would save his life must lose it. It appears that in order to save my life—that is to really live—I must lose that which appears to be my life, the system of mistaken ideas and values that embody my ego. Kunkel suggests that the way we do this always involves "finding one's place within the service of the we," that is through commitment to and engagement with others.

The way in which this is related to surrender to God is described by Kunkel as follows:

> The emptiness and indifference resulting from the collapse of the Ego and the complete loss of egocentricity enable the individual to discover the very foundations of his life and of human life in general. He sees that man is powerless and important at the same time, that he is part of a larger unit and responsible for it. Furthermore, he realizes—and this is the decisive insight—that he himself as well as the larger unit, the We, is created, sent, supported, endowed and used by a higher reality who rules the world and in whom he and others live and move and have their being. Thus he feels himself gripped, influenced by God and charged with a concrete task. He feels like a tool seized by a strong hand, or like a knight commissioned by his king.[11]

Kunkel's we-psychology does much to correct the most serious limitations of Jung's view of spirituality while at the same time retaining the richness of his understanding of the dynamics of inner life. Spirituality is here understood as self-transcendence and self-surrender, concepts much more central to Christian spirituality than self-fulfillment or individuation.

Existential Psychology

Existential psychology is not so much a specific set of theories or techniques as it is a general approach to psychology. Its beginnings are usually identified with the Danish theologian and philosopher Søren Kierkegaard (1813–1855). It has since evolved into a broad and diverse tradition—so broad that it defies easy definition. As a group, the existential approaches stand in opposition to those systems of psychology that view persons reductionistically. Ignoring human essence, the abstraction of certain schools of philosophy and psychology, existential psychologists focus on human existence and issues such as the establishment of meaning and purpose for life; freedom, responsibility, and choice; and a creative response to the reality of existential isolation and the inevitability of death. These and related issues move existential psychologists into the very heart of spirituality.

Søren Kierkegaard

Søren Kierkegaard's breadth as a thinker is reflected in the fact that his books continually cross the parochial boundaries that usually separate literature, psychology, theology, philosophy, and devotional writings. His most influential psychological writings were *Sickness Unto Death* (1849) and *The Concept of Anxiety* (1844). It is here that we find his most extensive discussion of the self and its role in spirituality.

Kierkegaard saw persons as spirit. By this he did not mean they are immaterial; rather, spirit is the absolute of all that a person can be. Each person is intended to become a self. Selfhood is not a given for Kierkegaard; it is an achievement. It is to become a self-conscious responsible agent. This is also what it means to be spirit.

Spirit is defined by Kierkegaard as the "self relating to itself."[12] By this Kierkegaard was referring to self-acceptance, self-understanding, and self-consciousness—all qualities of a growing self or spirit. But self cannot become all it is intended to be by itself. Ultimately self can only become a true self by relating itself to God. Kresten Nordentoft, the major systematizer of Kierkegaard's psychology, describes this aspect of Kierkegaard's thought as follows:

> Man always relates himself to God and man's existence is always determined by this relationship regardless of whether man acknowledges this relationship or not. . . . Man does not become free in an illusory attempt to emancipate himself from every relationship of dependence but by acknowledging to himself his real dependence, that is his createdness by God, and thereby, his relationship to the authority which liberates him. . . . If one does not become free in relationship to the Almighty, one makes oneself unfree in relation to other powers which one does not know.[13]

When the self is dependent on something outside itself (i.e., God) it can then serve as a point of integration for all other aspects of personality. In Kierkegaard's view, self is the synthesis of elements that are, and will always be, in opposition to each other. Self is the synthesis of the finite and the infinite, of the temporal and the eternal, of things possible and things necessary. These elements are held together by the self, and because of this, human life involves constant effort, vigilance, and courage to maintain itself as authentically human.

There is an ever present temptation to let go of the tension. But, according to Kierkegaard, this is the coward's way because it destroys the self in the effort to escape from anxiety. The result is a one-sided personality that lacks balance. This, according to Kierkegaard, inevitably leads to despair. Despair manifests itself in one of two forms: It is either not willing to be one's own self (despair of weakness) or willing to be oneself but in defiance of God (manly despair). In both forms, the true self is never fully developed or realized.

This understanding of spirituality bears striking resemblance to the two previous positions considered. For Kierkegaard, as for Jung, self is a synthesis of all parts of personality—even those that do not seem easily put together. The struggle to bring these discrepant parts together is a spiritual struggle in that in so doing we become the self we truly are rather than living out some false self.

Kierkegaard's emphasis on self-knowledge in this process is also consistent with Jung. Kierkegaard states that consciousness of self is the criterion of the self. The more consciousness, the more self. However, he makes much more explicit than Jung the way in which knowledge of God is a part of this process. Kierkegaard suggests that we begin with a lack of consciousness of being an eternal self and then come to a knowledge of this eternal element of our being. As our self is defined more and more in the awareness of existing before God, we become our true self. In Kierkegaard's words: "The more conception of God, the more self; the more self, the more conception of God. Only when the self as this definite individual is conscious of existing before God, only then is it the infinite self."[14]

Kierkegaard's assertion that self must be grounded in something outside itself and that true selfhood is only possible by being grounded in God is more in line with Kunkel than with Jung. Kierkegaard here recognizes the surrender of self to something greater than self that Kunkel described as being the only path out of egocentricity.

John Finch

John Finch, a spokesman for what he calls Christian existential psychology, is a contemporary author who is attempting to bring existential psychology back to its roots in Kierkegaard. He notes that existential psychology has abandoned any concern for an ultimate reference point of spirit or self and argues that unless spirit is grounded in Spirit, freedom, responsibility, and all the other transcendent qualities of self are meaningless.

Reviewing the points of dissension for the major Freudian revisionists, Finch notes that they all made their major quarrel Freud's elimination of some aspect of persons that did not fit into his mechanistic and naturalistic model. They labeled this aspect variously, calling it spirit, soul, and our capacity for self-transcendence, but each held that it is the one and only source of wholeness. Finch suggests that the human quality observed by these theorists is the *imago dei*, that is, our imaging of God. He offers the term *spirit* as the most suitable one to describe this aspect of persons, defining spirit as "that quality which characterizes man as self-transcendent, free, and responsible, and which is unique to man."[15]

Viewing spirit as the *imago dei* suggests to Finch why we are oriented toward God. This God-likeness, and our orientation toward God, is obscured by a network of defenses that, while purporting to protect the self, actually suffocates it. These defenses, which Finch calls the false self, are a result of sin, which he views as a sickness created by our egocentric tendency to assert that we are the captains of our fate, the masters of our soul.

Finch's major contribution may be his understanding of the way through the false self, back to spirit, and finally to the grounding of spirit in Spirit. His method is an intensive psychotherapeutic experience conducted within the framework of the traditional spiritual retreat. The process of this therapeutic retreat involves a dismantling of the false selves and a descent into the dread that the mystics have called the abyss. Finch describes this as a "radical and ineffable confrontation with one's own being which becomes at the same instant an experience of the infinite love of God. For, having abandoned one's feeble attempts to constitute one's own security, one finds that he or she is and always has been held."[16]

The goal of Finch's Christian existential psychotherapy is to encourage persons seeking help to find and develop their true self, this being their spirit. Finch describes this as a spiritual encounter, wherein the therapist attempts to "excavate and probe through the years of rationalized encrustations; lovingly appealing to the individual's carefully concealed sense of responsibility; fanning the little sparks of conscience back to flame; uncluttering the conscience and attempting to witness of the Spirit to the spirit . . . to encourage the spirit to emerge and be itself."[17]

Finch's therapy is reminiscent of Kunkel's emphasis on the necessity of crisis in the breakdown of egocentricity. For both Kunkel and Finch, spiritual growth necessarily involves crisis. The encrustations of the false self are not broken through easily, but until they are, true self (spirit) does not emerge. Finch also shares with Kunkel the notion of ego-centeredness as the enemy of spirituality. Both also affirm that only self-transcendence that is rooted in God can produce the wholeness of personality that we need.

Adrian van Kaam

The last representative of the existential tradition whom we shall consider is Adrian van Kaam. Trained as both a psychologist and a Catholic priest, van Kaam's writings have frequently focused on issues of spirituality and the way in which psychology can inform or assist spiritual growth.

Probably van Kaam's clearest statement on spirituality and psychology is found in his book *On Being Yourself* (1972).[18] Here he explores the relationship between spiritual growth and self-discovery. His major thesis is that spirituality is the attempt to integrate oneself in the light of one's presence to God. By this he refers to the attempt to live our life aware of the reality that we are in the presence of God, to see ourselves in the light of our Divine Origin.

Understood correctly, the spiritual quest can be described as the quest for self-discovery and self-fulfillment. It is the quest for the real me—the original me. However, this is not to be confused with self-enhancement or mere ego-fulfillment. It is not to be a search for self in isolation from God but a search for self-in-God. This is the difference between selfism as idolatry and Christian spiritual growth.

Van Kaam argues that when Scriptures speak of giving up myself or of denying myself, these should not be interpreted as losing our identity or fusing with the Godhead. Rather, their meaning is that "I should distance myself from false self images. I should not pursue after an isolated God-like self."[19] The search is for my original self as hidden in God, and only when I find this do I find my true self.

Christian spirituality is looking to God to find my meaning and integration point. This looking is not, however, primarily exterior. Rather, it is interior. Van Kaam describes the spiritual life as a life of inner direction, a life lived in contact with our deepest self. It is here that we find the most personal statement of God's will for our lives. It is here that we learn who God calls us, as unique individuals, to be. What we discover is that each of us is called to be a unique self, an original creation.

According to van Kaam, true spirituality excludes mere imitation or conformity. One's spiritual life can never be a carbon copy of that of another. Christianity has often missed this central truth, assuming that as we become more like Christ we become more similar to each other. Van Kaam asserts that this is a fundamental error; the more I grow in Christ, the more I should find and express the uniqueness of Christ in me.

Spiritual persons are characterized by direction and purpose to their lives. These are not superficial or arbitrary directions and meanings but rather they flow out from the center of personality. In contrast, nonspiritual persons may also have direction and meaning, but these do not flow out of their innermost selves. Christian spirituality flows out of our union with Christ. In van Kaam's words: "Spirituality in the most profound sense resides in the core of my being, in my deepest self or spirit, where I as willing unite my will to the will of God for me."[20]

Van Kaam's picture of mature spirituality being associated with meaning and direction that flow out of the depths of personality reminds us of Jung's differentiation between true and false spirituality. Both Jung and van Kaam see true spirituality as beginning with integrated interiority and moving toward meaningfully directed behavior. Van Kaam's view of spirituality also helps us understand the role of self-discovery in spiritual growth. When self is pursued in the presence of God, I am enabled to find my true and original spiritual self—something that will forever elude me if self-fulfillment is pursued apart from the Origin and Ground of self.

Contemplative Psychology

Not by any means a major system of psychology, contemplative psychology is the name Gerald May has given to his efforts to develop a spiritual perspective on psychological experience. Drawing particularly on the wisdom of the ancient contemplative literature of the Western and Eastern spiritual traditions, he has suggested the contours of a psychology that would rely on intuition while continuing to respect other traditional modes of knowing such as observation and logical inference. He suggests that the goal of contemplative psychology is not to solve mystery but to appreciate it; to seek to know, experience, love, and nurture it even in the absence of understanding it.[21] Contemplative psychology draws its name from contemplative spirituality, which May defines as the willingness and courage to open oneself to mystery.

Basic to May's discussion of the attitudes behind a contemplative approach to psychology or spirituality is the distinction he draws between willingness and willfulness. *Willingness* is openness to surrender to a reality greater than oneself and readiness to relinquish the idea that one can actually master life. As such it is a surrender of separateness. In contrast, *willfulness* is an attempt to master one's own destiny and control or manipulate existence. In brief, "Willingness is saying yes to the mystery of being alive in each moment. Willfulness is saying no, or perhaps more commonly, 'Yes but.'"[22]

The relationship between spirituality and mystery is important for May. He argues that spirit and mystery are closely related. Mystery may not always be spiritual, but there is no doubt that spirituality is always mysterious. The search for an experiential appreciation of the meaning of life is a spiritual quest, and if it is followed deeply enough, it will inevitably come upon mystery.

Religion and spirituality are also closely related. He suggests:

> Religion can exist without spirituality if it consists only of standards of conduct, non-experiential theology and rituals that are practiced for no felt reason. . . . A spiritual quest becomes decidedly religious only when one begins to identify a relationship with the Ultimate Spirit or Mystery and when that relationship begins to manifest itself in specific behaviors such as worship. . . . No spiritual quest can progress very far without becoming religious.[23]

May suggests that the keystone of contemplative spirituality is what he calls the "unitive experience." This is the experience of a momentary loss of self-definition accompanied by some degree of self-transcendence. In these moments, all mental activity seems to be temporarily suspended, and the person feels caught up in a state of awe or wonder and possibly fear or anxiety. However, there is also a pervasive sense of being-at-one. Unitive experiences appear to be a universal spiritual phenomenon. May reports that when interviewed in depth and asked the right questions, virtually everyone can report one or two such experiences.

The reason these experiences are important for spirituality is that they are an especially clear example of the difference between willingness and willfulness. Unitive experiences cannot be willfully produced; they can only be willingly accepted. They are a gift of grace. As such, they illustrate the surrender that characterizes genuine spiritual experience.

In its most basic form, May suggests the spiritual quest to be a search for our roots. Human spiritual longing is realizing that we have forgotten who we are, accepting that, and searching for our place. May points out that psychology cannot address this quest without reducing it to some kind of need-meeting, narcissistic process. Only religion can help us understand such spiritual questing. Then we understand "that the frenzy of searching is not really needed, that in fact we have already been found."[24] Searching will usually continue, but slowly searching comes to be superseded by surrender. May continues:

> The [spiritual] longing hovers around the edges of daily awareness, kept alive by occasional spiritual experiences and momentary recollections of the "home" that existed before self-definition and independent identity were established. The longing for reunion with this "home" is marginally available to awareness but most of the time we are so preoccupied with other issues that we fail to notice it.[25]

While not labeling his work as contemplative psychology, the writings of William McNamara closely parallel those of May. Drawing his psychological insights from the realm of Christian mysticism, McNamara defines the goal of Christian spirituality as the realization of union with God. He argues that in this alone lies the ultimate fulfillment of human personality; this is the answer to life's deepest yearnings.

Of particular importance is McNamara's discussion of the deep center of personality. Is it spirit, or is it Spirit? He answers:

> The centre of the soul is not God, but it is so intimately grounded in God that it can and sometimes is mistaken for God himself. The centre is the created ground of being grounded in God's Uncreated Being. . . . This most profound and sacred depth of the soul is the dwelling place of God. It is in this divine centre that we are made in his likeness. Nothing can fill or satisfy this centre except God himself. At this centre God is more real than man is.[26]

Drawing on the richness of Christian mysticism, McNamara and May offer us a perspective on spirituality that is compatible with and at the same time enriches that offered by the other theorists considered in this chapter. Once again we are presented with spirituality as deep longings that can ultimately only be fulfilled in self-transcendence. Humans in and of themselves appear to be incomplete. Our deepest yearnings appear to drive us beyond ourselves for their fulfillment. These yearnings are usually called spiritual yearnings because their satisfaction requires that we transcend the ordinary modes of life. They call us to something higher and yet something deeper at the same time. They call us into the depths of ourselves, and yet they call us out and beyond ourselves. These are the mysteries of spiritual longings.

Integrated Spirituality

This review of several of the systems of psychology that address spirituality demonstrates that spirituality does not need to stand outside the domain of psychology. Spiritual longings occur within the very heart of personality; they are not the stirrings of some part of persons independent of the rest of personality. They can, therefore, be studied psychologically. Even if this point of reference does not afford an ultimate or complete understanding of spirituality, it does contribute to our understanding of its nature and place within personality.

There is a surprising degree of consensus among the theorists whom we have reviewed about the nature of spirituality. All seem to agree that spirituality is associated with an integration of interior life (ideally including all the diverse aspects of personality) and external behavior. All also agree that this includes moving beyond the false selves that we create and then confuse with our true self. With the exception of Jung, all the others also agree that the transcendence of false selves and the integration of personality can only occur when the self is dependent on God. Only when self, or spirit, is grounded in Spirit do we find our true self, our self-in-God. The spiritual quest is thus understood as the quest for our place and for our identity—a quest that may not appear overtly spiritual but that is spiritual given what these theorists assert to be the only satisfactory solution to this quest.

How does this understanding of spirituality relate to historic Christian understandings? And how does Christian spirituality relate to other non-Christian, or even nonreligious, spiritualities? Even more basically, how are we to understand the concept of spirituality? These are the questions to which we now turn.

5

Christian Spirituality

In our review of psychological understandings of the spiritual dimension of persons, we encountered a variety of understandings of the term *spirituality*. Before developing a Christian perspective on the matter, it might be helpful, therefore, to be clear on what is meant by *spirituality*. Doing so should also provide a framework for understanding the relationship of Christian spirituality to other spiritualities.

Spirituality and Spiritualities

Most generally, *spirituality* can be defined as the human quest for and experience of meaning, God, and the other. Spirituality is an expression of a yearning for connections that we unconsciously recognize will clarify the meaning of our existence and secure our identity and its fulfillment. To be human is to be driven by a deep and foundational longing for coherence and purpose to life and one's identity. Spiritual longings arise out of our awareness that we have forgotten who we are and where we belong. We seem, however, to have a faint archetypal memory of the place where we belong, and it is somewhere other than self and involves a relationship with someone transcendent to self.

Spirituality is also, therefore, an expression of a yearning for surrender. We seem to need to be in the service of something or someone bigger than the self. At some deep level we appear to recognize the wisdom of Jesus' teaching that in order to find our life we must first lose it. Although we also are driven by a powerful egocentric desire to surrender nothing to anyone in our quest to construct our own autonomous self, at the same time, we seem to know that the places we can create through our own efforts are too small to afford either significant purpose or enduring identity. In self-transcendent surrender, we suddenly recognize that we have found both meaning to life and a framework for a cohesive identity; we suddenly recognize that we have found our place and our true self.

Put another way, spirituality can be thought of as a person's experience of and response to the Divine. All persons are created spiritual beings. This means that all persons have some awareness of the Divine. Their only choice is how they respond to this awareness. To be human is to face the inescapable challenge of working out our existence in relation to God. Created for relationship with, surrender to, and loving service of God, our only choice is to which god we give ourselves and our service. It may be that we serve the true God, our creator, or it may be that we serve an idol, whether this be ourselves or some part of the rest of creation. But serve we must, and our response to this call to service and surrender defines our spirituality and our identity. Choices of ultimate allegiance and surrender are spiritual choices, and life cannot be lived without making them. We are free in will and spirit only within the bounds of our heart's allegiances.

Spirituality is foundational to humanity. To describe someone as spiritual and someone else as nonspiritual is simply to acknowledge their differing awareness of and response to their inherent spiritual nature. A spiritual person is one who listens to the longings in the depths of his or her soul and seeks to respond to them. The nonspiritual person is not devoid of spiritual yearning but has merely chosen to ignore them. By means of any of the many available distractions that serve to cut us off from our depths, such a person lives his or her life in the external world with little attention to inner spiritual realities.

Not all spirituality is religious, however, and not all religious spirituality is Christian. Gerald May suggests that the spiritual quest only becomes religious when the individual begins to experience his or her self in relationship with some higher power and responds to this relationship with prayer or worship.[1] Christian spirituality, a subset of religious spiritualities, involves a state of deep relationship with God made possible through faith in Jesus Christ and the life of the indwelling Holy Spirit. The relationship of these various spiritualities is graphically represented in figure 1.

Figure 1
Types of Spirituality

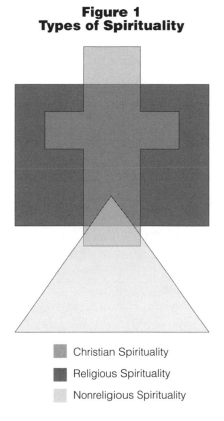

Christian Spirituality

Religious Spirituality

Nonreligious Spirituality

The most basic form of spirituality is what I would call nonreligious spirituality. This is the quest for self-transcendence and surrender—a quest that is a fundamental part of our being as creatures made in the image of God. It is quite possible to become aware of these longings and yet fail to recognize their ultimate significance, that is, the fact that they represent the voice of God within calling us back to relationship with himself. Persons who are aware of these longings and who are responsive to them are undoubtedly more alive, more fully human, and better off psychologically than persons who have no such awareness. However, from a Christian point of view, such persons are still outside the intimate relationship with God to which their longings were intended to direct them.

Religious spirituality involves a relationship with the power or being who serves as the focus of self-transcendence and meaning for life. Spirituality here explicitly includes prayer or meditation and worship. Contrary to their claims, much of what occurs within groups such as Alcoholics Anonymous appears to support a religious spirituality. Those seeking help are encouraged to turn over control of their lives to a higher power and then to develop a relationship with this power through meditation and prayer. While it appears possible to encourage a nonreligious spirituality, and some applications of the Alcoholics Anonymous concept may in fact be doing this, Gerald May notes that no spiritual quest can progress very far without becoming religious.[2]

In Christian spirituality, the probings and responses to the deep spiritual longings are carried out within the context of Christian faith and community. This allows the spiritual yearnings to be recognized as the call of Spirit to spirit and nourishes and directs the subsequent journey.

The essence of Christian spirituality is the deep relationship with God that occurs when the human spirit is grounded in the Holy Spirit. Spiritual growth is movement into a deeper and closer relationship with God. As this occurs, our wills and characters are increasingly conformed to God's will and character, and we become more whole. Contrary to some caricatures of Christian spirituality, as we become more like God we do not become less human. Rather, as we come home to God we find our true selves and become more fully human. Spiritual growth is thus closely related to psychological growth. To grow into a deeper relationship with God is to find our place, identity, and purpose and to discover a point of reference for the integration of our personality.

Christian Ways of Experiencing God

Even a cursory familiarity with the history of Christian spirituality demonstrates a great variety of understandings and experience. In fact, this history reveals such diversity that it is sometimes interpreted as a history of spiritualities in the plural. However, it is probably more accurately interpreted as reflecting different ways of experiencing God.

In his book *A History of Christian Spirituality*, Urban Holmes argues that the variety of ways in which Christians have learned to experience God can be profitably viewed in relationship to two bipolar scales: a kataphatic/apophatic scale and a speculative/affective scale.[3] The first two dimensions describe techniques of spiritual growth while the second two describe the primary focus of these techniques.

Kataphatic and apophatic refer to the two classic approaches to meditation. Kataphatic spirituality is based on the active use of the imagination. Within this tradition, the Christian identifies positive images of God and uses these images as a tool for meditation. For example, meditation might take the form of visualizing Christ as the Good Shepherd. Additional details in this image might possibly include his carrying a wounded sheep or his searching the lonely hills for a lost one. Other senses might also be involved by imagining the sounds of the hillside, the coolness of the mountain air, or the hunger experienced by the self-sacrificing shepherd.

Other images of God that could be used as a basis for kataphatic meditation are God as love, God as light, God as fire, God as father, God as mother, God as justice, or God as mercy. Christian traditions that have most closely been identified with kataphatic spirituality are medieval monastics (i.e., Gregory the Great), fourteenth century mystics (i.e., Richard Rolle and Julian of Norwich), and the sixteenth-century Spanish mystics (particularly Ignatius of Loyola and Teresa of Avila).

In contrast to the kataphatic method, apophatic spirituality is based on an emptying technique of meditation. Rather than focusing on images that symbolize some aspect of God, the emphasis in apophatic approaches is on what God is not. God is not merely a heavenly father; he is much more than this. Nor is he exhaustively represented by the imagery of the shepherd. These, and all other images, are judged to be imperfect and dangerous misrepresentations of his being. In the apophatic tradition, God is encountered as mystery. He is an elusive or hidden God who, while having revealed himself to us, is still only encountered in obscure awareness. While kataphatic spirituality affirms the knowability of God and the intimacy humans can have with him, apophatic spirituality warns of the dangers of glib overfamiliarity and the idolatrous assumption that the reality of God can be captured in words or symbols.

The goal of apophatic spirituality is to experience union with God. What is discovered in this experience of God is not so much knowledge as love. God is discovered to be incomprehensible to our intellects but not to our love. Examples of this tradition include Eastern Orthodox spirituality, the fourteenth-century Meister Eckhart, and from the same period, the unknown English priest who authored *The Cloud of Unknowing*.

The speculative/affective scale is the second dimension suggested by Holmes for understanding the variety of ways in which Christians approach God and expect to meet him in their lives. Speculative approaches to spirituality are those traditions that emphasize the illumination of the mind (or intellect) while affective approaches emphasize illumination of the heart (or emotions).

Speculative spirituality emphasizes encountering God with the mind and is thus usually associated with a rational and propositional theology. Speculative spirituality is seen in much of Eastern Orthodox Christianity and most Western Protestant Christianity. It is perhaps seen most clearly in Reformed (Calvinist) Christians who affirm the importance of knowing God through his self-revelation in Scripture. In this tradition, God is not primarily experienced in some nonrational or emotional manner. Rather, he is encountered with the mind and is known through the study of his Word, the Bible. Speculative approaches to spirituality tend to be strong on theology and often somewhat weaker on the direct experience of God.

Affective spirituality emphasizes a direct encounter with God in experience. God is met in the heart rather than in the head. Knowing about God is judged to be a poor substitute for actually knowing and experiencing God personally. Examples of such a "heart religion" can be found throughout the history of Christianity, ranging from the early Desert Fathers of the fourth and fifth centuries to modern-day neo-Pentecostals and charismatics, both Roman Catholic and Protestant. In all its manifestations, the affective approach to spirituality tends to be strong on the experience of God and somewhat weaker on theology or systematic biblical reflection on that experience. The study of doctrine and theology is secondary to the direct experience of God. When theology is emphasized, it focuses on the nonrational aspects of the experience of God.

It should be noted that the distinction between head and heart suggested by the second dimension of Holmes's model may be artificial and even misleading. Contemporary psychological understandings of emotions suggest that they include both cognitions and feelings; they are matters, therefore, of both head and heart. This is, in fact, born out by the examples associated with the speculative/affective dimension in the above paragraphs. Eastern Orthodox Christianity is not devoid of emotion, and John Calvin certainly had a religion of both heart and head. Thus, while attempts to classify religious experience by this dichotomy are common, the dangers of such distinctions should be kept in mind.

Holmes does acknowledge that two scales and four associated ways of experiencing God are closely interrelated. It is difficult to describe functioning on one scale without reference to the other. His depiction of their relationship is presented in figure 2. He suggests that full-orbed spirituality should ideally contain a balance of all four of these ways of experiencing God—represented by the circle in the center of the figure. Problems in spirituality are associated with movement beyond this circle of balance. Four specific dangers of such loss of balance are suggested by this model. Rationalism is the result of an exaggerated speculative/kataphatic spirituality,

Pietism of exaggerated kataphatic/affective spirituality, quietism of exaggerated apophatic/affective spirituality, and encratism (extreme asceticism) of exaggerated speculative/apophatic spirituality.

Figure 2
Ways of Experiencing God
and Their Associated Dangers

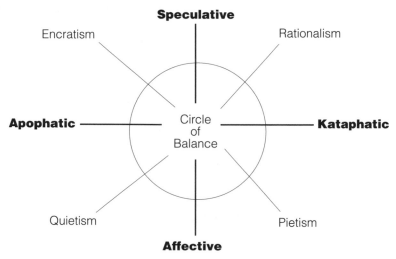

From Urban Holmes, *A History of Christian Spirituality* (New York: Seabury, 1980), 4.

Perhaps the value of this model is not so much its contribution to analysis and classification as its contribution to the understanding of the breadth of Christian spirituality. There is clearly no single way of encountering or experiencing the Christian God. Human personhood is too complex and diverse and God too big for our encounter with him to be simple, precisely patterned, or predictable.

What Is Christian Spirituality?

For all its breadth and despite important similarities that it shares with other spiritualities, Christian spirituality has a number of distinctive characteristics. Christian spirituality:

1. begins with a response of the call of Spirit to spirit
2. is rooted in a commitment to Jesus and a transformational approach to life
3. is nurtured by the means of grace
4. involves a deep knowing of Jesus and, through him, the Father and the Spirit
5. requires a deep knowing of oneself
6. leads to the realization of the unique self whom God ordained we should be
7. is uniquely developed within the context of suffering
8. is manifest by a sharing of the goodness of God's love with others and in care for his creation
9. expresses that goodness in celebration in Christian community

Let us consider each of these in turn as we attempt to better understand the spiritual context within which Christian soul care is offered.

1. *Christian spirituality begins with a response to the call of Spirit to spirit.* The essence of the Christian spiritual quest is eloquently summarized in St. Augustine's observation that "our soul is restless until it finds rest in thee, O Lord; for thou hast made us for thyself."[4] Made in God's image, humans are incomplete until they find themselves in relationship to the God who created them for intimate communion with himself. For Christians, this is the ultimate meaning and purpose of life.

The restlessness noted by St. Augustine is not always experienced as a response to the call of God's Spirit to ours. Sometimes we experience it as a quest for meaning, happiness, success, truth, perfection, place, fulfillment, coherence, surrender, belonging, transcendence, purpose, or the discovery of our deepest and truest self. At other times it is experienced more directly as a longing to know God or a desire to receive his forgiveness. But regardless of how we experience this restlessness, Christians affirm that the initiative in the matter is with God. It is his Spirit who calls to us, even when we experience the initiative as ours. Whether quietly and gently or with passion and immediacy, God's Spirit calls to ours, inviting us to turn to him and discover our true place, purpose, and identity.

The first step in a spiritual response to these yearnings involves learning to be still. The divine advice to "be still, and know that I am God" (Ps. 46:10) reminds us of the necessity of quietness and solitude in the discernment of the spiritual call. This also remains important for all subsequent steps on the journey, but the journey never begins if we fail to stop and listen to the messages from the depths of our soul. It is here that we encounter God, for it is here that we discern the call of his Spirit. If we are incapable of being quiet long enough to hear his still, small voice, we will remain victims of our compulsive busyness, which is always the enemy of spiritual depth.

The fact that our spiritual yearnings are often not obviously spiritual in nature has important implications for soul care. Issues that appear to be primarily psychological in nature often have a deeper spiritual significance. The first steps of response to the call of Spirit to spirit are often not consciously spiritual. But when we experience these yearnings and begin to respond to them, we are responding to the call of God's Spirit and are taking the first steps on a journey that may, if guided by his Spirit, turn out to be a journey of Christian spirituality.

2. *Christian spirituality is rooted in a commitment to Jesus and a transformational approach to life.* Christian spirituality is not a philosophy, religious posture, or psychospiritual technique. Nor is it something that can fit comfortably with the rest of one's life without changing the whole. Radical transformation is at the very core of life in Christ, and Christian spirituality is rooted in a commitment to Christ and an openness to the transformed life he offers to and expects of his followers.

Christian spirituality is, thus, well represented not only by the image of a journey but also by images of growth, development, and transformation. Christian spirituality is not simply a state; it is better thought of as a process. The process of Christian growth is empowered by the Holy Spirit—the Spirit of Jesus—and is directed toward the transformation of one into his image. This transformation begins with repentance and commitment to Christ, who is made an integral part of one's inner and outer life. The Spirit of Christ then becomes the engine of the spiritual change that subsequently begins to occur in both these inner and outer aspects of self.

3. *Christian spirituality is nurtured by the means of grace.* If we stay for a moment with this organic image of Christian spirituality as a growth process, the nourishment for spiritual growth comes to us by what are called the means of grace. Scriptures, prayer, the sacraments, and Christian fellowship all serve as media through which grace may be uniquely received. Properly understood, it is important to recognize that none of these things mechanically transmit God's grace in and of themselves. To be rightly received, they must be received with faith and gratitude. When received in this manner, they become channels of God's grace that nourish our spiritual growth and direct our spiritual journey.

The primary means of grace is Scripture. This is where we receive the communication of the gospel as well as where God's revelation of himself and of ourselves to us both begin. Engagement with Scripture is, therefore, essential if we are to know God, ourselves, and his will for us.

Prayer builds on and flows naturally out of an engagement with God as he reveals himself in Scripture. Prayer is not simply talking to God. More fundamentally, it is the attunement of the heart to his presence. Prayer is the place in which the deepest part of us touches and is touched by God. In prayer, God's Spirit prays in and through us. Even our response to God requires his grace and reflects the empowering of his Spirit.

The two other major means of grace are the sacraments and Christian fellowship. With a few minor exceptions, almost all Christian traditions celebrate at least baptism and communion. When these practices are viewed as sacraments, they are understood to be an outward and visible sign of an inward and spiritual grace. This is what it means to speak of them as means of grace.

Finally, the important place of fellowship in Christian spirituality reminds us that the Christian's relationship with God is not a personal possession. Christian spirituality is corporate spirituality, and fellowship with other Christians is one of the means of receiving divine grace. Do-it-yourself spirituality, so common in much contemporary Christianity, is not biblical Christian spirituality. Life in Christ is life in Christian community.

4. *Christian spirituality involves a deep knowing of Jesus and, through him, the Father and the Spirit.* Christian spirituality is not simply a knowing about God, it is knowing God. Familiarity with ideas about God is no substitute for direct experiential knowing of him. Christian spirituality is grounded in knowing, not knowledge.

Because God is love, to know him is to love him and to love him is to know him. Knowing God, therefore, is not simply a matter of the head. It is also a matter of the heart. The foundation of this heart knowing must be personal knowledge of God's love. To know God's love personally is to be filled with his nature (Eph. 3:19). This is the transformational knowing that Scriptures tell us is the essence of eternal life (John 17:3).

Knowing God requires that we believe that God wants to be known. God does not hide from us but continuously reaches out to us, seeking to communicate with us. One of the great surprises in the character of the Christian God is that he tells us that he desires to know us and be known by us.

While God reaches out to us, he is also boundless mystery. There is no one else like God. To describe God as holy is to note that he is separate, wholly other. Mystery makes some people uncomfortable. They want a tidy God who is easily confined within dogmatic formulations. However, such a God of our own making evokes no wonder, and the lives of his followers are empty of both surprise and awe.

Knowing God starts with knowing Jesus. Jesus was described by the apostle Paul as "the image of the invisible God . . . in him all the fullness of God was pleased to dwell" (Col. 1:15, 19). Through both word and deed, Jesus introduces us to what God is really like. Archbishop Michael Ramsay has been quoted as saying, "God is Christlike and in him is no un-Christlikeness at all." This means that every idea of God must be measured against the person of Jesus, for to know Jesus is to know his Spirit and his Father.

Christian spirituality involves the grounding of the human spirit in the divine Spirit. Spirituality that is not rooted in the Holy Spirit is not Christian. This is consistent with the biblical use of the term *spirituality*, which implies life in and of the Spirit. Spirituality that does not ground spirit in Spirit is not Christian.

God is only known through openness, surrender, and receptivity. He is not known through logic, analysis, or control. Knowledge about God may be subject to logical analysis, but knowing is more than knowledge. It is this personal knowing of God that is essential for Christian spirituality. Theology is a poor substitute for direct experience of God, as are ideas about someone for personal encounter with him or her.

5. *Christian spirituality requires a deep knowing of oneself.* John Calvin begins book 1, chapter 1 of his *Institutes of the Christian Religion* with a bold assertion. He argues that knowing God and knowing self are very closely connected. In fact, he goes so far as to assert that without knowledge of self there is no true knowledge of God, and without knowledge of God there is no true knowledge of self.[5]

The radical nature of this assertion lies in the prominence it gives to the knowing of self in Christian spirituality. This has often been a neglected component of the Christian spiritual journey. But how frightening the consequences have been when people have thought they could know God apart from any real knowing of themselves. The result has been outward postures of piety that are dramatically incongruent with the actual state of the inner world. This lack of authenticity is usually apparent to everyone other than the individual, who defends against such awareness by an increasing reliance on denial and projection. This, in turn, leads to rigidity and an ever widening gap between inner reality and outer appearances.

Genuine Christian spirituality takes very seriously the knowing of oneself. This is the deep connection between spiritual and psychological wholeness. Calvin asserts that the limits of self-knowledge will be the limits on one's knowledge of God. This reflects sound psychology. People who are afraid to look deeply at themselves will of course be equally afraid to look deeply and personally at God. For such persons, ideas about God provide a substitute for direct experience of him.

How do we come to know ourselves? First, self is ultimately only intelligible in relationship to both God and other people. Created for relationship with God, any self we think we discover apart from this relationship is ultimately a false and incomplete self. Discovery of this true self, our self-in-Christ, is made possible by God knowing us. He then reveals our true self to us.

The first step to knowing myself in relation to God is knowing myself as known by God. How does God see me when he looks at me? The answer to this question will determine a great deal about the rest of my relationship to God. The biblical answer is that first and foremost we must realize that God views us with love. Fearfully and wonderfully knit together in our mother's womb by the hand of God, watched over so that not a hair of our head falls out without his awareness, pursued when we ignore and reject him, and deeply loved even while we were yet sinners—in these ways, God assures us that he is unequivocally for us. He loves us with a depth and faithfulness that we cannot imagine. This must be the foundation of our knowing of our self.

But knowing our self as known by God also forces us to acknowledge the reality of our sin. Much more than the things we do, the core of our sin is based in the mistaken belief that we can be like God without God. Repeating the mistake of our first parents, we all seek to be like God without submission to him. We all want to live our life independent of God and total surrender to his will. In so doing, we seek to be our own god; we seek to be as God. James Finley notes that

> any expression of self-proclaimed likeness to God is forbidden us, not because it breaks some law arbitrarily decreed by God, but because such an action is tantamount to a fundamental, death-dealing ontological lie. We are not God. We are not our own origin, nor are we our own ultimate fulfilment. To claim to be so is a suicidal act that wounds our faith relationship with the living God and replaces it with a futile faith in a self that can never exist.[6]

Genuine knowing of self also requires that we experience ourselves in relationships with other people. Some people approach the knowing of self like the peeling of an onion. Examining the self in isolation rather than within relationships, they try to peel back its layers, ultimately resulting in its dismantling, not its discovery. Self is a gift that is given to us by others; it is not a creation of our own. When we set out to discover a self apart from relationships with others, we are setting out to create a false self. Genuine self-knowledge will always involve knowing ourselves in relationships. This requires being in intimate relationships and knowing how to reflect on our experiences within them. It also involves deep knowing of others.

The Western psychology of the self has been greatly influenced by Descartes's dictum, "I think, therefore I am." This makes self dependent only on the self and its capacity for thinking (self-reflection). In contrast to this, the African spiritual philosophy of Ubuntu states, "I am because we are; we are because I am." This makes self dependent on other selves. It means, "I am a person because there are other persons around me." In such a view—a view much closer to the Christian understanding of self than that of Descartes—selfhood, personhood, and humanity itself are gifts received from others. There is no meaningful development, discovery, or actualization of the self apart from intimate relationship with these significant others.

A deep knowing of ourselves also requires that we come face-to-face with the shadow aspects of our personality. In any genuine encounter with the self, we will encounter much that is unpleasant and some things that will be quite frightening. Christian spirituality involves acknowledging our many part-selves and exposing them to the light of God's love. There, God is able to embrace them with his grace, gather them together around himself, and slowly weave them into the new person he is making.

Furthermore, deep knowing of self also requires that we embark on a journey of understanding and undoing our characteristic strategies of self-deception. Scripture affirms what psychology demonstrates: "The heart is deceitful above all things" (Jer. 17:9). It is hard to overestimate the human capacity for self-deception. Our ability to deceive others is noteworthy but retreats into insignificance when compared to our ability to deceive ourselves. How is it that pediatricians can sexually abuse children in their care while remaining in practice and active on medical ethics task forces? Or how can church treasurers steal from congregational offerings, or televangelists so easily and habitually commit the very sins they most denounce?

That which shocks us in others is typically overlooked in ourselves, even if what we face in ourselves may appear to be of a lesser magnitude. If we are honest, we too must admit that we routinely lie to ourselves and bend the truth to reshape reality into a form we find more acceptable. Whether by means of rationalizations (plausible but not actual reasons for behavior), repression or denial (an outright refusal to accept something unpleasant), or projection (the attribution to others of motives and feelings we refuse to accept in ourselves), we attempt to deceive ourselves. Understanding the characteristic ways in which we do this is an essential part of knowing ourselves. It is also, obviously, a first step toward living our lives in the light of truth rather than the darkness of illusion.

Finally, a genuine knowing of the self only comes from engaging with, rather than running from, experiences of darkness, suffering, and struggle. If we run from pain, we run from knowing ourselves. Similarly, if we run from our anxieties, compulsions, and depressions rather than entering into them and wrestling with God in the midst of them, we never know ourselves in a true and deep way. Symptoms are the voice of the soul. Learning to prayerfully listen to them, along with our dreams and patterns of reaction to people and events, is an important means of attending to our soul. Deep knowing of self is impossible without learning to listen to these messages from the deepest recesses of our inner world.

It is important to remember that self-knowledge is simply the means, not the end, of Christian spirituality. The goal of self-knowledge is self-transformation. There are no shortcuts to such self-transformation. In the final analysis, it is the result of a lifelong commitment to honesty, self-examination, prayer, and growth. This is the only route to a genuine knowing and growth of self, and this is an essential part of any spirituality that seeks to integrate our religious life with the rest of our being.

6. *Christian spirituality leads to the realization of the unique self whom God ordained we should be.* The goal of Christian spirituality is fundamentally at odds with that of spiritualities that lead toward a fusion of self with the Divine. This ultimately results in a loss of self. In sharp contrast to this, Christianity calls for a discovery and actualization of our true self—a self we can only find in Christ.

Christians believe that we originate in God as unique persons and that God calls us in Christ to be ourselves. The problem is in discovering our true self. God leaves us free to be real or unreal. He leaves us free to be any self we choose to be, but we cannot make these choices with impunity. Thomas Merton points out, "If we lie to ourselves and others we cannot expect to find truth and reality whenever we happen to want them. If we have chosen the way of falsity we must not be surprised that truth eludes us when we finally come to need it."[7]

The goal of Christian spirituality is sometimes presented as the denial of self. Properly understood, the denial that is a part of Christian spirituality is not of self but of false selves. False selves are the egocentric, willful ways of being that we create in an attempt to live life independent of God, apart from his love, and beyond the reach of his will. As such, they are ultimately illusions, but they are illusions that block us from psychospiritual vitality. To crucify our false selves is to give up our attempt to be master of our own destiny, captain of our own ship. It is to surrender to God's will for us and to his love.

Our Christian calling is to work with God toward the creation of our true self. The exciting thing about this work is that we do not know beforehand what the result will be. Our true self is hidden in Christ. But we do know that this true self-in-Christ will enhance our originality, fulfill our humanity, and satisfy our search for identity.

Adrian van Kaam speaks most eloquently about the way in which the call to be like Christ is a call to originality. He states:

Each person is called to become his own self and yet to become at-one with God. I must become the unique person I am meant to be. The more I become what my Creator called me to be originally, the more I will be united with my Divine Origin. This union with my Origin deepens my originality. Mine is an originality that God wills from eternity. He originated me as precisely this person and nobody else.[8]

My life in Christ will be an original one, absolutely unique. It will be based on the distinctives of the temperament, interpersonal style, and personality that God has already given me. And it will be the unique reflection of his image that he has designed from eternity that I should be.

It is also important to note, however, that my true self-in-Christ will fulfill my humanity. Christian spirituality does not call for the renunciation of humanness, trading humanity for divinity. It does not make us less human but more. There is great potential danger in losing sight of our humanity as we strive to be more like God. Not accepting the limitations of humanity and striving to be like God was the sin committed by our first parents in the Garden of Eden. God does not ask that we become God. Instead, he offers his help to become fully human.

Finally, we should note that the discovery and actualization of our true self-in-Christ will satisfy our search for our identity and vocation. Dag Hammarskjöld, former Secretary-General of the United Nations, describes this as follows:

> Body and soul contain a thousand possibilities out of which you can build many I's. But in only one of them is there a congruence of the elector and the elected. Only one—which you will never find until you have excluded all those superficial and fleeting possibilities of being and doing with which you toy, out of curiosity or wonder or greed, and which hinder you from casting anchor in the experience of the mystery of life, and the consciousness of the talent entrusted to you which is your I.[9]

7. *Christian spirituality is uniquely developed within the context of suffering.* Christianity does not promise health, wealth, and prosperity. It is much more realistic than that. God does not promise to remove trouble from us but to be with us when we experience either suffering or blessing. Consequently, Christian spirituality not only embraces success but also suffering. In fact, it points out

that experiences of suffering and struggle often contain unique opportunities for spiritual growth.

In baptism we identify with Christ, and in profession of faith we declare ourselves to be a Christ follower. But who was this Christ whose life we take as ours? The Apostles' Creed reminds us that he suffered, died, was buried, descended into hell, and on the third day rose again. The life with which we identify in baptism is, therefore, a life of suffering, death, hell, and resurrection. It is within the context of struggle, not success, where we should expect to primarily meet the God who comes to us as the Suffering Servant.

In Christ's cross we confront a God who seeks to be known as a broken being—suffering, destitute, humiliated, and abandoned. Christopher Levan asks, "Can we put our faith in a God who so loves the world that participation in its pain is the starting point of divine revelation and action?"[10] If we rightly understand the revelation of the cross, we will understand that it is within suffering— our own and that of others—that Christ reveals himself. Martin Luther emphasized that the road to a genuine knowing of God must always start with knowing God's suffering in the world. Only when we stand with those who suffer pain, humiliation, starvation, and poverty and look at the world through their experience will we truly know the God who came into the world to share human pain.

Openness to suffering is really openness to life. Suffering is an inevitable part of life, and if we are to be open to any of life, we must be open to it all. If we run from pain in ourself and others, we will never know peace or joy with any real depth. Openness to life means living it with willingness, not willfulness. Willingness involves surrender to a reality greater than oneself and relinquishment of the idea that a person can actually master life. As such it is the surrender of separateness. In contrast, willfulness is the setting apart of oneself from the deepest reality in an attempt to master one's own destiny and control and manipulate existence. Christ is the epitome of life lived with willingness. Christian spirituality invites us to take up his attitude: "Not my will but thine be done."

8. *Christian spirituality is manifest by a sharing of the goodness of God's love with others and in care for his creation.* Christian spiritual-

ity is not a private religious experience but participation in God's redemptive plan for creation. It will be marked, therefore, by love for God and others and care for God's creation.

Alistair Campbell notes that a proper understanding of Christian vocation is always

> a response to grace which takes us back to our place in the world and to a joy in caring for others. It is the response of people who were once captive but now released (redeemed), who were estranged but now find closeness (reconciled), whose world was shattered, but is now made whole (saved). This response rediscovers the goodness in creation and so restores a sense of vocation based on gifts and gratitude.[11]

Christian spirituality moves us into the world. Spirituality that is oblivious to the suffering and injustice of the world is not Christian spirituality. Christians who experience God deeply in their lives do not just pray and worship, they also care for the poor and the disenfranchised and seek the correction or amelioration of social evils. And they do so as a response to love, not as a legalistic obligation.

We are not called to give to the poor or love those who are unlovable simply because they are less fortunate than we are. Condescension or pity are not the motives of Christian charity. Christian charity is grounded in the theology of the cross that, we just noted, means that God is somehow particularly present in those who suffer. Christian charity is offering a cup of cold water to my fellow human who thirsts, knowing that in some mysterious way it is Christ who thirsts and it is Christ who receives my gift of love.

Christian spirituality is also manifest in care of God's creation. Questions about how best to respond to global crises of pollution, biological depletion, overpopulation, and resource scarcity are all spiritual questions. Christian spirituality involves participation in God's kingdom plan for the restoration of the totality of his creation. It should include an environmental ethic that flows out of a commitment to justice, peace, and stewardship. It should also be directed toward the biblical standard of shalom, that is, peace and wholeness. This standard applies to the natural world as well as to humans and their relationships.

9. *Christian spirituality expresses that goodness in celebration in Christian community.* Celebration and community are the context of mature Christian spirituality. Not only does Christian spirituality move us from the sanctuary to the world, so too it moves us from self-encapsulation to engagement in Christian community. One cannot be spiritually whole without a relationship to a faith community. The church protects and affirms spiritual growth and is an indispensable part of its nurture and celebration. Acts of corporate worship have the potential to be profoundly powerful resources for soul care.

In summary, it should be apparent that Christian spirituality relates to all of life and should affect all of life. As noted by Dallas Willard, "Spirituality in human beings is not an extra or 'superior' mode of existence . . . a hidden stream of separate reality, a separate life running parallel to our bodily existence."[12] Spirituality is as basic to humanity as embodiment. Created of dust and the breath of God, we cannot escape from either. Our spirituality cannot be divorced from any aspect of life; it infuses and permeates all aspects of our being. Our work, our play, our sexuality, our prayers, our humor, our passion, and our aggression all are part of our spiritual life, this being a relationship with God that allows us to find our true identity, our meaning, and our life.

It should also be apparent that our spirituality is situated right in the heart of what we usually think of as the psychological aspects of our functioning. If spirituality is our response to deep foundational yearnings for meaning, identity, connections, and surrender, what part of our psychological functioning could possibly be excluded from such a quest? As we will see more clearly in the next chapter, the spiritual and the psychological interpenetrate so fully that one cannot be meaningfully separated from the other.

Christian spiritual formation has too often neglected the psychological and biological aspects of our existence. When this occurs, people are given a spirituality that is pathological and destructive. Our spirituality is the relationship of our total selves to God. If anything is excluded from our spirituality it will, by necessity, become a dissociated part of self, detached from the rest of our life. Whether this be our body, our unconscious, our emotions, our intellect, our sexuality, or any other part of our self, the result is always the same—a fragmentation of person-hood and an encapsulated spirituality. Christian spirituality either makes us more whole or, if it is contained in some limited sphere of our being, furthers our fragmentation. Only the former is worthy of being associated with the Spirit of Christ who empowers, directs, and gives name to the experience we have been calling Christian spirituality.

6

The Psychospiritual Focus of Soul Care

We earlier noted that while soul care involves the care of whole persons, it is the nurture of the inner psychospiritual life of those persons that is its special focus. Without neglecting the way in which the person's inner life is lived in and influenced by the external world, those who care for souls make the inner world of psychospiritual longings, needs, and problems their primary focus. Working toward the health and well-being of the whole person, they seek to nurture the growth of persons at the core of their being. Health and well-being that begins in the psychospiritual core of personality will affect the whole person, just as unaddressed pathology in this core produces problems throughout the rest of one's being.

Psychospiritual Dynamics of Personality

As we noted in the conclusion to the last chapter, our spirituality is situated right in the heart of what we normally consider to be the psychological aspects of our functioning. Spirituality, even our uniquely Christian spirituality, does not involve some new, extra part of personality through which we relate to the Divine or establish meaning for life. The response that we make to the deep longings for coherence and connectedness that shape the human psyche are spiritual responses, regardless of whether they include overtly religious elements or not. The totality of our being is involved in whatever relationship to the Divine we adopt or posture of meaning and coherence we discover. Furthermore, our relationship with the Divine is mediated by the same psychological processes and mechanisms as those involved in relationships with other people.

The term *psychospiritual* refers to the fact that the inner world has no separate spiritual and psychological compartments. Humans are, in their inner persons, psychospiritual beings. No problem of the inner person is either spiritual or psychological; all problems are psychospiritual. Psychological and spiritual aspects of human functioning are identical. Any segregation of spirituality and psychology is, therefore, both artificial and destructive to the true understanding of persons.

When we speak of the spiritual, we must understand, therefore, that what we refer to is the spiritual face of these psychospiritual dynamics, a dimension that is typically ignored in truncated psychological discourse and analysis. Similarly, when we speak of the psychological, we must understand that what we refer to is the psychological face of these same psychospiritual dynamics, a dimension that is equally neglected in truncated spiritual discourse.

Any psychology that seeks to understand the human condition must address this total range of psychospiritual dynamics. And any theology that seeks to be relevant to the human condition must understand how the Christian spiritual life is, in fact, profoundly relevant to this same total range of psychospiritual dynamics. Psychological and spiritual categories are human inventions, and relatively recent at that. They distort the biblical understanding of the holistic nature of human personhood that we reviewed in chapter 3. The essential assertion of biblical anthropology is that human personhood is of one piece; we are not composed of separate or independent parts, whether these be body and soul, or soul and spirit.

Those who seek to care for others in their depths and totality must unlearn all the false distinctions they have made between psychological and spiritual aspects of persons. They must also learn to recognize and understand psychospiritual dynamics as they emerge in both health and pathology. Most importantly, they must learn to discern the spiritual face of those things that may appear to be simply a psychological matter and the psychological face of those that appear to be simply a spiritual one. So-called "spiritual" needs and problems manifest themselves in and through psychological symptoms and mechanisms, just as so-called "psychological" needs and problems manifest themselves in and through things that are apparently more spiritual. If the focus of soul care dialogue is to be on the inner psychospiritual world, those who care for souls must understand the workings of this world.

Learning to Discern the Spiritual in the Psychological

The understanding of spirituality developed in the last chapter suggests that everyone experiences spiritual longings in one form or another. When they are not consciously experienced as having to do with the Divine, they usually take the form of psychological needs. If we examine these needs carefully, however, we can often discern a spiritual quest at their core. Recognizing this spiritual core then allows us to nourish a response to the needs that is spiritual, not just psychological.

The Quest for Identity

It used to be common to think of the search for identity as an adolescent phenomenon. Yet, while it is true that this is the period of life when identity issues first emerge into the foreground of experience, children also experience identity questions, and many adults go through much of their life continuing to struggle with them.

If in childhood the quest for identity typically takes the form of "Who will I be when I grow up?" in adolescence the search moves from the future to the present. The question in this stage of life is usually, "Who am I?" or even, "Is there a real me?" The panic that often characterizes the asking of these questions is what we tend to associate with the adolescent identity crisis. However, over the course of the next few years the urgency of these questions subsides. An identity of some form is found, and the late adolescent launches into young adulthood caught up with jobs, careers, relationships, and sometimes marriage. These foci allow identity issues to recede from the foreground for a while. The identity question has been temporarily answered by the circumstances of life. I now define myself in terms of my roles: I am my job, my marital status, or possibly my economic status.

Midlife frequently calls for a readjustment of the answers we have previously adopted to core spiritual questions. Identity once again often becomes an issue. After having invested fifteen years in their children or a career, many people begin to ask if that is all there is to life for them. Could they, perhaps, be some quite different person, maybe unmarried, or maybe in a different career, or maybe in a different part of the country? These longings are identity longings. The question is once again, "Who am I? Am I to be defined by the circumstances of my life, or is there something else to me? Could I change my circumstances and fit them to who I feel myself really to be? Would changing the external aspects of my life perhaps be a way to discover the real me?" These questions are spiritual questions, and the search for identity, regardless of the stage of life in which it appears, should be understood to reflect the spiritual quest.

The search for identity is intimately connected with the search for purpose, which is much more visibly a spiritual search. In fact, Victor Frankl argues that the quest for meaning and purpose is the primary manifestation of the spiritual quest.[1] "Who am I?" is only satisfactorily answered when it is answered within the context of a philosophy of life. Existence then has direction, and this is ultimately necessary for stable identity. When the forty-five-year-old businessman asks if there might be any other way to live his life than as that of an identity exclusively wrapped up in his business, he is questioning the purpose of life and, in particular, the purpose of his life. Similarly, when the adolescent asks who she is, she is also asking about the meaning and purpose of her life. The question "Who am I?" is always closely related to the more basic question "Why am I?"

The quest for identity is also a manifestation of the quest for place. "Who am I?" is another way of saying, "Where do I fit in? Where do I belong?" If we look at the pattern of the restlessness of our lives, it is often possible to discern an underlying search for our place as a basic and fundamental theme. Some people change jobs every few years, others change churches, communities, spouses, or lifestyles. Others do not make these changes in their external circumstances but continue to experience themselves as not in their place. They may feel the place they have created for themselves is not where they really belong, but they may not have any idea how to find their way home.

We have forgotten who we are and where we belong, and most of the time we have forgotten that we have forgotten. Our restlessness, however, betrays the presence of this search. We need to feel that we belong somewhere. We are all searching for home, and this search is a very central part of our spiritual questing. Paradise has been lost; only a faint memory of it remains. We long to return but no longer remember the way.

Another aspect of the quest for identity that demonstrates its essentially spiritual nature is the quest for values. To ask, "Who am I?" is to ask, "What do I believe? What are or should be my values?" Values are personal. My values define who I am and serve as central planks in my identity. Only moral philosophers work with values in the abstract. The rest of us relate to values as parts of self. But values, like purpose, clearly move us into the realm of spirituality. Value questions demand that we have a big framework for life, an overall philosophy of life. Whether I value honesty over self-interest and how far I go in pursuing this value depends on how I answer questions about the nature of the ultimate good for myself and others.

Thus we see that one important way in which many people experience their spiritual quest is in terms of a quest for identity and the associated quests for purpose, place, and personal values. While failing to recognize these as part of the spiritual quest, people do, nonetheless, shape their spirit by the answers and solutions they adopt. The pursuit of identity is, therefore, a spiritual pursuit. Because it has implications for the structure of personality, it is also appropriately viewed as a psychological pursuit. However, its spiritual nature is clearly reflected in the manner in which identity, purpose, place, and values all define the direction of personality.

The Quest for Relatedness

The need for relationships is as deep as anything humans experience. Infants who are given adequate amounts of food and water die if they do not receive human contact. Adults surrounded by people all day cry out inside for friendships that will break down the walls of loneliness that imprison them. Although some people seem to function without intimacy or personal relationships, we all yearn for deep and meaningful connections with others.

In the absence of intimate and satisfying personal relationships, our quest for relatedness turns us toward things. We may form attachment to possessions. Money, homes, clothes, cars, and many more things all offer possibilities for attachments. One way or another we seem to need to be related to someone or something outside ourselves. It is as if we recognize at some deep level that we are incomplete in ourself. The self needs people and things outside itself for wholeness.

Technology sometimes forms an interesting bridge between people and things. Males in particular sometimes form a primary attachment to mechanical or technological things, often subsequently using them as a bridge to connect with other men who share their interest. Hobbyists of all sorts connect with each other around common interests, first being connected to things and through them subsequently connected to people.

Computers often form a particularly fascinating bridge in this manner. Many people spend more time each week with their personal computer than they do with all the other people in their life put together. While the computer may appear to be simply a tool to do their job, this does not tell the whole story. If we look carefully, what we are forced to recognize is that such people often relate to their computers in the ways in which others relate to friends. If truth is told, their computer is their closest friend. Interestingly, computers also allow people to connect with each other.

Internet friendships and even courtships are no longer uncommon. Virtual sex has come to replace the real thing for some people. Technology offers the possibility of not just connections to things but also through it, connections to other people. Often technology makes these interpersonal connections safer by rendering them less personal. Nonetheless, it does offer another means of establishing interpersonal relatedness.

Is this need for relatedness psychological or spiritual? Obviously, it is both. Christians affirm that it is a reflection of our having been made in the image of a relational God. We are incomplete in ourselves, and our spiritual yearnings manifest themselves in part as a quest for relatedness. We need to be connected to other people, and we need to be connected to the world around us. Connectedness is basic to spirituality.

The Quest for Happiness

The search for happiness is riddled with paradoxes. Happiness appears to be forever elusive when its attainment is the primary objective. However, when other goals are pursued, happiness is often a by-product. To pursue happiness as a primary goal appears to be a self-defeating venture. We are more likely to find happiness when we forget about it and pursue other things.

Also somewhat paradoxical, it seems that those who experience themselves as continuing to search for happiness are often more in touch with their underlying spiritual yearnings than those who feel satisfied. Those who continue to seek happiness remain sensitive to a longing for fulfillment, a longing that derives from their deepest spiritual needs. On the other hand, those who feel they have found happiness and who feel satisfied with their life are often those for whom the spiritual longings are less intense. Satisfaction breeds complacency, and this is always the enemy of the spiritual journey.

The search for happiness is something with which most people can easily identify. We seem to feel sure that we will recognize happiness when we find it and feel it to be our undeniable right. We certainly seem to know when we don't have it. At those points we feel we have been dealt an unfair deal by life, and we raise our clenched fist to the heavens, demanding a better lot in life. This reveals the extent to which we define happiness in terms of the circumstances of our lives. We feel we would be happy if our cancer was cured, if we had more money, if we had a spouse or a different spouse, or if our kids would stop messing up their lives and ours.

This external focus on the source of happiness is the reason happiness is so elusive. To be cured of our cancer is only to later discover a heart illness. To double our income is to still feel dissatisfied, now seeing that we underestimated how much money we need to be happy. To divorce and remarry is frequently to find oneself facing the same problems and dissatisfactions. This focus on externals is part of the reason some people get depressed on vacations. They spend months telling themselves they are unhappy because of their work, the cold weather, or their boss only to discover that even on the beaches of their vacation paradise, happiness is still elusive.

The search for happiness is a spiritual search. It is a longing for all there is to life, for fullness of life and fullness of personhood. It is a longing born in the deep call from within to live life on a higher plane. It is a call to self-transcendence and to spiritual surrender. Happiness was never meant to be found in things. Ultimately, the call of happiness is a call to the deep joy in life that is found when one discovers one's place, purpose, and identity in relationship with God.

The Quest for Success

Closely related to the search for happiness is the search for success. For many, the two are synonymous. For these people, both tend to be elusive.

Success is defined in many different ways. Undoubtedly, the most common way is to equate it with financial status. Success is to be richer, regardless of whatever net worth is at any given point. Another person may define success more in terms of social or occupational status. Yet another may define it in terms of power. But lurking behind the specific definition of success is usually a comparison with someone whom we regard as being successful. Note, however, that we tend to choose our comparison points above rather than below us. This means that we compare ourselves to someone we judge to be more successful than ourselves. Therefore, if I am to be a success I must be at least as successful (and usually more successful) than him or her. Success, thus defined, is hopelessly elusive. What I may really be experiencing is competition with another person, not a drive to meet some personal goal or standard. Often this competition is fueled by anger or resentment, and such feelings are never assuaged by accomplishments.

Success, like happiness, is an illusory goal when defined in terms of accomplishments or possessions. However, because of its ambiguity, it serves as an excellent screen for the spiritual quest. Instead of experiencing a call to self-transcendence and surrender, I define the place for which I seek in terms of external things. However, this place is much too close to where I already am; it is not the place where I will find my true identity or rest from my searching.

In and of itself, the quest for success is not a bad quest; it is merely misdirected. Like all human strivings and longings, the quest for success is reflective of a basic desire that is good but has become distorted. The quest for success can be understood as the spiritual longing to be all we can be. But when this longing is directed toward accomplishments rather than a quality of life or state of character, it is a false spiritual direction that ultimately proves unsatisfying.

The Quest for Perfection

While none of us has ever experienced anything that is absolutely perfect, pure, or right, we all seem to have some idea of the existence of these states. Our internalized image of the ideal serves as a pull toward perfection. As such, the quest for perfection is one of the greatest sources of ennoblement in human experience. However, it also rubs against the constant reminders of the imperfections of our lives and has the potential for being a source of great torment.

Perfectionism is not usually seen as a virtue by psychologists. At least in the people we see professionally, perfectionists are usually tight, rigid characters in whom the perfectionistic longings serve to strangle creativity and energy. Such people are driven to the obsessive pursuit of standards that, while they might be attainable by virtue of talent and opportunity, are made unattainable by the person's rigidity. Psychologists working within a psychodynamic orientation tend to view such people as being terrorized by harsh introjects of parents who, at least in the child's experience, were critical, demanding, and never satisfied with their performance. These people usually come for professional help because of the frustration and misery produced by their unrealistic perfectionistic longings. It is easy, therefore, to understand why mental health professionals have come to view the quest for perfection as almost invariably a symptom of neurosis.

More benign forms of perfectionism undoubtedly exist. These, in contrast, may be both adaptive and even virtuous. Perfectionists are persons with admirably high standards of excellence, who are not easily contented with sloppiness or halfhearted effort. Their efforts must be maximal, and until the results meet their standards, such persons will continue to try to improve themselves and their performance.

Perfectionism, like idealism, has a quality that suggests the presence in some dim corner of the unconscious of a faint memory of paradise lost. Perhaps by means of an archetype of paradise residing in the collective unconscious, we seem to recall the values and possibilities of life in paradise, and we long to return. The desire to be perfect, thus viewed, is a good and basic aspect of our humanity. However, the road to perfection is fraught with frustration unless we operate within a framework of grace wherein we are afforded some enablement as well as tolerance or forgiveness for failure. Apart from such grace, our ideals are so hopelessly beyond our ability to perform that we will forever be caught in frustration and a sense of failure.

The quest for perfection is, therefore, a spiritual quest. It is the quest for wholeness. Much more than the absence of mistakes, it reflects a longing for the ideal, for that which is right, beautiful, and pure. While it is easy to view these as naive expressions of innocence, a person who has lost all idealism and all drive for perfection is a person to be pitied. Perfectionistic longings continuously remind us of our failings and limitations, but without these reminders, we would more easily forget the paradise that, while lost, is the place for which we long.

The Quest for Truth and Justice

Many in our age have become so cynical as to view the quest for truth or justice as naive. We are told there is no ultimate truth. Truth is what we make it, whatever we believe it to be. Similarly, justice is viewed as a utopian concept. The preservation of self-interest is viewed as so basic to human personality that justice is perceived as unattainable apart from a total equalization of power, and this, everyone recognizes, is most improbable. Yet the search for truth and justice is very real to a large number of people who have not yet succumbed to this message of relativity and despair.

Many who still search for truth are young people who have not yet lost their idealism. Consider the passion of the university student who devours the classic writings of philosophy and religion in a search for what life is all about. Or consider the many thousands of young people in cults in America. These young men and woman will do whatever their messianic leader asks of them, regardless of how little sense it makes to their otherwise rational minds, because of their conviction of the truth of his message and the utopian hope of his ideals. Behind this hope and fervent pursuit of truth is the human spiritual quest.

Not only young people pursue truth, however. Consider the plodding and relentless investigation of the scientist who views his or her research not merely as a job but as a personal attempt to unravel the mysteries of the universe and thus come one step closer to truth. Or consider the psychotherapist who patiently sifts though distorted memories and misperceptions searching for the truth—truth that holds the promise of setting the patient free. Or consider the psychotherapy patient. Here the pursuit of truth may be a quest to make sense of personal experience and penetrate the web of falsifications and confusion that have permeated life. In whatever form it appears, the quest for truth is a spiritual longing.

Similarly, the pursuit of justice is a spiritual quest. Consider the excitement of the student who first discovers Marx and feels hope and vision for the correction of the social ills of which he or she is painfully conscious. Or consider the politician, social security administration clerk, or inner-city social worker whose motivation for daily tasks is fueled by the hope of bringing those within his or her sphere of responsibility the justice they deserve. The hope for justice and the belief that things should be and can be better is once again a faint memory of paradise lost. It is reflective of the basic human spiritual longing.

Viewed thus, the cry of the oppressed is a spiritual cry, whether understood as such or not. It is a longing for a redeemer who will save them from their plight and rule justly. Comfortable, middle-class, Western Christians are often puzzled by the numerous Old Testament psalms that cry out for justice. Perhaps we sometimes find ourselves shirking from justice, fearing that we may not fare so well under a truly just administration; our self-interests might be jeopardized. However, the oppressed psalmist—along with the oppressed millions of the world today—cries out for justice, seeing his only hope to lie in a fair judge who will recognize the unfairness of the present situation and bring justice. The search for justice is the quest for the kingdom of God, a kingdom where shalom will be the result of the just reign of God.

The Quest for Beauty

In the movie *Amadeus*, Salieri cried out to God with distress because he saw his passion for music not being equaled by his abilities. Salieri's appreciation for great music moved him to tears when he listened to Mozart perform or even when he read the scores of his music. It also forced him to attend every one of Mozart's concerts, as painful as this was for him because of his rivalry with the younger but more talented man. This passion for music was an expression of Salieri's spiritual questing in that it reflected his longing for self-transcendence. Jealousy dulled and eventually killed this spiritual flame as he came to renounce God and give expression to his hatred for Mozart—all this a result of his perception of the great discrepancy between his immense appreciation for beauty and his mediocre talent.

Aesthetic appreciation is a spiritual experience. Consider the experience of being emotionally stirred by a magnificent performance of some great opera or piece of music. Or consider the response to a great work of art. On the part of one who has learned to appreciate such expressions of beauty, these experiences are as moving and possibly as deep as any in life. They lift us out of and beyond ourselves.

If the appreciation of beauty created by others is a spiritual experience, how much more can it be to create such works of beauty ourselves. In her book *The Mind of the Maker*, Dorothy Sayers says that human creativity reveals the fact that we were made in the image of God.[2] She goes on to argue that as we discover and express our creativity, we participate with God in creation. God created from nothing; we take what he made and creatively refashion it in order to make and enjoy beauty.

Abraham Maslow describes the quest for beauty as a need of humans, noting that aesthetic appreciation seems to be a necessary component of self-actualization.[3] He classifies aesthetic appreciation as a higher-level need, noting that until lower-level needs (such as needs for safety, sustenance, and security) are consistently met, higher-level needs will not even be experienced. However, to fail to experience the appreciation of beauty is, according to Maslow, to be less than fully human.

The Quest for Stimulation

Augustine spoke of our hearts being restless until they find their rest in God. While the source of the restlessness is usually quite unclear, the experience of restlessness is perhaps the most common experience of the spiritual quest encountered by people today.

Stimulation is the most readily available diversion from restlessness. Our society provides an almost endless variety of such sources of stimulation. Television, books, travel, music, sporting events, alcohol, drugs, food, gambling, the Internet, consumerism, exercise, and a large number of other activities all serve as excellent sources of stimulation and escape from our restlessness. Through such stimulation we speak of being able to relax and let go of the pressures of our busy lives. To some extent this is accurate. However, we also tend to become addicted to these stimulants or, more correctly, addicted to the state of being stimulated. The escape is then not simply from our pressures but from our inner selves. Thus, these sources of stimulation come to eventually deaden our spirituality.

To grow spiritually we must be able to be still. In order to hear the quiet voice of our inner self, we must turn down the volume of the external sources of noise in our life. We must be able to experience solitude. In fact, Henri Nouwen argues that the pursuit of what he calls "solitude of heart" is the first step in spiritual growth.[4] By this he refers not primarily to physical solitude, although he notes that we do not progress far with solitude of the heart unless we can welcome and use physical solitude, but rather to a sensitivity to our inner voices. It is precisely our desire to run from these voices that fuels our pursuit of stimulation.

Our quest for stimulation is not, therefore, so much the direct experience of our spirituality as it is the experience of our attempts to run from our spirituality. The pursuit of stimulation is the way in which we drown out the quiet inner voice that speaks, never yells, from deep within. The restlessness that drives our need for stimulation is a more direct expression of the spiritual call. However, unless we listen to rather than run from this restlessness, we never will understand its ultimate meaning or be led by it in a direction of spiritual growth.

The Quest for Mystery

We live in an age that attempts to eliminate mystery. We no longer experience the unexplainable as mysterious but rather as not yet understandable. Today's unexplained event is assumed to be tomorrow's new discovery. We have forgotten how to stand in awe of those things that transcend our understanding.

Yet in this world of nonmystery, we find occasional experiences breaking though our defenses against awe. On a starry night we momentarily find ourselves asking questions about a universe that is expanding at the speed of light. Or studying the workings of the brain, we continue to return to the haunting question of whether mind is adequately explained by electrochemical reactions in the brain. We may even begin to wonder if science really eliminates mystery or merely covers it up with theories, which while possibly even true, are not complete explanations.

Rudolf Otto, in his classic book *The Idea of the Holy*, labels our awareness that reality transcends rational or scientific explanation as our encounter with the "numinous."[5] Otto describes the major element of the experience of the numinous as creature-consciousness, that is, the awareness of our smallness when up against an awe-inspiring, absolute, overwhelming might of some kind. This experience, according to Otto, involves both fear and fascination. Much like and related to the experience of the young child frightened and yet fascinated by a ghost story, encounter with the numinous is encounter with the *mysterium tremendum*. Otto goes on to describe this further:

> The feeling of it may at times come sweeping like a gentle tide, pervading the mind with a tranquil mood of deepest worship. It may pass over into a more set and lasting attitude of the soul, continuing, as it were, thrillingly vibrant and resonant, until at last it dies away and the soul resumes its 'profane,' nonreligious mood of everyday experience. It may burst in sudden eruption up from the depths of the soul with spasms and convulsions, or lead to the strangest excitements, to intoxicated frenzy, to transport, and to ecstasy.[6]

The experience of the numinous is the experience of being up against something that is wholly other—something inescapably above or beyond ourselves. The experience of *mysterium tremen-*

dum is a spiritual experience, and the call we experience within it is the call to self-transcendent surrender to God.

Mystery surrounds us. We can ignore it, get angry at its continued presence, or learn to love it and allow it to lead us into a deeper experience of life. Spirituality and mystery are closely related. Mystery may not always be spiritual, but a spirituality that does not have room for mystery is shallow and impoverished.

Learning to Discern the Psychological in the Spiritual

While it is important to learn to discern the spiritual significance of matters that appear to be simply psychological, it is equally important to learn to discern the psychological dimension of matters that appear simply spiritual. The spiritual is always imbedded in the psychological. Spiritual experiences occur within the same psychological structures and mechanisms that mediate our relationships to ourselves and other people. There is no distinctively "spiritual" part of personality. Personality, in its totality, is spiritual. Those who seek to care for the souls of others need to learn to understand the broad psychospiritual foundations of spiritual experience.

Trusting God is not simply a spiritual matter because God is the focus of our spirituality. Trust in God is a psychospiritual commitment, made possible by the development of the capacity for trust and facilitated by the gift of faith. The point is that trust is trust. The person whose psychological development has been so profoundly impaired that he or she has no capacity for trust in others will be equally incapable of trust in God. The gift of faith will need to be accompanied by the experience of psychospiritual healing, healing that will usually first involve experiencing the trustworthiness of at least one other human.

Similarly, the experience of receiving God's forgiveness is inextricably connected with human experiences of forgiveness. The person who has never known the forgiveness of a human will have a hard time experiencing God's forgiveness. But if he or she is given the gift of being able to do so, this is a matter of psychological, not simply spiritual, significance. The experience of grace has effects on psychospiritual functioning that can never be contained within artificial spiritual or psychological compartments of personality.

Christians often hide behind God-talk. In doing so they use religious language to avoid more direct, personal, and honest communication about themselves. The discerning soul friend will be able to hear the psychological significance of such talk and assist the one they seek to help in doing the same. Discussion about why God does not seem to be answering one's prayers may obscure a person's experience of depression. Similarly, talk about how one can know God's will can be simply a distraction from anxiety that should possibly be the real focus of the dialogue. Unfortunately, religious or spiritual language can be both a means of communicating our deepest longings and most profound experiences and, at other times, a means of avoiding an honest encounter with our deepest self.

Bringing a psychospiritual focus to our soul care dialogue means learning to discern the psychological face of spiritual discourse and gently helping the person also explore this face. Some people need to be helped to talk more about their earthly father, not simply their heavenly father. Others need help to talk about themselves, not just their theology. A psychospiritual focus to soul care means that those who care for souls must be continuously active in grounding spirituality in embodied personhood. Recall that our spirituality is the relationship of our total selves to God—our feelings, our thoughts, our bodies, our sexuality, our unconscious, our passions, and our anxieties. A psychospiritual focus means that those who care for souls seek to engage with others holistically, refusing to see their problems and experiences as simply associated with one or another so-called part or aspect of personhood.

Psychospiritual Health and Growth

We earlier described the goal of soul care as the support and restoration of the well-being of persons in their depth and totality, with particular concern for their inner life. Having examined the way in which the psychological and spiritual interact in the soul, we can now also describe this in terms of fostering psychospiritual health and growth. But how does such health and growth manifest itself? And how can we know if we are proceeding in the right direction?

Psychospiritual health is seen in every aspect of a person's life. First and foremost it is reflected in movement from egocentricity and self-preoccupation to self-sacrificing love. Learning to be fully human is learning to love, and the school of psychospiritual health is the school of love. But being in the school of love is learning to be more fully human, for love is the fulfillment not just of God's law but of our being. This means that increasing psychospiritual health also involves becoming more fully alive and living life with more passion, sensitivity, integrity, authenticity, and immediacy. Change that is not characterized by increasing love and more vital living has nothing to do with genuine psychospiritual growth.

In addition, psychospiritual health is also reflected in movement from willfulness to willingness, that is from a life of control to one of surrender to the will of God. We want to be masters of our own fate, to be in control, but Jesus invites us to relinquish the controls of our lives to him. He invites us to surrender our desperate and illusory striving after autonomy. He also invites us to surrender the isolation and rigidity associated with our egocentricity. In their place he offers rest, fulfillment, and the discovery of our true and deepest self-in-Christ. When we take this step of surrender, we suddenly discover the place for which we have been unconsciously longing. Like a tool seized by a strong hand, we know we are at last where we belong; we know we have been found. Paradoxically, the abundant life promised us in Christ does not come from grasping but releasing. It does not come from striving but relinquishing. It does not come so much from taking as from giving. Surrender is the foundational dynamic of Christian spirituality—surrender of my efforts to live my life outside the grasp of God's love and surrender to God's will and gracious Spirit who now becomes an abiding inner presence.

Psychospiritual health is also reflected in increasing personal freedom—freedom from guilt and excessive anxiety, freedom from bondage to the past, and freedom to be fully alive to the present. It is also reflected in increasing intimacy with other people, an ever expanding knowledge of self, an open relationship between the conscious and unconscious aspects of self, an actualization of one's unique and most deeply true self, and an ever increasing integration of personality. Finally, it is also seen in what Kierkegaard called purity of heart, that is, the ability to will one thing and live life with the single-mindedness and clarity of direction that comes from such focus.[7]

In all of this, psychological and spiritual growth are inextricably intertwined. That which genuinely helps our psychological growth has the potential to be equally good for us spiritually. Similarly, genuine spiritual growth should be good for us psychologically. Spiritual and psychological health are intimately related. Speaking of this relationship, Howard Clinebell states that "spiritual health is an indispensable aspect of mental health. The two can be separated only on a theoretical basis. In live human beings, spiritual and mental health are inextricably interwoven. What hurts or heals one's relationship with oneself and others will tend to hurt or heal one's relationship with God and vice versa."[8]

Notice, however, that I describe growth in one area as having the potential to produce growth in the other. However, it does not guarantee it. By means of the psychopathological process known as dissociation, we can artificially split apart things that should go together. Feelings can be split from thoughts, memory from experience, and the spiritual from the psychological. The sad truth is that we can experience growth in psychological health and maturity that has no spiritual impact. Similarly, spiritual experiences that should transform us to our very depths can leave us relatively unchanged. It is obviously possible to have a degree of psychological health and still not have an inner world that is integrated around and oriented toward some self-transcendent reference point that affords meaning, purpose, place, and identity. Similarly, it is possible to experience a degree of spiritual growth that is not translated into psychological health. The ideal, however, is that the effects of growth in the inner self be experienced throughout personality.

Those who care for the souls of others seek the preservation and restoration of the well-being of persons in their depth and totality. But how exactly do they do this? As we now turn our attention to this important question, we shall see that soul care is delivered through a relationship that is based on dialogue. An examination of this demanding and yet uniquely rewarding form of interpersonal engagement is the focus of the next chapter.

Part 2

Giving and Receiving
Soul Care

7

Dialogue in Soul Care

Few things seem more natural and yet in actuality are more challenging than dialogue. When dialogue is reduced to conversation, or even further to talking, it is quite a simple matter. Most people are capable of carrying on a conversation, and even more are capable of verbal communication, at least at some basic level. Properly understood, however, dialogue involves much more than either of these simple activities, and it forms the foundation for the engagement between those who care for souls and those who receive such care.

The English word *dialogue* comes from two Greek roots, *dia*, meaning "with each other," and *logos*, meaning "word" or "speech," suggesting the core meaning of shared speech or conversation. But most use of the term *dialogue* involves richer connotations than this minimalist definition. As commonly employed, dialogue refers to deep or significant conversation. Dialogue is more than advice giving, information exchange, or the communication of something already known. Properly understood, dialogue is exploration and discovery through conversational engagement. It is shared inquiry that is designed to increase awareness, understanding, and insight.

Physicist and communication theorist David Bohm suggests that in genuine dialogue, participants access a larger pool of meaning than that which is held by any one member.[1] By means of deep sharing within a context of empathic listening that brings to the surface the tacit assumptions that are normally taken for granted, dialogue offers the possibility of going beyond the understandings held by the individual members of the dialogue. This is, in fact, the goal of dialogue—the creation of understanding that supersedes that which existed in the individual participants prior to the onset of the dialogue.

Dialogue demands reciprocity and always involves synergy. In this regard, dialogue can be thought of as collaborative creativity. Something new is created or discovered, this being a new understanding of some aspect of reality. This understanding is developed collaboratively and is shared by the participants in the dialogue. When it involves genuinely meeting another person and ascertaining something of the truth of his or her life, this understanding holds transforming possibilities for all members of the dialogue.

Dialogue can, therefore, be thought of as conversational engagement that expands understanding of self, others, and the world. It expands, therefore, the self. In genuine dialogue, I attempt to share how I experience the world and seek to understand how you do so. In this process, each participant touches and is touched by others, this resulting in a change to each. One cannot help but be changed by genuine dialogue.

Debate, Discussion, Conversation, and Dialogue

Dialogue both shares important features with other forms of verbal interaction and has significant distinctives. While differentiating it from the other modalities of communication runs the risk of creating artificial boundaries, it does assist us in our effort to identify the distinguishing features of dialogue.

On a number of dimensions, dialogue and debate anchor opposite ends of a continuum on which discussion and conversation hold more intermediate positions—discussion being closer to debate and conversation being closer to dialogue. This can be seen in table 1, which summarizes some of the most important differences between these four forms of communication.

Table 1
Forms of Verbal Interaction

	Debate	Discussion	Conversation	Dialogue
Content	Regulated	←	→	Unregulated
Outcome	Win/Lose	←	→	Win/Win
Trust	Low trust	←	→	High trust
Respect	Intolerant of differences	←	→	Embraces differences
Interchange	Facts and arguments	←	→	Feelings, values, and construals
Format	Statements	←	→	Questions and statements
Focus	"What do I know?"	←	→	"What can I learn?"
Questions	Used to disarm and disguise opinions	←	→	Used to deepen understanding
Knowledge	Used as a weapon	←	→	Used as a gift
Risks	Avoid risks	←	→	Take risks
Goal	Prove	←	→	Explore
Listening	Rehearsal and preparation to pounce	←	→	Active empathy
Volition	Willful control, unwilling to change	←	→	Willing surrender, willing to change

Adapted from material developed by David Gouthro, a Vancouver-based consultant with the firm The Cutting Edge. Used with permission.

Differences between these four forms of interaction are most apparent when we consider the extreme positions of dialogue and debate but are also readily discernible between dialogue and discussion or debate and conversation. Because the boundaries between these four verbal forms of interaction are far from rigid, differences between adjacent positions on the continuum are often less clear and sometimes more arbitrary.

The core difference between dialogue and discussion can be seen by noting that the English word *discussion* comes from the Latin *discutere*, a word that means "to smash to pieces."[2] Discussion, which has the same roots as *percussion* and *concussion*, is a conversational form that often promotes fragmentation. Participants approach discussions recognizing that such encounters involve the advocacy of ideas and positions with resulting winners and losers. Listening in discussions often takes a distinct second place to rehearsing one's own upcoming contribution, and the overall objective is usually less one of increased understanding than of making points.

These differences are, of course, even more pronounced when we consider debate. No one who understands the rules of debate approaches such an encounter expecting to deepen their understanding on the matters being discussed, to shift their position during or as a result of the interchange, or to learn from the other. Debates are a civilized form of combat—sometimes less civilized than others. They are not forums for free exchange of ideas as a means of encounter and discovery.

Debate, and to a lesser extent discussion, also differs from dialogue in that it has both a focus and implicit rules that encourage participants to stick to the understood topic. Debates are about formally agreed-upon topics, while the focus of discussions is identified more informally. When viewed in relation to conversation or dialogue, however, there is little question that discussions operate with some regulation of content. Discussions are about something. Good discussions maintain some sort of a focus on the understood topic, never wandering from topic to topic in the way in which a good conversation typically does. Discussions can, therefore, be described as seeking convergence, even though in reality they often produce divergence.

In contrast, conversations and dialogue operate with great tolerance for divergence. In fact, divergence is often taken to be a hallmark of engaging conversation. Conversations and dialogues do not have intended outcomes, nor do they usually have implicit or explicit rules about content. They are simply the free exchange of thoughts and feelings. This is why we become annoyed when someone initiates what we take for conversation only to discover that this is but the opening ploy of a sales pitch or act of religious proselytization. Conversations and, to an even greater extent, dialogues involve higher levels of interpersonal trust than debates and discussions, and for this reason they involve the exchange not just of facts and arguments but also of feelings, values, and construals. Rather than a focus on "What do I know?" and "How can I most convincingly present it?" the challenges of conversation and dialogue are "What can I learn?" and "How can I understand the other most fully?"

Dialogue is always a win/win encounter. In relation to discussion and debate, it is more about exploring than proving, discovery than making points. In dialogue, knowledge is employed as a gift, while in debate it is used as a weapon, but the true gift in dialogue is not simply one's knowledge but one's self. This is why dialogue can only occur within a context of trust and respect. One may require some degree of safety to share one's opinions and knowledge, but how much more must the environment be free of threat if one is to feel safe enough to share one's deepest self?

Dialogue strives for the engagement of two or more persons in ways that honors both their separateness and their connectedness. Dialogue also supports the development of each participant's ever deepening understandings of self, others, and the issues being explored. When it is pressed into the service of more specific tasks, such as solving problems or effecting changes desired by one of the participants, dialogue runs the risk of losing its potency as an opportunity for the free and mutual sharing of selves. This is particularly true when one of the participants in the dialogue has a goal of doing something with or to the other—even something as benevolent as promoting their growth. However, when dialogue is entered with more mutuality, goals of growth and development are quite compatible with the nonmanipulative ideal of the inter-personal engagement I am calling dialogue.

The distinction between these four forms of verbal interaction can, perhaps, be represented in the following way: Picture conversation as two people chatting about whatever comes into their minds. They may speak of feelings, thoughts, the weather, upcoming plans, their relationship, politics, mutual acquaintances, books read, or movies seen. Good conversation is not measured by outcome but entirely by process; it is conversation that is mutual and engaging.

In contrast, while any of the topics casually touched upon during the conversation just described would be suitable as a focus of discussion, good discussion is more restricted than good conversation. The focus of discussion is something about which one can take a position. This means that discussion is more about opinions than feelings, positions than perceptions. In discussion, one says to the other, "So tell me, what do you think about X?" (the upcoming election, a current movie, some sociopolitical issue, or a point of theology). But a good discussion can only explore one of these topics at a time, and while the exploration that occurs in discussion involves more risk taking and sharing of self than in debate, discussion still involves less interpersonal trust and less risk taking than dialogue.

Debates are, of course, the most structured and combative form of verbal interaction. The topic is established, the rules of interaction are clear, and the interchange is understood by all participants as about winning or losing, not about discovery and exploration.

In contrast, dialogue involves two or more people talking with each other for no other purpose than to deeply meet each other. In dialogue each says to the other, "This is how I experience the world. Tell me how you experience it." Good dialogue involves sharing of the self, deep engagement with another self, and the resulting expansion of both selves.

Martin Buber described dialogue as the mode of exchange in which there is a true turning toward and engagement of another person, including a full appreciation of the other not as an object but as a genuine human being.[3] Buber described such engagement as "I-Thou encounters," this in contrast to "I-It encounters" in which the other is engaged as an object. Dialogue within an I-Thou relationship yields personal knowledge that is quite different from the impersonal knowledge produced by I-It encounters. Personal knowledge is knowledge *of*, whereas impersonal knowledge is knowledge *about*. It is personal knowing that is at the core of genuine dialogue.

According to Buber, all real living exists in meeting others, and the place where we meet them is in dialogue. In genuine dialogue the other becomes present, not merely in the imagination or feelings, but in the depths of one's being. This requires that each person be a person in his or her own right. Meeting, under these conditions, results in each participating in the life of the other. What was between two people is now within each of them. This is the mystery of dialogue.

Therapeutic Conversation

One important aspect of Buber's vision of dialogue is his suggestion that true dialogue can only occur in a relationship between equals. This has important implications for nonreciprocal soul care relationships such as that between psychotherapist and patient. In fact, in conversation with Carl Rogers, Buber argued that because of this requirement of equality, therapeutic conversation necessarily remains inferior to genuine dialogue because therapist and patient can never be equal partners in the relationship.[4] Buber claimed that as soon as you professionalize a helping role, you create an inequality between people—an inequality that makes the free encounter that is a part of genuine dialogue impossible.

While psychotherapists sometimes use the language of dialogue, more commonly they speak of conducting an interview. This does not mean they simply ask questions. Therapeutic soul care has come too far in its understanding of the importance of listening to tolerate simple interrogation. But while therapeutic conversation has much to contribute to the understanding and practice of soul care dialogue, it is a very restricted form of such dialogue. Before examining those restrictions, let us first consider its potential contributions.

Each of the major psychotherapeutic traditions has tended to emphasize different aspects of therapeutic conversation. The first to do so, psychoanalysis, has focused on how and to what we listen. Freud himself made two very important contributions to the understanding and practice of listening. The first of these was his emphasis on the importance of attending to nonverbal as well as verbal communication. Listening, he asserted, has as much to do with observing as hearing. His comments on this are instructive.

> When I set myself the task of bringing to the light what human beings keep hidden within them, not by the compelling powers of hypnosis, but by observing what they show, I thought that the task was a harder one than it really is. He that has eyes to see and ears to hear may convince himself that no mortal can keep a secret. If his lips are silent, he chatters with his finger-tips; betrayal oozes out of him at every pore. And thus the task of making conscious the most hidden recesses of the mind is one which is quite possible to accomplish.[5]

Making the hidden recesses of the mind conscious is not a standard part of soul care dialogue. Nevertheless, Freud's emphasis on the importance of attending to nonverbal communication has great value for all who seek to listen to others. Human language includes verbal (the actual words), vocal (such things as intonation, rate, pitch, inflection, etc.), and behavioral components (including such things as facial expressions, posture, gestures, mannerisms, etc.). Good listening involves attending to all three channels.

Freud's second major contribution to the understanding and practice of therapeutic conversation is of even greater importance. This was his advice to listen with what he described as "evenly suspended attention."[6] Noting the common tendency to focus attention during a conversation on things that strike us as most relevant or interesting, he suggested that we listen with a somewhat softer, more diffuse focus. The goal of such listening is to be open to the experience of the other with as little focusing of attention as is possible. The risk of concentration during conversation is, according to Freud, the risk of hearing only what we already know and being open to that which we have already anticipated.

Freud also drew attention to the way in which a therapist's desires can disrupt deep engagement. Even such apparently benevolent desires as the desire to remember or the desire to listen well can, according to Freud, become a disruption to listening. Freud's somewhat surprising advice to psychoanalysts was to approach therapeutic conversation with an absence of desire, memory, or even understanding, simply trusting that a deep receptivity of the person and his or her experience affords the best understanding of and engagement with him or her. Many people have found this to be singularly helpful advice regarding listening.

The major contribution of Carl Rogers to the practice of therapeutic conversation was unquestionably his identification of what he described as the three necessary and sufficient conditions of therapeutic change.[7] According to Rogers, these three conditions are therapist characteristics—namely, empathy, respect, and congruence. Empathy is the ability to enter into the experience of others, or, better, receive their experience as they share it with you, holding it within you in such a manner as not to confuse it with your own. Respect is described by Rogers as unconditional positive regard. It is a deep valuing or prizing of the other that is communicated by an absence of judgmentalism or conditions of worth. Rogers also referred to this quality as nonpossessive warmth. Congruence refers to being deeply one's self—not playing a role and not expressing anything that is incongruent with one's deepest self.

Although Rogers focused on empathy, respect, and congruence as ways of being, not techniques, it was inevitable that others would turn them into therapeutic techniques. The resulting implication for therapeutic conversation was a focus on feelings and inner experience of the other and the tendency to communicate this empathic understanding back to the one being listened to by such expressions as, "What I think I hear you saying is . . . ," or, "It sounds as if you are feeling . . ." One could describe this focus of listening as the phenomenological experience of the other. It is an empathic attempt to understand the inner experience of the other.

The major contribution of Harry Stack Sullivan to the understanding and practice of therapeutic conversation was to debunk the myth of objectivity in clinical interviews.[8] He asserted that the psychotherapeutic interview did not yield objective information about patients, only information about their encounter with a particular interviewer in particular circumstances at a particular time. In his view, the psychotherapeutic interview is shaped by and affects each of its participants. It is, therefore, not a clinical tool that leaves therapists unaffected, but an encounter.

To what do psychotherapists listen in their conversations with those they seek to help? While somewhat dependent on the approach to psychotherapy adopted, therapists typically listen *through* the framework of their implicit or explicit theoretical assumptions about the nature of personality, psychopathology, and psychotherapeutic process *for* problems and confirmation or refutation of hypotheses to help explain these problems. Integrating the major psychotherapeutic traditions, we can identify four foci of listening in therapeutic conversation: the manifest content of the conversation, the phenomenological experience of the other, the latent content of the conversation, and one's own phenomenological experience.

All good therapeutic listening begins with serious attention to the actual words spoken by the other. This is what is meant by listening to the manifest content. In listening at this level, one attends to the direct and explicit meaning of the words used by the other in an attempt to understand what they are trying to communicate. Listening at the level of the manifest content involves avoiding the temptation to get at deeper, unspoken meanings of what is being said. The story that is told is assumed to be the story that is important.

Listening in such a manner is more demanding than first meets the eye. It requires active engagement and some inner, silent processing of what is being heard. While listening at the level of the manifest content, the therapist must ask of all statements, "Could this mean anything other than what first occurs to me?" This question is not verbalized; it is asked of the therapist, not the patient. To ask it is not to doubt the sincerity of the other but to doubt conventional language. In fact, the more conventional the language, the more the need to ask, "Am I sure I know what this person means by this word or expression?"

To listen at the second level, that is at the level of the other's phenomenological experience, is to listen empathically in the manner described by Carl Rogers. This is listening designed to allow one to understand the internal frame of reference and experience of the other. Such listening begins with what I am calling the manifest content but also includes all available nonverbal information. The goal of such listening is to allow the therapist to experience the world as it is experienced by the patient or client, which is what it means to empathically grasp the other's phenomenological experience.

Listening to the latent content involves listening for the story behind the story. Such listening attempts to go beyond the conscious experience of the one who is talking by listening for clues about the deeper unconscious levels of meaning that are presumed to lie behind the words. Thus, for example, Freud pointed to the value of attending to such things as slips of the tongue, unusual or inappropriate feelings, and patterns of resistance as potential routes to an understanding of what he called the latent content in the communication. Psychoanalysts suggest that the latent content is encoded in the manifest content and have developed elaborate clinical strategies to help therapists listen to this deeper level of meaning.

The final level of psychotherapeutic listening is listening to one's own phenomenological experience. It might seem strange to suggest that in listening to and attempting to understand what you are saying to me at least part of my attention should be directed to my inner experience. Yet this is the logical outgrowth of the principle articulated by Sullivan, namely, that clinical conversation is not an objective means of assessment but a subjective process of personal encounter. The assumption is that as my conscious mind attempts to listen to the expressions of your conscious mind, unconscious levels of my mind are also listening and responding to the unconscious level of your communication. This is what Theodore Reik called listening with the third ear.[9] In practice it requires that the therapist attend to his or her vagrant thoughts, fantasies, intuitions, associations, and feelings, searching inner experience for clues to help interpret latent content.

While psychotherapeutic understandings of listening and talking can inform soul care dialogue, therapeutic conversation is, as was stated earlier, a very restrictive form of dialogue. Because of the ease with which psychotherapists slip into emphasizing doing over being and the technical over the personal, the listening that therapists offer is often quite limited. Psychotherapists cannot afford the luxury of dialogue as we have defined it. (Perhaps it would be better to say their patients cannot generally afford such a luxury, purchasing instead more limited symptom-focused conversation.) Therapeutic conversation is, and must be, more focused than the free and mutual expression and engagement of people that occurs under conditions of dialogue. Only psychoanalysts offer the possibility of exploring absolutely whatever comes into consciousness. In reality, however, the psychoanalytic conversation is much more a monologue than a genuine dialogue.

Psychotherapists are trained to use conversation to achieve therapeutic ends. This training typically includes learning such molecular conversational skills as attending, the reflection of feelings, the encouragement of concreteness, the use of confrontation, and the formulation of questions. But the broad and ambitious goals of genuine dialogue are easily sacrificed at the altar of carefully rehearsed listening postures and intervening strategies. Maintaining good eye contact, offering carefully timed and thoughtful reflections of what has been heard, and identifying discrepancies and thematic links can contribute to genuine dialogue but are, in themselves, a poor substitute for it.

The clinical nature of therapeutic soul care also threatens genuine dialogue by predisposing those who offer such care to focus on problems and their solutions. If the goal is the alleviation of problems, dialogue is simply a tool—a means to an end. Problem alleviation, however, is much too narrow an end for dialogue that is directed toward the care and nurture of persons in their psychospiritual core. Problems can be addressed as part of such dialogue, but a narrow focus on difficulties always compromises the richness of such dialogue.

In Buber's view, the alternative to dialogue as a personal encounter between people who meet each other as humans is an impersonal encounter wherein the other is engaged as an object. No matter how good the intention, such objectification of a person inevitably dehumanizes them. Unfortunately, therapeutic conversation too often involves such objectification and dehumanization of persons. Whenever we encounter a case, a diagnostic category, an example of a particular problem or coping strategy, or even a patient, we fail to encounter a human being. Worse, in relating to others in such ways, we actually diminish their humanness. We may help them with a dysfunction of some part of their self, but we do not enhance the vitality and robustness of that overall self. Persons, not problems, should be the focus of soul care, and it is these persons whom we should seek to engage in dialogue.

Describing the difficulty of achieving genuine dialogue within therapeutic conversation, Maurice Friedman notes that "psychotherapists often give others technical aid without entering into relationship with them. Help without mutuality is presumptuousness. . . . It is an attempt to practice magic." He goes on, "We attain genuine dialogue not by aiming at it but by allowing the other to exist in his or her otherness and not just as a content of our experience and thought. We can perceive the other person as whole and unique only through the attitude of a partner and not through that reductive, analytical and derivative look that prevails today."[10] The challenge for psychotherapists is to settle for nothing less than the deep meeting that Buber described as the place of real living and all genuine healing and growth.

Pastoral Conversation

If the challenge of therapeutic conversation is not to allow reductionistic analysis, clinical techniques, or therapeutic roles to impair the genuine and deep encounter of two people, the challenge of pastoral conversation is to find a path between listening to the other and speaking for God that does not confuse dialogue and preaching. Whereas dialogue was earlier described as a posture of, "Here is how I see the world; tell me how you see it so I can see more clearly," at its worst, pastoral conversation has sometimes been little more than, "Here is how God sees the world; what more is there to say?"

This is obviously not a posture of genuine dialogue. Nor is it an accurate picture of typical pastoral conversation. Under the influence of the clinical pastoral education movement, pastoral care, conversation, and counseling have been sensitized to the importance of listening, not simply proclaiming God's Word. But in being reminded of the value of listening, pastoral caregivers are not simply being offered the latest distillations of therapeutic soul care, they are more properly being called back to the best of their own tradition. Consider, for example, the advice of the seventeenth-century French pastor François Fénelon, advising others on the provision of spiritual counsel:

> Speak little; listen much; think far more of understanding hearts and of adapting yourself to their needs than of saying clever things to them. Show that you have an open mind, and let everyone see by experience that there is safety and consolation in opening his mind to you.[11]

Several centuries later, Dietrich Bonhoeffer emphasized the same point, but with even stronger words:

> Many people are looking for an ear that will listen. They do not find it among Christians because Christians are talking when they should be listening. He who no longer listens to his brother will soon no longer be listening to God either. . . . One who cannot listen long and patiently will presently be talking beside the point and never really speaking to others, albeit he be not conscious of it.[12]

The pastor's call to proclaim God's Word is associated with what is probably the greatest contribution that pastoral conversation can make to nonpastoral soul care—the reminder of the importance of moral inquiry in soul care dialogue. Although pastoral care has at times been unclear about its moral framework, of all the contemporary forms of soul care, it has remained most faithful to the awareness that the care of souls must include a moral perspective. The challenge is to conduct this moral inquiry without resorting to moral manipulation or offering mere moralisms. The best pastoral care does this quite routinely. Others who seek to rediscover a moral framework for the soul care they offer have much to learn from examining such care.

Morality forms such a deep and foundational part of human personality that it necessarily structures all of life. Life can never be lived in a place that makes moral judgments inappropriate. Many people, however, think of certain aspects of life as belonging to a value-free sphere. As noted earlier, some erroneously argue that psychotherapy operates in such a sphere. Others might argue that the conduct of basic scientific research, or the repair of a radio, or the word processing of a letter excludes appropriate moral reflection. As noted by C. S. Lewis, however, right and wrong form such a deep and enduring part of how we are programmed to engage with the world that its presence must be interpreted as evidence of the deep structure of reality or, in his words, as a "clue to the meaning of the universe."[13]

This makes moral reflection a valuable part of any dialogue. If the goal of dialogue is the deep engagement of two or more people who seek through conversation to work together toward shared and truthful understandings of themselves, each other, and the world, morality has an important place in such conversation. Truth cannot be pursued or apprehended apart from morality; truth does not exist outside of rightness. This is what Christians understand by the theological assertion that Christ embodies both truth and righteousness.

If moral reflection has an important place in dialogue in general, it has an indispensable place in soul care dialogue. In the earlier discussion of the history of soul care, we noted that until the rise of therapeutic psychology, soul care always included a moral dimension. When we examined the history of Christian soul care, we again noted that care worthy of being called Christian always operated within a moral context. Not only should Christian soul care be associated with love, forgiveness, and grace, it should also provide an opportunity for exploration of how life should be lived. This is moral inquiry. The presence of a moral component to soul care does not make it the same as moral instruction or moral persuasion. What soul care offers is a context for moral reflection.

Among those who offer soul care, clergy are unique in their social and symbolic role. They are religious authority figures who, like it or not, symbolically represent religious values. The great advantage of this is that people approach clergy knowing that their encounter will occur within a moral framework and that the moral dimension of life will be a part of their dialogue. Some people seek out clergy because they want advice that flows out of this mutually accepted moral framework. Others may seek out clergy simply because they view them as offering a moral perspective on life. Such people may not want advice and may not even accept the moral framework adopted by the cleric, but they still desire care from clergy who are recognized as offering the possibility of moral reflection.

Clergy are often avoided, of course, for precisely the same reason. Experiences of emotional manipulation by guilt motivation lead some people to conclude that a moral perspective is the last thing they need. They think they know what such a perspective on their life would be, and they reject it and those whom they associate with it. This reveals the dark side of moral discourse. When it is offered with judgmentalism, emotional coercion, or any form of moral bullying, it is always destructive.

Christ was clear about his moral framework, and yet his dealings with people were consistently characterized by grace and an absence of coercion. His was a moral perspective that was consistent with genuine dialogue because it offered freedom of expression and supported freedom of choice. Christian soul care is not the place for doing whatever has to be done to ensure that others see and respond to the matters at hand as you do (or as you assume God does). It is, however, an excellent place to offer an opportunity for an examination of life from a Christian perspective and to consider the light that such a perspective sheds on life and its choices.

In his book *The Moral Context of Pastoral Care*, Don Browning notes that a temporary suspension of moral judgments is both possible and appropriate when the moral framework is clear. This was the case in Jesus' dialogical encounters. Because his value framework was very clear to all who met him, Jesus had the freedom to sometimes leave his moral judgments unstated. When the moral framework is apparent, there is no need to always state the obvious; judgments can, in such a situation, often be assumed. Browning goes on to argue that it is precisely because clergy work in the context of a community that is engaged in attempts to clarify its value commitments that on many occasions they have the privilege of temporarily bracketing moral issues of those in their care.[14]

What of those who do not work out of such a context and who do not offer a moral framework for their care? An absence of such a framework can easily be construed as suggesting that moral considerations are not important. Such a moral vacuum ultimately leads to a disintegration of the value framework of the individual and of society. It also contributes to moral confusion. Unfortunately, it is not just psychotherapists who have fallen into the trap of thinking that an absence of judgmentalism requires an absence of moral reflection and inquiry. Under the influence of therapeutic psychology, pastoral counselors have too often succumbed to the same folly.

An absence of a moral framework for soul care suggests that morality is a private and personal matter—a position that when taken to the extreme suggests that each person is ultimately only accountable to himself or herself. The privatization of morality has been a consequence of the secularization of the West. Most people acknowledge that moral decisions have to be made in life but seem to operate with the assumption that because these decisions have to be made personally and individually, there is no significant role for shared inquiry on the matter. This is most unfortunate; morality is much too complicated to be left to any of us alone. We desperately need relationships in which we can engage in careful reflection on the moral dimension of our life.

Where does one find such relationships? Where can people turn to reflect on the ethical and moral issues of their business and personal lives? To whom can a person talk about questions of how to balance work and personal life? Where do people go who wish to explore their response to issues of injustice in their communities? The available contexts for shared inquiry into the moral issues of life are quite limited. At one time, the church played this role for the majority of the members of Western society. Unfortunately, its role has been seriously limited by virtue of the marginalized place it now occupies in secularized society.

Psychotherapists and counselors who are willing to engage with others around these moral questions have been a resource for some people. As noted earlier, however, the majority of mental health professionals have been seduced by the erroneous view that psychological problems are unrelated to morality and that moral considerations are, therefore, inappropriate in the therapeutic context. For most people, the most available context for moral reflection is their friendships. In fact, probably the majority of soul care that is provided is that which is offered by friends to friends without any idea that what they are doing is offering *cura animarum*. Unfortunately, however, friendships often operate with the same understanding of privatized morality. Consequently, friends often accept arbitrary limits on conversation that make moral discourse and ethical reflection awkward.

Soul Care Dialogue

There is a great need for soul friendships that afford opportunities for reflection within the context of a genuinely dialogical encounter. But can exploration and discovery be a part of conversations that operate within a framework of Christian moral reflection, or must the goals of such conversation be the more limited ones of moral persuasion? Can soul care ever meet the ideals of mutuality suggested by Buber as necessary if we are to describe it as involving dialogue? Why is dialogue so difficult and rare in soul care? These are the questions to which we must now turn as we seek to place the concept of dialogue back within the soul care relationship.

It is somewhat distressing to discover how many Christians feel that dialogue, as it has been described in this chapter, is neither possible nor desirable in soul care. Viewing soul care as a relationship of spiritual direction or counsel, they suggest that the intent of aiding the spiritual growth of another is, to some degree at least, incompatible with ideals of mutuality, exploration, and discovery. Soul care is, in such a view, a relationship wherein one person is acknowledged as being responsible for providing assistance to the other and wherein anything that the first party gets from the relationship is a fringe benefit, certainly not part of any reasonable expectation. Feeling a degree of certainty about their perception of truth, such people also have very limited expectations about how their own understanding of matters might change as a result of their interactions with those for whom they care. Mutuality has, therefore, no significant place in soul care for such people.

Such a vision of soul care shares very little with that which is being developed in these pages. Anyone who assumes they have nothing more to learn has no business being trusted with the enormous responsibilities of soul care. And anyone who is afraid to meet another in such a way that would allow for the possibility of their own self being changed should be kept as far as possible from soul care responsibilities.

Mutuality does not require symmetry of roles. Even in situations in which I am recognized as having the primary responsibility for the care of another person, mutuality can be present if I am able to answer in the affirmative to the following three questions. Am I willing to bring myself, not just my care, to the encounter? Can I accept the other as a whole and separate person, as he or she is? And am I willing to be open enough to his or her experience and ideas that my own may change as a result of our interaction? If I can answer yes to these questions, dialogue can be present. If not, it may be a relationship of care, and it may even be a relationship of help, but it will not be an encounter that is worthy of being called dialogue.

Many things keep us from such encounters. People who are overly rational often structure dialogue in ways that leave only very restricted room for the exploration of emotions. Such a process also excludes or minimizes anything that appears to be either nonrational or irrational. Unconscious processes and products will be shortchanged, as will be longings, dreams, intuitions, peak experiences, and dark nights of the soul. Also, the prizing of mystery is not likely to occur in dialogue with someone who is overly impressed by rationality.

Similarly, intellectualization also limits dialogue. While abstraction and analysis have a definite capacity to enhance understanding, their excessive use quickly strangles genuine dialogue. They do so by transforming personal knowledge into impersonal knowledge. Intellectualization places a great distance between the observer and the observed and between the analyzer and that which is analyzed. It thus distorts the experience it seeks to understand by excluding that which is most distinctly personal. When this is the dominant way in which a person engages with ideas, feelings, and experiences, the result will always be truncated exploration. The conversation between such a person and others will also seldom be worthy of being called dialogue.

Analysis is often a response to low tolerance to mystery or ambiguity. People who experience such a low tolerance respond to something that is ambiguous as, at best, a challenge and, at worst, a threat. Their response in these two situations is, however, the same; that is, they attempt to eliminate the mystery by analyzing whatever it is they cannot understand. Thus understood, analysis is often an emotional response to threat or insecurity, not simply an intellectual response to a problem. But one person's problem is another's opportunity for psychospiritual growth. Mystery should not be uniformly either worshiped or abhorred. It should, instead, be viewed as productive ground for dialogical exploration.

A lack of genuinely knowing one's own self is also a major barrier to dialogue. Dialogue is the meeting of two or more selves. What I have to give to others is directly proportional to the extent of my genuine and deep knowing of myself. All I have to give to others is self—either one of many available false selves (my personae) or my true and real self. If I do not know my self, the only self I have to offer in dialogue is a false self—some egocentric creation of my own construction. If I offer a false self to another, it is extremely hard for that person to offer his or her deepest and truest self. Instead, false selves invite engagement of false selves. True and most authentic ways of being cannot emerge under conditions of an encounter with a false self. However, to the extent that I am genuinely and deeply congruent, authentic, and my true or real self, others who meet me are afforded an opportunity to be a true or real self themselves. They may not know what makes that possible, but at some deep level, they recognize possibilities for deep encounter that are remarkably rare.

Apart from a deep knowing of self, I remain unable to separate the one I seek to meet in dialogue from myself. In dialogue I meet the other within myself, not in some external place. This is the difference between personal knowing of someone and impersonal knowing about him or her. Dialogue is not an encounter with information about another person; it is a direct engagement with the person. Because the place where we meet is somewhere deep within the self, it is essential that I be able to distinguish him or her from me—the individual in his or her separateness from that individual as an introject in my inner reality. This is why this personal knowing of another in dialogue is so dependent on my deep knowing of myself. I know my self so that I may know other selves, and in knowing other selves, I come to know my own self more deeply.

A lack of courage and a fear of intimacy also both block dialogue. It takes courage to respond to the invitation to share myself with another person. If I am afraid of genuinely meeting another self, I will prefer a conversational form that makes less demands on its participants. Genuine dialogue is an intimate encounter; it is not for those who lack the courage to honestly engage with another.

Finally, dialogue is also impaired by a need for control. One can control interviews and conversations, but one must surrender to and embrace dialogue. Much like moving into a flowing stream of water, one must enter dialogue ready to let go and be carried along on a journey. We create *opportunities* for dialogue, and we participate in it; we don't create dialogue or control it. If I must control where I go and where the conversation or relationship goes, I cannot afford dialogue. If, on the other hand, I can temporarily relinquish my need to control myself, others, and my relationship with them, dialogue offers me and them a unique opportunity for an experience of surrender that produces an enlargement of the self for all participants.

Practical Suggestions for Providers of Soul Care

Approaching a relationship of soul care with the understanding that the essence of what this involves is dialogue may be both liberating and terrifying. On the one hand, it may imply less need to worry about mastering theory or doing clever things, but on the other hand, it also means there is nothing to hide behind.

The encounter of selves called dialogue is not so much about *doing* as *being*. Properly understood, it is more of a privilege than a responsibility, a gift than an accomplishment. The potency of dialogue, according to Buber, is that relatedness is the essence of life. To be is to be related. Dialogue is, therefore, the heart of personal life—something that offers us a glimpse into eternity. It is "the unpredictable, unpossessable meeting with the other."[15] By the grace of God, not our own skill or cleverness, such a meeting affords profound possibilities of living life with more self-awareness, vitality, wholeness, and purpose. This is the miracle of dialogue, and it is the core of soul care.

How does the one providing soul care facilitate the possibility of dialogue? What should be discussed, and how should the conversation be directed? Several practical suggestions follow:

1. *Dialogue is facilitated by personal preparation.* Although dialogue can occur spontaneously, it is facilitated by a degree of personal preparation. Preparing for soul care dialogue is preparing a place of quiet within myself, a place into which I can invite and meet another person. It is hard to enter into genuine dialogue when I am distracted by external pressures or preoccupied with internal issues. Quiet, prayerful reflection stills my own soul, puts me in touch with God, and helps clear an inner space for the other. It also prepares me to meet the other person as he or she is—sepa-

rate from me, from my ideas about him or her, and even from my previous experiences of that person.

2. *Dialogue is also facilitated by setting aside all desires except love.* Desires, other than love, get in the way of soul care dialogue. Even such benign desires as the wish to be helpful or to be experienced as a good listener tend to be distractions from genuine dialogue as they encourage me to focus on myself. Only love leaves me free to set myself, including my needs and desires, to the side. Only love allows me to temporarily stand apart from my own experiences and construals of the world and enter deeply into those of the one for whom I seek to care.

As noted earlier, dialogue is even interrupted by the desire for memory or understanding. Freud's advice to listen without attempting to remember or understand contains much wisdom. A need to remember or even understand tightens one up, whereas the listening that occurs under the conditions of evenly suspended attention leaves one open and maximally receptive to the other person.

3. *The focus of soul care dialogue should be the inner experience of the one receiving care.* Soul care dialogue does not follow a rigid script. The intent is to allow the one receiving care to tell his or her story and for the one offering care to listen and interact in ways that help him or her do so. The aspect of the story and experience that is the special focus of soul care is inner experience. This includes such things as the person's feelings, struggles, hopes, values, and desires. It also includes the experience of God and other aspects of his or her spiritual life. Listen, therefore, with the goal of entering into the person's experience and being able to see the world from his or her frame of reference. This is the ideal of empathic listening.

4. *Listen for the imbedded spiritual significance of whatever is being discussed.* It is quite misleading to expect that Christian soul care will always or even usually involve conversation about religious or explicitly spiritual matters. Such conversation is certainly appropriate, but it need not be forced. Instead, those who offer Chris-

tian soul care should learn to listen for the spiritual significance of whatever it is that is being discussed. Such discernment is a gift of the Holy Spirit, upon whom, therefore, those who offer Christian soul care must be dependent.

5. *Listen with respect.* Christian soul care cannot be offered apart from deep respect for the one who is receiving care. This respect is grounded in a recognition of that person's value as another human created in the image of God and an expectation that a genuine encounter with him or her holds possibilities of learning and growth for both parties. It also includes a recognition of the immense privilege that is involved in being invited into the inner garden of another. Entrance into that inner sacred space should be undertaken with respect and care. This includes being slow to judge.

6. *Attend to your own experience in the dialogue.* While the primary focus of the one offering care is on the words of the other, a low level of attention to one's own inner experience is often helpful in understanding the experience of the other. Attention to one's inner experience often suggests metaphors that may prove helpful in the dialogue. For example, if while listening to someone's report of work pressure you discern increasing tightness within your chest, consider the possibility of making the notion of "tightness" part of your empathic response. Or, if as you listen to someone describe his or her fear or other painful emotion you suddenly get a mental image of someone curling up in a ball, crawling into a hole, and pulling the hole in after him or her, trust this intuitive metaphor and draw from it in your response.

Good communication touches more than our conscious minds. It also touches the depths of our unconscious minds and, through that, touches our bodies. Good metaphors can be generated by simply thinking about what is heard. However, the best metaphors, like the richest of all human creative efforts, come from tapping into deeper levels of one's experience.

7. *Invite moral reflection on the matters under discussion.* Moral reflection is best initiated by inviting the one seeking care to engage in

such reflection himself or herself. Questions such as, "I wonder how you judge the appropriateness of . . . ?" or, "How have you approached the ethical or moral aspect of . . . ?" are often helpful. Care must be taken, of course, not to raise this moral perspective in a judgmental manner. Moral reflection is not the same as preaching.

8. *Don't be afraid of judicious advice, suggestions, or offerings of direction.* The ideals of soul care should be respect, not passivity or nondirectiveness. While an authoritarian style is almost (if not always) inappropriate, this does not mean that the one offering care should never give advice, make suggestions, or offer direction. If the dialogue is to be genuine, the one offering care must be a real person. This means that he or she is expected to engage as a person, not simply as a listening machine. Offering self includes a measured offering of one's ideas and suggestions.

8

Dreams, the Unconscious, and the Language of the Soul

In the last chapter we noted that dialogue involves engagement with another person at a deep level of shared experience. Readiness for dialogue involves readiness to listen and respond to the expressions of the soul of the other—to his or her deepest longings, needs, anxieties, hopes, values, and beliefs. But what is the language of the soul? And how can we help another person better know his or her own inner world?

As Daniel pointed out to the ancient Babylonian king Nebuchadnezzar, dreams play a potentially important role in knowing our inner world. King Nebuchadnezzar had a dream and wanted it interpreted. Like most people in the premodern world, he believed that dreams were God's means of communicating with people, and he did not want to miss God's message. The problem was that he had forgotten his dream. So he went to the court dream interpreters, whose job was normally to reveal the meaning of reported dreams, and asked them to tell him his dream and then interpret it. When they were unable to do so, he ordered them killed. On hearing this, the Hebrew prophet Daniel prayed to God that he would know both the king's dream and its meaning. God answered his prayer. Daniel then went to the king and spoke these words: "This mystery has been revealed to me, not that I am wiser than any other man, but for this sole purpose: that the king should learn what it means, and that you should understand your inmost thoughts" (Dan. 2:30 JB).

As noted by John Sanford, Daniel presented King Nebuchadnezzar with a one-sentence summary of the essentials of the understanding of dreams offered by modern depth psychology.[1] He asserted that dreams come to us with a purpose, namely, to help us know our innermost thoughts. These innermost thoughts are what modern psychology calls the unconscious. Daniel's words reflect an awareness of the presence of the unconscious and of dreams as one of the ways in which it reveals itself. Here Daniel presented what is probably depth psychology's single most important insight related to dreams, namely, that behind them we can often discern a purposive, intelligent, revelatory action.

Dreams are not the only way of knowing our innermost thoughts and feelings. Quiet, regular reflection on our daily experiences, including an examination of our emotional reactions, and prayerful attending to our anxieties and compulsions affords a great deal of information regarding the state of our inner world. But dreams are unique in the direct access they give to this world and for this reason are often a very appropriate and helpful part of soul care dialogue. Before turning more directly to this, however, it may be helpful to first reflect on the place of the unconscious in Christian spirituality and in psychospiritual wholeness.

The Unconscious and Christian Spirituality

It is quite apparent that Christians sometimes relate to the unconscious with a good deal of suspicion. Viewing it as the dark and sinful aspect of self, they equate the unconscious with our fallen nature—the conscious mind being judged to be higher and, therefore, less affected by sin. Biblical references to the deceitfulness of the heart are taken as support for such a view.

Upon closer observation, this suspicion of the unconscious can be seen to be more a result of the Age of Enlightenment, with its emphasis on rationality, than of biblical teaching. The central place that dreams, visions, and other ecstatic experiences play in both Old and New Testaments clearly demonstrates the spiritual value of nonrational experiences that are mediated by the unconscious but have God as their source. A respect for the unconscious is also seen in the content and process of Christ's teachings. He urged his followers to be as little children, implying, among other things, that they rely less on rationality and more on faith. Furthermore, his extensive use of parables, metaphors, and paradox illustrated his awareness that good communication often bypasses the conscious mind and directly engages the unconscious. His was a call to a spirituality of the heart, not simply a religion of the head.

The valuing of rationality that was so central to the spirit of the Age of Enlightenment resulted in a mistrust of the unconscious and all its fruits (i.e., the mystical, the intuitive, and the ecstatic). This was further reinforced by the Freudian vision of the unconscious, which emphasized it as the seat of sexual and aggressive urges. Salvation was, under these influences, seen as a response to a personal, conscious decision and action on the part of an individual. Similarly, Christian growth came to be associated with a suppression or crucifixion of the unconscious world in favor of the conscious world of thought, volition, and behavior. It is no wonder that under such influences, spirituality was often sacrificed on the altar of religion.

Theologically, it is quite problematic to equate the unconscious with sin. Some who do so consider the unconscious to be a result of the fall. However, nothing was created by the fall. *Ex nihilo* creativity belongs to God alone. Sin merely distorts God's original good creation. Others who equate the unconscious with sin think of the unconscious as the part of personality most contaminated by sin. Viewed in such a way, it is also thought to be dangerous and untrustworthy. In reality, however, sin is a disease that afflicts all aspects of personhood, including both the unconscious and conscious mind. Sin cannot be localized in any part of personhood.

The unconscious was every bit a part of God's good creation as the conscious. Both are wonderful gifts. The gift of the conscious mind brings awareness. The gift of the unconscious mind brings the capacity not to be limited by awareness.

Christian religion that is devoid of the unconscious is inevitably shallow, insipid, and rational. The experience of worship, although often conducted by Protestants as if it were strictly a rational, conscious matter, clearly engages us at the level of our unconscious. Experiences of the presence of God, the fear of the Lord, the mystical union with Christ, or the leading of the Holy Spirit, all involve the unconscious. God is far too big for our engagement with him or response to him to be adequately contained within consciousness. If God is the creator of both our conscious and unconscious minds, surely he would speak to us and expect to meet us in the depths of our unconscious being.

Properly understood, the unconscious can be seen to be the source of spiritual experience: of visions, of prophecies, of "the still small voice," and of the sense of the presence of God. The unconscious is the place wherein we have our primary meeting with God. It is the quiet, inner garden wherein he walks and seeks communion with us. We may think conscious thoughts and confess consciously held beliefs about God, but our actual experience of him is primarily unconscious. Only secondarily does it become conscious. While the unconscious mind is far from a perfect medium of encounter with God, in many ways it is the preferred one.

The unconscious should, therefore, not be seen as a closed system driven by previous experience and instinctual urges but rather as an open system that is uniquely receptive to and expressive of creative, nonrational, and spiritual matters. It has, therefore, an indispensable role in our spiritual life. Religion is the achievement of consciousness; spirituality is the gift of the unconscious. God calls us to meet him and respond with the totality of our being. Richness of spiritual life occurs when our encounter with God is not limited to the rational, propositional, and volitional modes of being that are associated with consciousness but also incudes the intuitive, symbolic, emotional, and creative modes of being that emerge from the soil of the unconscious.

The Unconscious and Wholeness

Not only does the unconscious have an important role to play in facilitating our experience of and response to God, it also has a crucial role to play in our health and wholeness. The English word *health* is derived from the old Saxon word *hal*, from which we get *hale* and *whole*. The greeting "hello" is an expression of a wish for wholeness for the one we meet, and such wholeness is the essence of health.

Wholeness implies not just an absence of symptoms of disease but, much more importantly, integrality. The body is a good example of something whole: When one part suffers, the whole suffers. I may speak of a pain in my leg, but it is I who suffer, in my totality, not simply my leg. This is also emphasized in Jesus' parables of the lost sheep and the lost coin (Luke 15:3–10). Wholeness demands that all members be present and well. Becoming whole does not mean being perfect, just complete.

One of the most important things we have learned from depth psychology is that there can be no wholeness apart from the redemption of the unconscious. This insight was expressed in Freud's observation that our capacity for freedom of choice and action is limited by our bondage to personality factors that operate beyond our awareness. In other words, it is that which we choose not to know or acknowledge about ourselves (i.e., that which we repress, deny, or in other ways relegate to the unconscious) that has the most power over us. To the extent to which we experience bondage of will and action, it is bondage in relation to things we are unwilling or unable to face. The more such things exist and the more unwilling we are to face them, the greater the bondage.

Jung's vision of psychospiritual growth as accessing the unconscious and forging a relationship with it built on Freud's insight and significantly extended it. According to Jung, psychospiritual wholeness requires a partnership between the conscious and unconscious aspects of being. The idea of such a partnership may be quite frightening as the unconscious contains much that is dark. We are tempted to think that we should eliminate these aspects of ourself by denying their existence. However, to do so is to increase their power. To deny the existence of the inner world is not to escape its frightening aspects but to render oneself more vulnerable to them. John Sanford notes, "Evil gains power when its existence is denied, or when we have become used to it and no longer are aroused by it. To deny the reality of the unconscious is not to know oneself, and not to know oneself is to risk becoming possessed by that which we have ignored."[2] The most basic rule of the unconscious seems to be that the more split off something is from consciousness, the more malignant it will be. The best way to eliminate aspects of ourself that should be crucified, not actualized, begins, therefore, with an acknowledgment of their presence.

Listening to our dreams, or any other form of attending to the messages of our unconscious mind, will inevitably confront us with things that will be unpleasant. There is no way to bargain with the unconscious, seeking access to only positive things and not to those that are experienced as negative. This is the reason why openness to the contents of our unconscious requires courage. It remains, however, indispensable to wholeness.

The goal of a relationship with the unconscious is to redeem that which has been lost, restore that which has been left in an imperfect condition, and then eliminate anything that is truly evil or sinful. But the sinfulness or evil of the contents of the unconsciousness cannot be determined until they are faced head-on. Many things that look monstrous in the dark shadows of the inner world take on quite different proportions when exposed to the light of day. Fragments of personality, isolated from the rest so as to render them more benign, need to be brought to consciousness, have their connections to the present and the rest of personality restored, and have decisions made about how to relate to them. "To make something conscious is an act of redemption. Redemption means to win something back from an imperfect to a perfect condition."[3] By the grace of God and with his help, this is what we seek to do as we engage with others in ways that encourage listening to messages from the unconscious.

Dream Work in Soul Care

While dreams are not the only way in which we can begin to listen to our unconscious and its messages to us, they are the means with which we have the most regular contact. Approximately one-quarter of our total sleeping time is spent in dreaming. This equals two hours of dreams during every average eight-hour night of sleep. What a source of information about the state of our inner world we would have if we could begin to attend to those messages.

Learning to listen to dreams in ways that foster psychospiritual growth is like any other skill—it takes practice and discipline. Numerous books exist on the theory and techniques of dream interpretation,[4] a number of these written on the use of dreams for specifically Christian spiritual growth.[5] But just as reading books is not the best way to learn to speak a foreign language, neither is it the best way to learn the language of the soul. For most people, learning to work with dreams requires that they discuss their dreams with someone who has experience in dream work.

Dreams are usually first discussed in soul care as part of the encouragement of regular journal writing. One of the easiest ways to begin to attend to the messages of the soul is to keep a journal. This is not the same as a diary, which, as the term is usually understood, focuses more on external events. To be useful for psychospiritual growth, journal writing needs to focus on inner life, that is, on such things as feelings, fantasies, reactions, intuitions, vagrant thoughts, troubling attitudes or behaviors, and puzzling experiences. Keeping such a journal begins to build the discipline of regular, prayerful, reflection on the events of the day, and regular journal writing provides a wonderful way of beginning to attend to dreams.

Journal writing need not be undertaken on a daily basis. While such a highly disciplined approach works well for some people, many others find it impossible to do daily. The challenge is to establish a habit of reflection and writing that fits with the rhythms and demands of one's life. Typically this begins with the purchase of a bound book of blank pages or by starting a journal file on a computer. This is a signal to the unconscious of a commitment to begin to take seriously the matters of the inner world. Entries then should be made as time for reflection is available. People who have regular times for prayer or Bible study often find it ideal to make their journal work a part of such times. The key, however, is not when or how often the work is done but that it is done. Almost invariably, people who actually try journal writing report that it pays significant psychospiritual dividends.

The possibilities for what is written in one's journal are considerable. Some people include Bible study insights; others include written prayers. Some organize their reflection in terms of the experiences of the previous day, while others focus more on what is anticipated in the upcoming day. Some focus on moods and emotions, while others focus on reactions and behaviors. Some include written dialogue with parts of self being engaged in examination, and others use their journal primarily as a place to record and reflect on dreams. What is important is that the reflection and writing be undertaken within a context of prayer and that the exercise be understood as a dialogue between self and God. This is unquestionably the framework within which dream work is most fruitful for psychospiritual growth. Beyond this there is room for a good deal of flexibility.

Principles of Dream Work

Advice about how to actually work with dreams differs substantially between proponents of the various major approaches to dream work. Freudians look for evidence of unconscious conflict, Jungians for underdeveloped aspects of personality and guidance for living from the wisdom of the collective unconscious, Adlerians for compensations for inferiority feelings, and object relations theorists for introjects of significant others that have become problematic fragments of self. One's theory of dreams, therefore, influences one's techniques in significant ways.

While there is, as yet, no comprehensive theory of dreams, there is a general consensus on the basic principles and techniques of dream work. Before considering these techniques, eight basic principles for the use of dreams in Christian soul care dialogue can be identified.

1. *Welcome dreams as a gift from God.* There are several important components of welcoming dreams as a gift from God. The first is to receive them with gratitude and expectancy. This means that dreams should be viewed as something worthwhile, meaningful, and given for our benefit. An unknown Jewish rabbi is reported to have compared an unexamined dream to an unopened letter. This nicely captures the meaningfulness of the dream. If it is a communication, receive it with expectation. View it as a gift.

The significance of this gift is, of course, even greater when we consider the possibility that the dream was given by God. Until the eighteenth century, almost no one would have ever seriously doubted this. Dreams were accepted as having spiritual significance and were received as messages that either foretold the future or pointed to some aspect of the past or present that required attention. Accepting that dreams are given by God does not require that we interpret them as literally being his voice. Forged in the heart of the unconscious, dreams can be thought of as a combination of messages about the state of the inner world and fragments of life experiences that are shaped by God as a communication designed for our well-being. In other words, instead of positing some impersonal part of self as the source of the dream, God can be thought of as the one who gives us dreams. He is the benevolent source of all good gifts, so why should he not be the source of messages that come via our unconscious?

If we can accept that God is more desirous of communicating with us than we could ever be of communicating with him (this being a central part of the Good News of Christianity), and if we can affirm that he is sovereign over the totality of his creation, including the unconscious, then we will be ready to accept the possibility that God may speak to us through our dreams. Dreams should not be expected to replace God's communication to us through his Word, through the sacraments, or through prayer.

But dreams personalize God's communication with us in a way that helps us know ourselves and grow.

Viewed in such a manner, dreams can be seen as gifts of a God who seeks to use them to help us know what Daniel called "our inmost thought" (Dan. 2:30 JB). Dreams are, therefore, a way in which God offers to help us know ourselves. We also come to know ourselves through our relationships, by reflection on our actions and reactions, and by prayerful meditation on Scripture, but dreams complement these means of knowing ourselves. They bring us personalized messages from God, forged in the hearth of our unconscious.

2. Recognize that some dreams are more profitable for dream work than others. Dreams differ tremendously in terms of their usefulness for dream work. Some dreams are a fairly direct replaying of the events of the previous day. For example, I may dream of myself giving a lecture or of running late for my appointments. However, even here, if one or more significant details differ between the dream and the reality of the day, such dreams may still have great significance. Other dreams may offer more of a comment on the day's events, thus increasing their importance. For example, I may have felt that the amount of preparation for the lecture the previous day was quite adequate but dream about turning up with no notes and no preparation. Such a dream suggests a fairly transparent message that some important aspect of my life may not be receiving sufficient attention. John Sanford describes these dreams as "daily housekeeping" and sees them as containing a wisdom that helps us live our lives on center, even if their message is relatively transparent and their significance not usually profound.[6]

Dreams that are most profitable for dream work are those that are most shaped by the unconscious. These generally occur late in the night, often just before waking, and are usually longer than average. They also usually have strong feelings attached to them. Feelings of wonder, awe, terror, or deep peace are particularly indicative of a significant dream, but any strong feeling is significant. Feelings that stay with the dreamer for some time after awakening are always indicative of a very significant dream.

The most significant dreams are those that have an incongru-
ous element or puzzling quality to them. Dreams with people fly-
ing, animals talking, mythological creatures, larger-than-life figures, extraterrestrial aliens, or anything that does not come from
the events of our daily lives indicate that the dream has arisen
from the deepest levels of the unconscious. Such dreams often
are charged with psychic energy. Sometimes they are described
as "numinous" dreams because they seem to partake of an
autonomous spiritual reality that transcends our own personal
nature. The clearest numinous dreams are those involving a direct
encounter with God or his angels. Frequently such dreams are
associated with deep and remarkably powerful feelings of wonder or awe. Their vividness often lasts a lifetime.

One woman in her late forties, reporting a dream from age
eleven, indicated that the details remain as vivid as if it were from
the previous night. In this dream she saw herself walking down
a street near a magnificent, large church. Suddenly, the sky behind
the church was rolled back, and she was swept up into heaven.
There she saw a scene with Mary, Joseph, and Jesus, who talked
with her and invited her to engage in their conversation. The emotions accompanying this experience were those of profound awe
and blessedness. It gave her, she reports as an adult, a lifelong
sense of her specialness to God.

In another, a man reported that he was toiling in a factory, making things that he then placed on a conveyor belt. Allowing his
eye to follow the incline of this belt, he saw that it led to a rec-
tangular mouth of a gray, monolithic facade with no other features than the mouth and a large sign that said DUTY. Suddenly
he heard his name called and turning, saw a soft, billowy, white
curtain extending from horizon to horizon on his left and right
and out of sight into the sky above him. The voice then called his
name again and invited him to lift the curtain and enter. Doing
so, he was immediately confronted with a large banquet hall, filled
with people eating, drinking, and enjoying themselves. Jesus was
at the front of the hall, his arms outstretched, and calling him forward to the one remaining empty chair, which had his name on
it. On seeing this, he was filled with unspeakable joy and a never-
before-realized sense of peace.

Numinous dreams of this sort are often associated with major life changes and, not infrequently, with religious conversion. The one that was at the core of the conversion of the slave trader John Newton is a good example of such a dream. In this dream, Newton saw himself on a sailing ship in Venice suddenly being approached by a stranger who gave him a ring and told him that his life would be full of happiness as long as he had this ring. Newton was delighted with the gift and kept it in his possession until a friend ridiculed him for his superstition. He then threw the ring into the sea. Immediately, however, he saw a great fire on shore and knew instinctively that he would be drawn into that fire. Deeply regretting having thrown the ring away, he stood looking at where the ring had sunk into the sea. Suddenly someone stood at his side and asked him why he looked so sad. He told the stranger how he had been given the ring and then stupidly thrown it away. At this point, the stranger jumped into the sea, disappeared into the depths, and reappeared with the ring. Newton then demanded the return of the ring, but the stranger's reply was, "I will keep it for you. But whenever you need the power of the ring, remember I will always be at your side."

Throughout the rest of his days John Newton described this dream as the most important event of his life. He stated that at the moment of awakening from the dream he felt like a piece of wood that had just been rescued from a ravaging fire. As a result of this dream, he ceased being captain of a slave trading ship and became an Anglican clergyman, known throughout Christendom today as the author of the popular hymn "Amazing Grace."[7]

3. *Recognize that, with the help of God, the dreamer is the one best able to discern the significance of the dream.* Too often dream work involves someone listening to the dreams of another and simply declaring what they supposedly mean. While this may be appropriate in some contexts, such an authoritarian approach does not fit well with the ideals of soul care dialogue presented in chapter 7. When dream work is made a part of soul care, it seems much preferable to assume that the dreamer is in the best position to determine the significance of the dream. This does not mean that there is no role for another person. The mere telling of one's dream to another

often places the dream in a much different context, and restrained probing of the dream by the other can also open up its possibilities. Ultimately, however, the dream belongs to the dreamer, and it seems safest to treat it as an interaction between him or her and God.

This means that the dreamer should be encouraged to prayerfully reflect on the dream and wait upon God for help in hearing what, if anything, God wishes to say through it. There is no need to rush to closure on the determination of the dream's significance. What is required is an attitude of prayerful reflection and an expectation that God will illumine the significance of the message he has given.

Affirming that the dreamer is ultimately the one best able to determine the significance of the dream also suggests the unhelpfulness of cookbook approaches to dream interpretation. While certain dream symbols may appear to carry specific meanings, it remains most useful for the dreamer to be the ultimate interpreter of them. Some dream symbols may be totally unfamiliar to the dreamer and yet common to mythology, fairy tales, or folklore. Suggestions of possible significance and indications of ways to further explore these possibilities can be very helpful, but authoritarian translations are seldom useful. Dreams are given by God to empower the recipient of the gift. Dream work must, therefore, be conducted in ways that support this.

4. *View the dream as offering questions rather than answers, advice, or prophetic revelations.* This principle cuts to the heart of the differences between the major ways of thinking about dreams.

Some people relate to dreams as prophetic revelations. Dreams about weddings, for example, may be interpreted as meaning that someone close to them will soon get married, while those of accidents or funerals suggest impending misfortune or death. Such a view is easily described as superstitious. However, large numbers of people, many of them highly educated and of above average intelligence, acknowledge one or more experiences of such dreams as a source of extrasensory knowledge that later turned out to be valid.

A more common approach is to view the dream as giving advice on some aspect of living. In such a view, when faced with a decision between two jobs, a dream in which the dreamer has chosen one of them might be interpreted as advice on the decision at hand. Or, a person whose lifestyle reflects a high degree of consumerism and materialism might interpret a dream involving an extremely simple lifestyle as advice about changes that need to be made.

In contrast to these two interpretative postures, I have found it most useful to view the dream as offering a question to be asked of self. Understood in this more conservative way, the dream suggests something we need to think about or reflect upon. Thus, a dream about war suggests questions such as, "What inner enemy am I facing?" or, "In relation to whom do I feel either threatened or hostile?" Similarly, a dream of falling might suggest questions such as, "Of what am I afraid of losing control?" or, "What aspect of my life is out of control?" In such an approach, the task is not to find the one true meaning of the dream but to reflect on the questions it raises.

5. *View dreams as parables.* While it is not useful to approach a dream seeking its one true meaning, it is useful to attempt to discern its one basic point or question. When viewed as a parable, we are better able to realize that amid the often puzzling array of details, the dream contains one overall theme. Parables are interpreted too literally when we seek to translate every element in the story into an implication. Parables, like dreams, make essentially one basic point.

Like parables, dreams are a form of communication that are initially provocative, sometimes even troubling. They are not passive communications that simply present information; rather, they invite engagement. Both dreams and parables also give returns that are proportional to the investment of interest and effort.

Viewing dreams as parables helps the dreamer not to become overly literal in his or her interpretation of them. Dreams are not secret messages, cleverly encoded so their true meaning will not be readily available to anyone by chance stumbling on them. They are stories that engage the self in an experience that, upon reflection, yields important information. This is what both dreams and parables do. They draw one into their story until suddenly, their message is quite clear and usually remarkably simple.

6. *Pay particular attention to repetitions.* People sometimes worry that if they miss the significance of a particular dream, that message is lost for all time. This never seems to be the case. God appears to be highly redundant in his communications with us in dreams—at least until we finally get the point. When examined carefully, dreams involve a great deal of repetition at the level of overall theme. Because of this, paying particular attention to these repetitions, both within dreams and between dreams within a night, is very important. Reflecting on similarities between dreams over a longer course of time is also, of course, very important.

A participant in a dream workshop described a dream of the previous night that she suddenly realized contained important elements that had been present in several recent dreams. In the dream of the previous night she had been in a library when suddenly books began to tumble off the shelves onto her. Before she knew it, she was up to her waist in books and unable to move. On reflection, she recalled that books and libraries had been in a dream earlier that week and in at least two other recent dreams, fragments of which she could still remember. The significance of this repetition had eluded her until she began to understand the principle of redundancy in dreams as a means of catching our attention. As she began to explore the question being posed by these dreams, she first identified books with her love of knowledge and her investment in the life of the mind. Scenes of books falling on her and, in one dream, being eaten and then vomited out at a dinner party led her to ask, "In what ways am I hiding behind knowledge and ideas?" and, "At what cost have I sold my soul to intellectual pursuits?" This was to be the beginning of significant exploration for her—growth that was catalyzed by a repetition of an element of a dream until it finally caught her attention.

7. *Recognize that people and objects in dreams usually are best understood as representing parts of self.* Most people dream, at least occa-

sionally, of friends and family members. Because a dream is coming from within me, however, it is most useful to understand it as about me, not others. In the view of object relations theory, internal representations of significant others are a part of the deepest strata of our psyche, actually forming a part of our self.[8] At a minimum this means that the element of my dream that presents itself as my father is not really my external father but the internal father who lives within me. Appearing in my dream, this element profitably tells me something about myself. In terms of my external father, the most it tells me is something about my experience of my relationship with him.

In a similar way, all the objects and people in a dream, coming from within me, reflect more about me than any people or objects in the external world with which they may be readily associated. Thus, while on one level a dream of a fight with a friend may reflect the experience of a recent interchange or feelings about an impending one, at a deeper level it is most usefully viewed as information about me. Both parties to the interaction in the dream are parts of me, as is their interaction (the fighting).

Viewed in such a way, a dream of an authoritarian boss invites me to reflect on the bossy parts of my own self, while one of an innocent and frightened child invites me to reflect on the innocent and frightened part of my self. Carefully observed, dreams will invite similar reflection on our masculine and feminine parts, our deceitful parts, our playful parts, our seductive parts, our masochistic parts, our narcissistic parts, our grandiose parts, our competitive parts, and our exhibitionistic parts. The creativity of the mind in finding appropriate representations for the various parts of our self is hard to underestimate. Behind the incredible richness and diversity of human dreams lies an even greater complexity and diversity of our selves.

8. *Undertake dream work within a context of the Christian disciplines and community.* Dream work calls for discernment. Dreams bring us into contact with both lost or underdeveloped parts of self that should be integrated and sinful or evil elements that should be eliminated. This need for discernment underscores the importance of approaching dream work fully equipped with the re-

sources of the Christian life. Dream work should, ideally, be done within the context of prayer and as a part of a life that includes corporate worship, the sacraments, and the study of Scriptures. When it is conducted as a part of Christian soul care, these resources can be supplemented by the spiritual guidance that can be mediated by another Christian. Although such relationships are sometimes referred to as spiritual guidance, the true guide is always the Holy Spirit. The soul friend is merely the companion on the journey.

Techniques of Dream Work

Preparation for work with dreams begins before falling asleep by inviting God to speak in whatever way he chooses and by expressing a desire to hear what he has to say. Just as the young boy Samuel mistook God's voice in the night for that of the prophet Eli, so too, we often fail to recognize God's nighttime voice. Samuel's words, "Speak for thy servant heareth" (1 Sam. 3:10 KJV) can be ours as we prayerfully prepare for sleep and express our desire to do so in the presence of the God who has no more ceased being Revelation than he has ceased being Love.

Readiness to receive dreams as communications from God is evidenced by having a journal and pen readily available. Because dreams fade so fast from memory, it is necessary to record them as soon as one awakens. Having a journal and pen by the bedside tells God that you are serious about your desire to hear and obey his word.

If an unexamined dream can be compared to an unopened letter, dream work can be thought of as opening the letter, reading, and reflecting on it. There are a great many ways of doing this. We will concentrate on the techniques that seem to have the most promise for dream work conducted within the context of Christian soul care.[9] The first three of these are basic ones that should be the starting point for anyone new to dream work. Most people find these immediately useful, and many never have occasion to go beyond them. After these, we will briefly consider several more advanced techniques.

Basic Techniques

1. *Immediately upon awakening after significant dreams, write a dream report.* Writing the dream down in as much detail as can be remembered on awakening is the first and most essential step to dream work. This record of the dream then becomes the data for the work of all subsequent steps. The dream report is not the place for reflection on the significance of the dream. It is simply a statement, as thorough as can be produced, of the images, actions, reactions, thoughts, feelings, conversations, characters, character development, attitudes, colors, sounds, and sensations experienced in the dream. The dream report should be written quickly, without concern for grammar, spelling, or punctuation. Everything remembered from the dream should be included without any censoring or editing. The date of the dream should also be noted.

Following the recording of the dream, you should also note any reactions that you have upon waking. Feelings that have carried over into consciousness, immediate questions raised by the dream, first associations to any of the images, and any other initial reactions should be noted here. This is not yet the formal dream work. However, these initial reactions are often very helpful in the subsequent dream work and will usually be forgotten if not written down immediately.

To illustrate a dream report, consider the following, a dream we will further explore as we subsequently add additional techniques of dream work.

Dream Report:

In the dream I was walking toward a house that I had apparently just bought. It was a late-nineteenth-century Victorian home with a large veranda, turrets, gables, and a most interesting roof line. Entering it I was immediately impressed with a large, circular staircase, mahogany flooring, and especially the high ceilings. My eyes were drawn up by the light on the ceiling and upper parts of the rooms. I then noticed windows just under the ceiling in each room. I thought this somewhat odd but appreciated the light it allowed in. For some reason I felt particularly excited by the high ceilings and kept looking at them. Going from room to room, I then discovered that the previous owners had left most of their clothes, which were in excellent condition and of impeccable quality, and I immediately thought that many of them would fit me quite well. I then noticed that the high windows in each room were open, allowing a pleasant breeze to enter the house.

Reaction:

Feeling of excitement from dream still with me on awakening. Surprised I liked an old house so much given that I have always preferred new houses and new things. Most striking feature of dream was high ceilings and light. Pleasant but curious.

2. *At the earliest possible good time for reflection, give the dream a title and identify its theme, dominant affects, and the major questions that it raises.* Known as the TTAQ (Title, Theme, Affect, Question) technique, this simple activity is perhaps the single most useful technique of dream work. Many people do nothing more with their dreams than record them and complete these four tasks. The dividends from this can be extremely rewarding.

First, give the dream a title. This helps you focus on its essence and provides a handle for subsequent reference to it. Think of this title as that which an artist might give it if it were a painting hanging in a gallery. If you have trouble finding this title, think of the title the dream may have given itself if asked. Or ask God for help in entitling his gift to you.

Then, identify the dream's main theme. This answers the question, "What is the dream principally about?" If there are several themes, list them in the order in which they appear in the dream. After doing so, consider again if one overall theme lies behind these. Again, don't fail to use the opportunity to ask for God's help in identifying this overall theme.

Identifying the overall affect (or feeling) expressed in the dream is usually the easiest of the four tasks. Sometimes no feeling was experienced in the dream, but most dreams involve feelings of some sort. What feelings did the principal character, the one with whom you most identify, have in the dream? What other feelings were experienced by or suggested by the behavior of other characters? After noting your reactions to the dream report, what feelings were present when you awoke in the morning?

Finally, what questions does the dream seem to be asking of you? The authors of this technique suggest that you "listen to the dream as if it were a friend asking you a meaningful question."[10] Again, do not hesitate to bring prayerful reflection to this question, asking what precisely God is trying to draw to your attention.

In terms of the dream of exploring the old house with the high ceilings and rooms filled with light, the following were the results of the TTAQ exercise:

Title: Exploring my new old house
Theme: The old holds promise of new discoveries
Affect: Excitement, wonder, lightness
Questions:

- *What new parts of self am I on the verge of discovering that open up exciting possibilities and hold the promise of raising my ceilings and allowing new light and fresh air to enter my life?*
- *What is old and familiar in my life but holds the possibility of offering new vitality?*
- *I have usually turned away from the old to the new and innovative. What have I missed in the old? in my own traditions? in my own story?*

3. *Make opportunities for prayer, Scripture study, and reflection on questions suggested by the dream.* Prayerful reflection on the themes and questions raised by the dream is the heart of the basic dream work. Now that the dream is recorded, there is no time limit on such reflection. It is not uncommon to return to particularly rich dreams again and again. Such reflection often suggests new questions and richer possibilities for unpacking the significance of the

dream. When one returns to earlier dreams, the possibilities of identifying themes and questions repeated between dreams is greatly enhanced.

Incorporation of Scripture study on issues raised by the dream can also be a powerful adjunct to this reflective work. Such thematically guided study demonstrates the psychological richness of Scriptures and shows their relevance to the issues of the inner life in a manner that is often not identified by sermons or conventional Bible study. Issues of loss, the management of anger, control of self and others, the fear of intimacy, trust of intuition, the limits of rationality, the discovery and actualization of one's truest self, or the possibilities of surrender all are richly addressed by Scripture study.

Discussing the questions and issues identified by the dream with a close and trusted friend can also be of great help in unpacking the dream's significance. This is, of course, the resource that is available in a soul care relationship. Things that are often quite opaque in personal, even prayerful, reflection sometimes become quite lucid when they are discussed with another person.

Results of Initial Reflection:

Prayerful reflection on the dream reinforces the initial impression that it is about the discovery of new possibilities in old, previously dismissed, and undervalued parts of my experience. The focus of reflection has been on redemption of parts of my religious heritage that have been discarded. I discovered that I have, in certain matters, thrown out the baby with the bath water.

Prayer on these matters suggested exploration of the scriptural theme of remembering the past. I have discovered rich insights in the ancient Hebrew understanding of the role of memory in identity. I recognize that I have very much tried to make my identity, like a new house, out of new materials. But new houses usually lack the elegance and grace of older ones, and I pray that God will begin to show me more of what he would have me redeem from the old materials of my life.

177

Advanced Techniques

Advanced techniques of dream work are best employed after experience with the more basic ones. There is no danger in employing them immediately; however, they generally detract from rather than facilitate dream work until one is thoroughly familiar with the basics. Once this experience has been acquired, the following techniques will be found to add significantly to the richness of working with dreams.

4. *Pay careful attention to the details of the dream and write down your associations to each major symbol.* In the work with the dream to this point, details have been ignored in favor of major themes and broad issues. This is what it means to treat the dream as a parable. Subsequent to such a broad-focus engagement with the dream, however, it is also appropriate to examine its details, provided the details were recorded in the dream report. The goal is not to interpret the details, simply to note them. Allow them to form their own story or to change your understanding of the themes or questions raised by the story you have to this point encountered. Then allow your mind to freely develop associations to each of the major symbolic elements of the dream. To illustrate this, let us again return to the dream we have been following through the various stages of dream work.

Major Symbols	Details	Associations
house	late-nineteenth-century Victorian, large veranda, turrets and gables, interesting roof, circular staircase, mahogany flooring, high ceilings, windows near ceiling, pleasant breeze	house = self, many rooms = many parts of self; this particular house reminds me of a small castle—something of architectural beauty, grace, and elegance; high ceilings and light suggest endless possibilities of expansiveness; breeze seems to be warm and nurturing. Overall, this house offers a wonderful place to live—incredible opportunities for discovery, growth, and enrichment.

Major Symbols	Details	Associations
clothing	good quality, good condition, would fit	Discarded by previous owner but of obvious great worth. Dare I take these discards and make them mine?

5. *Identify and pay particular attention to your dream ego.* As indicated earlier, it is helpful to think of each part of the dream as reflecting some part of self. But one part of self that usually appears in every dream is of particular importance—the ego. As this term is usually understood, the ego is the conscious, decision-making, executive part of self. It is assumed to hold the responsibility for the reconciliation of the demands of the inner and outer worlds. Because of these responsibilities, the ego is assumed to play an important role in dream formation. Its presence can, therefore, almost always be discerned in our dreams.

The dream ego is the character or characters in the dream who feel most like the dreamer or with whom the dreamer can most identify. The dream ego may be of the same or different sex, age, or race, and may even be an animal or a plant. But usually these disguises are quite transparent; the dreamer usually is quite capable of recognizing himself or herself in one (or occasionally more) of the symbols. Closely studying the attitudes, choices, actions, and reactions of the dream ego has great potential in understanding the state of one's inner world and in taking steps toward psychospiritual growth.

In particular, pay attention to the ways in which the dream ego is different from the waking ego. Noting these, ask if you are pleased with how the dream ego behaved. Ask if the dream ego may be demonstrating a way of being that should be considered. Then pray for discernment in recognizing what God may be saying to you through the actions of your dream ego.

Actions of Dream Ego:

Dream ego quite easily identified in this dream. He differed from me in only one significant way—he walked much more slowly and seemed more fully present in enjoying the house. In contrast, I seem to always be going somewhere else, moving through whatever room I am currently in to get to another. Dream ego took his time, both while approaching the house and while in it. Reflection on this suggests an interesting invitation–to stop and smell the roses, to linger in the places where I spend my time in both the inner and outer worlds.

6. *Conduct an imaginary conversation with the dream ego.* Almost everyone knows what it means to engage in a conversation with themselves. Some people do it quite frequently and even audibly. There is nothing abnormal about such inner dialogue. In fact, it is both normal and has the potential to be quite transforming.

Two things make such inner conversations pathological. The first is when they drown out messages from the external world. In such a situation, the person is so internally preoccupied that contact with the external world is impaired. This is seen most clearly in certain forms of psychosis. The second is when, by virtue of what is being said to self, inner conversations have the effect of impairing functioning in the external world. Negative, self-directed statements such as, "What's the use of trying; you are going to fail anyway?" or "Things are never going to get any better" form a stable part of most experiences of depression and clearly perpetuate feelings of depression. Changing such statements to more positive ones (e.g., "It's not true that you are no good at anything and that nobody likes you. For example, think of . . .") usually leads to dramatic improvements in emotional functioning.

Such conversations are not substantially different from those proposed with the dream ego. Both involve an imaginary conversation between different parts of self. Both are, therefore, conducted with one's imagination. The dream ego does not really speak or answer questions in the way in which an external person does. But, nonetheless, the conversation can be equally productive.

The only significant way in which dialogue with one's dream ego differs from the sort of conversations people typically have with themselves is that the dream work conversation is less under rational control. This affords greater room for imaginative development. In a typical inner conversation, a person may attempt to think through what diverse parts of self want out of some situation. ("On the one hand, I'd like . . . , but on the other hand, I'd also really like . . .") Dialogue with the dream ego invites the other part of self to speak for itself, that is, to suggest its own answer. While the answer comes from the imagination, this does not diminish its value. When Joan of Arc was asked at her heresy trial if the voices she heard and attributed to God were not really her imagination, she reportedly replied that of course they came from her imagination because how else could one possibly hear the voice of God?[11] Just as our dreams happen in our imagination and yet hold the possibility of carrying messages from God, so too dialogue with an element of our dreams may occur in our imagination and still be guided by God.

Jacob's wrestling with God illustrates many of the principles of dream work dialogue. As recorded in Genesis 32, Jacob was on his way to meet his brother Esau, whom he had not seen since he had betrayed him in order to steal his birthright blessing. On the final evening before Jacob's arrival, he sent the rest of his party ahead and spent the night alone. During the night, God appeared to him in a vision in which he and God wrestled until daybreak. At the end of the vision, we are presented with an interesting interaction. God asked Jacob to release him for it was almost daylight. But Jacob refused to do so until he was given a blessing. Jacob recognized that his nighttime visitor had something for him, and he was unwilling to let him go until he received what was to be his gift. God agreed to these terms, gave Jacob a new name as his gift, and Jacob released him.

If our dream characters can be interpreted as coming from God to bless us with a gift for our well-being, we too should be prepared to wrestle with them and not let them go until we have received the gift they bear. This is the basic principle behind dialogue with dream characters.

It is often helpful to begin this dialogue with prayer. This might then be followed by a question about what the dream ego brings as a gift, what it has to offer as advice, or, most simply, why it appeared as it did in the dream. One way in which such a conversation can develop is illustrated in the following:

Dialogue between Waking Ego (Ego) and Dream Ego (DE):

Ego: In the dream I noticed that you were taking your time exploring the house, not seeming to be in a hurry to get somewhere else. Is there something I should be learning from that fact?

DE: Well, that's part of what you should be thinking about, but what else did you notice about how I behaved?

Ego: Frankly, I'm not sure I noticed anything else.

DE: Try to picture how you saw me in the dream. What do you notice?

Ego: I'm not sure this gets us anywhere, but you were always looking up.

DE: Okay, but what else?

Ego: Well, maybe that you were very aware of a range of sensations—the lightness, the motion of the air in the breeze, the warmth of that air, etc.

DE: But you are still missing the most obvious.

Ego: Do you mean that you were appreciative of the old house?

DE: Of course.

Ego: So what am I to learn from that?

DE: What have you learned so far?

Ego: Well, maybe that I should take another look at things in my heritage that I have dismissed. Perhaps there are things of undiscovered value there.

DE: Okay. But it wasn't just anything old that I discovered in the dream; it was a house and clothes. Wrestle with that a bit more.

The result of this dialogue is that I am driven back to do more work on associations to the house and clothes.

house
A house is where one lives; it's one's private place and space. For me, a house is a castle—a refuge, a fortress, a place of retreat.

clothes
Clothes are what we put on for public places; how we present ourselves to others. My clothes are my public self.

old house
An old house is a house like I used to live in when I was growing up. It was always full of people, and yet it always had enough room for private space.

old clothes
Old clothes are humbler ways of engaging with others. Not putting on as much of a pretense; maybe, less investment in image.

Many other dream work techniques are available, but these six should provide more than enough for all but those who are highly experienced in dream work. The great danger of techniques is that they can depersonalize and mechanize dream work. At their best, they are ways of structuring an encounter with one's deepest self guided by the Spirit of God. Dreams are not objects for analysis but parts of self to be embraced in an I-Thou encounter. Such an engagement can happen on one's own, but it is almost always facilitated by dialogue with another. This is the wonderful and rich role of dream work in Christian soul care.

9

Forms of Christian Soul Care

To this point we have described the focus and some of the activities of Christian soul care but have not discussed who provides such care. In reality, a great range of people are involved in the Christian care of souls—parents, friends, teachers, clergy, psychotherapists, authors, lay counselors, health care professionals, chaplains, laity providing pastoral care, and spiritual directors being among them. Some of these groups provide such care for remuneration and, for that reason, can be described as professionals in soul care. Others provide soul care without remuneration and may, therefore, be thought of as nonprofessional or lay soul guides. One group is not superior to the other. Each fills a niche, and each is afforded possibilities of care not available to others.

Christian soul care is much too important to be left to any one group of people. For too long it was primarily the responsibility of clergy. Then, under the influence of the rise of therapeutic soul care, it increasingly became the responsibility of those trained in the psychotherapeutic arts and sciences. More recently we have witnessed a resurgence of interest in the ancient tradition of spiritual direction, this involving both clergy and laity. We have also seen, at least in some church traditions, the rise of fellowship groups as a form of mutual soul care.

What is important is that those who offer Christian soul care should do so in response to God's call to such service. The legitimacy of soul care as a Christian vocation is not effected by the presence or absence of financial remuneration nor by formal training in soul care. It is solely dependent on the call of God to such service, and such a call comes to a great variety of people.

At least nine forms of contemporary Christian soul care can be identified: family soul care, mutual soul care, pastoral care, lay counseling, Christian counseling, pastoral counseling, spiritual direction, Christian psychotherapy, and intensive soul care. While the boundaries between these activities are somewhat arbitrary, there are important distinctions and relationships between them. As graphically represented in figure 3, placing these forms of care in relation to the nurturing and healing components of soul care begins to show these distinctions and relationships. In this figure, approaches that share the same potential for both cure and care

Figure 3
Forms of Christian Soul Care

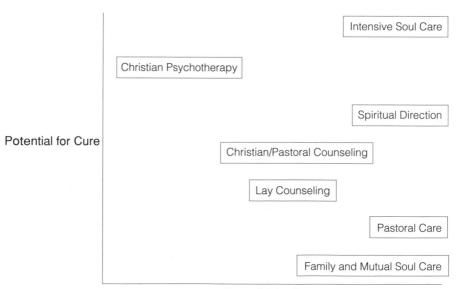

are combined. Those farther to the right have greater potential for nurture and support while those higher in the figure have greater potential for healing and restoration.

Family Soul Care

The most basic, and in some ways most important, form of Christian soul care is that provided by family and friends. When people care for each other within these intimate personal relationships, they do not usually think of themselves as providing soul care. They are simply caring for those they love. But if all of us could be in relationships in which friends and family care for us in the ways we have been describing, the need for more formal soul care would be greatly reduced.

At its best, the care that family members give to each other has unique potential to facilitate deep psychospiritual growth. Parents nurturing the psychospiritual development of their children have opportunities to influence their children in ways that no one else will ever have. So do people who make a genuine effort to know and support the growth of the inner life of their spouses. The same is true of siblings who move beyond rivalry to intimacy and soul friendship. While family care also offers some degree of healing and restoration of damage, the potential for this is much less than that which exists in other forms of soul care. However, the potential for deep soul friendships within families makes the family the primary and most important context of Christian soul care.

Unfortunately, however, families often fail to live up to the ideals of soul friendship. Parents content themselves with discipline and instruction, failing to also offer themselves in a gift of friendship. Tragically, spouses regularly do the same. Too often those who are active in caring for others outside the home offer little genuine soul friendship to those within their own family. The demands of such friendship are enormous, and chief among these are the demands of genuine dialogue.

If Christian soul care is to start at home, there is a great need for people to learn the art of dialogue. For many, this starts with developing the skills of deep empathic listening. Some seem reasonably capable of listening but fail to bring themselves to the relationship. For others it is primarily a matter of not spending sufficient time with their spouse or children. Regardless of what steps need to be taken, most families can readily identify things they need to do to move toward making the family a network of deep soul friendships. Sometimes all it takes is a reminder of how important it is to do so.

Mutual Soul Care

For many people, the most significant soul care relationships lie among friends. Like family soul care, friends providing psychospiritual nurture to each other do so in ways that are informal and seldom, if ever, thought of as soul care. Unlike the care given by spiritual directors and psychotherapists, the care friends give to each other does not constitute the totality of their relationship. Also unlike the professional caring relationships, the care that is given is generally much more mutual.

Everyone needs such friendships. We all need others who will take the time to listen to us and help us express ourselves at the level of our deepest psychospiritual longings, needs, and struggles. We also need people who, by the way they relate to us, help us learn how to attend to our own deepest selves in the same manner.

Mutual soul care is people caring for the significant others in their lives and thereby helping them care more adequately for themselves. Such relationships involve friendship, but not all friendships involve mutual soul care. The ideal of deep dialogical engagement marks the vast majority of friendships as falling short of genuine soul care relationships. Many others involve little mutuality; they are the one-sided helping relationships of people who seek to give care to others but who do not expect much in return.

Mutual soul care involves reciprocal intimacy and vulnerability. It also involves balanced and alternating giving and receiving.

At any given point in time, the relationship may not feel balanced in terms of who is primarily giving and who is primarily receiving. But over time, mutual soul care demands that the giving of care be bidirectional and roughly balanced.

Such relationships can involve as few as two people but can also occur within small groups. Fellowship groups are ideally suited to providing such care, which may easily be combined with other activities such as Bible study or prayer. However, not all Bible study or prayer groups are mutual soul care groups, which give primacy to the care and nurture of the inner life of participants in the group.

While mutual soul care can occur in the absence of any training, anything that enhances the understanding of the psychospiritual dynamics of the inner life enhances people's ability to both offer and receive such care. Those who are most able to care for the souls of others are those who most know their own inner worlds and who possess the psychospiritual health and maturity to reach out to others with love. Fortunately, we can learn these things with others. This is the exciting potential of relationships of mutual soul care.

Pastoral Care

The first of the more formal expressions of Christian soul care that we will consider is pastoral care. As this term is commonly employed, pastoral care refers to the total range of help offered by pastors, elders, deacons, and other members of a congregation to those in need of care. Pastoral care is a ministry of compassion, its source and motivation being the love of God. It includes such things as visiting the sick, attending to the dying, comforting the bereaved, supporting those who are struggling or facing difficulties of any kind, preaching, and administering the sacraments. In its most basic form, pastoral care is simply any Christian reaching out with help, encouragement, or support to others in times of need.

Pastoral care includes but is much broader than pastoral counseling. Pastoral counseling is usually initiated by the one seeking help and is typically problem focused. In contrast, pastoral care is more often initiated by the one offering care and does not usually have as narrow a problem focus. Pastoral care offers the gift of Christian love and nurture from one who attempts to mediate the gracious presence of God to another who is in need.

As its name suggests, pastoral care has more potential for soul care than cure. For many people, it is God's lifeline bringing them encouragement, support, and hope in times of crisis. However, seldom is it structured in a manner to allow for extended dialogue, and because of this, its potential for repair of psychospiritual damage and pathology is modest. Although it may initiate and stimulate movement toward greater psychospiritual growth, it is not usually all that is needed to sustain and direct such growth. It does, however, nicely complement other forms of soul care, and when offered alongside them, enhances the total spectrum of helping relationships that are available.

Unfortunately, episodic pastoral care is the extent of the soul care received by many Christians. They listen to sermons, engage as spectators in services of worship, periodically receive the sacraments, and may occasionally have a visit from a pastor, elder, or someone from the congregation. Is it any wonder that they feel the church has little relevance to the inner life of their soul? And can we really be surprised that they have so little awareness of the needs and realities of that inner life?

Lay Counseling

The rise of professional counseling has spawned the development in some sectors of the church of a phenomenon known as lay counseling. Lay counselors are usually people who are neither clergy nor professional counselors. Typically they are volunteers who are identified on the basis of their gifts and personality and who receive training in the basics of therapeutic communication. While this training can be quite extensive, sometimes it is quite minimal. For this reason, what lay counselors actually do varies considerably.

As usually practiced, lay counseling generally has a fairly clinical or psychological focus. This means that people come to lay counselors with problems for which they seek help, and lay counselors approach these people seeking to offer support and suggestions regarding ways of coping with the problems. Prayer and the use of other religious resources may form a part of some of these interventions. However, typically, lay counselors function as their generally more qualified Christian counselor counterparts, that is, as clinical therapists offering psychological assistance for problems in living.

When positioned as a form of soul care and placed within the continuum of soul care possibilities we are presently reviewing, lay counseling takes on a slightly different emphasis. Because of the limited training lay counselors have in therapeutic methods, they are really not well qualified for the deep reparative work of soul cure. However, since they are generally sincere Christians and caring, sensitive individuals, they can play a very significant role in a soul care that is primarily directed toward spiritual growth. If lay counseling could be understood in terms of helping people experience the presence of God and discern his will for them in the midst of whatever problems they are facing, the primary goal would become spiritual growth rather than psychological problem resolution. It would still be appropriate for people to seek their help in times of trouble. However, rather than approaching them as counselors who are expected to solve their problems, they would approach them as mature, caring Christians who are willing to share their journey for a while and help them grow. As such, lay counseling would form an important component in the spectrum of soul care, offering greater potential for soul cure than that typically associated with pastoral care, but less than the other more specialized forms of counseling and psychotherapy.

Christian Counseling

Christian counseling has been a major growth industry of the past few decades. With its own journals, professional associations, training programs, and credentialing organizations, Christian counseling has quickly made its mark on churches around the world. Publishers, authors, consultants, and workshop leaders have very much been a part of this phenomenon.

Practitioners of Christian counseling are highly diverse: Some have masters and even doctoral degrees in psychology, social work, or marital and family therapy, while others have no more than a course or workshop in counseling. Some have theological training and even pastoral experience, while others have neither. Some have a clear vision of their work as Christian soul care, while others simply have a vision of offering counseling services to an available market.

Christian counselors offer their soul care on a variety of bases and within a range of contexts. Some practice on a fee-for-service basis within private practice contexts (either group or individual). Others are on salary within churches, offering their services as part of a pastoral ministry team. Yet others work in centers supported by a number of churches, fees sometimes being waived for those coming from such churches and on a sliding scale for others. Still others offer their services on a volunteer basis without fee.

With such diversity, generalizations about Christian counseling are hazardous. However, it seems that generally the counseling that this group of people provides is psychological in nature, problem focused, and offered within the context of Christian values and understandings of life. Often this results in counseling that is highly directive, such as giving advice that is judged to be biblical. At other times, it differs little from intensive psychotherapy, exploring and treating the root causes of problems. It also seems safe to suggest that Christian counseling is generally more concerned with soul cure than care. Christian character formation may sometimes play a part in it, but generally the goal is problem amelioration.

Christian counseling has great potential as a component in the spectrum of Christian soul care options. Its practitioners generally have more understanding of psychological dynamics and better training in therapeutic dialogue than lay counselors and those offering pastoral care. Consequently, the care Christian counselors offer has the possibility of considerable depth and efficacy. However, too often Christian counselors do not have either the psychological training necessary to allow them to offer the deep psychotherapeutic soul cure to which they aspire nor the theological and spiritual preparation necessary to allow them to offer the spiritual direction that may be needed. With great potential to bridge the gap between clergy and psychotherapists, they too often fall between the extremes of these groups without carving out a distinctive domain that best utilizes their skills.

When understood as soul care and contrasted to the other major forms of such care, some potential repositioning of Christian counseling is suggested. The most important component of this would be to supplement its current clinical emphasis with a spiritual one, shifting it in the direction of spiritual formation. The problem focus would remain, since problems are the reason why most people seek out counselors. However, rather than simple problem amelioration, the goal of Christian counseling would be that of psychospiritual growth. If the understanding of psychological dynamics typically possessed by Christian counselors were enhanced by a clearer focus on goals related to spiritual growth, Christian counselors could offer care that would be more intensive than that typically associated with lay counselors and other providers of pastoral care. Their care would also be more psychologically oriented than that typically associated with pastoral counseling. This would allow Christian counselors to fill a gap that exists in the current spectrum of Christian soul care services rather than merely duplicate the services of Christian psychotherapists.

Pastoral Counseling

Soul care offered under the rubric of pastoral counseling is at least as diverse as that associated with Christian counseling. In general, pastoral counseling may be distinguished from more general Christian counseling by the fact that pastoral counseling is provided by someone who is or was a pastor. This means that such a person is explicitly identified with the church, not just with Christian values. As such, like it or not, pastoral counselors are representative of the Christian church, sought out as such, and related to as such.

Pastoral counselors have a number of advantages over other counselors. Their training typically contains not just broad theological preparation but also often includes supervised clinical pastoral education. At its best, such clinical training provides opportunity for deeper knowing of self as well as acquisition of counseling skills. Pastoral counselors also usually offer their counseling within the context of the church, thus affording a network of other resources that can be incorporated into their soul care. Taken together, these distinctives give the pastoral counselor an opportunity to offer care that is both psychologically and spiritually well informed and that is enriched by the resources of the local congregation as well as the broader Christian tradition of the care of souls.

Unfortunately, not all pastoral counselors meet these ideals or utilize the full range of resources at their disposal. Too many lose the distinctives of their pastoral identity while clamoring after clinical credentials and competencies. Others distance themselves from psychology and offer counseling that is little more than preaching to captive audiences of one.

Pastors who resist the temptation to take their counseling vision and norms exclusively from the clinical psychotherapies and yet who manage to redeem some of the best insights from these therapeutic traditions are in a unique position to offer distinctively Christian soul care. They are much more likely than any of the groups discussed thus far to both understand and be in a position to offer full-orbed soul care. Unlike those offering noncounseling forms of pastoral care, pastoral counselors usually meet with those they counsel over a series of sessions. This affords the opportunity for dialogue that is often missing in pastoral care services. Unlike Christian counselors who do not work out of a church, they have the unique opportunity to utilize the healing and sustaining resources of the Christian church.

In order to do this, pastoral counselors need a distinct vision of the counseling they provide—a vision that situates their counseling within the broader spectrum of other pastoral responsibilities they hold and that directs them in a form of counseling that takes advantage of the unique resources of their training and role. One such model is my own short-term, structured approach known as Strategic Pastoral Counseling.[1]

Spiritual Direction

Although relationships of spiritual direction predate those of psychotherapy and either pastoral or Christian counseling by centuries, this form of soul care is still less common and considerably less well understood. Sometimes called discipleship, spiritual mentoring, spiritual friendship, soul friendship, or shepherding, the overall goal is the same—to aid spiritual growth. Usually this involves such things as learning to discern God's will and the leading of his Spirit, growth in prayer and in the life of the Spirit, dying to sin, the experience of God's forgiveness, the discovery and actualization of our unique self in Christ, and experiencing union with God. In short, Christian spiritual direction helps people pay attention to God's call to them and respond with a life of prayer, obedience, holiness, service, and love.

The focus of spiritual direction is experience not ideas. This means that the experience of God is the goal, not developing certain understandings of that experience. Moreover, experience of God is understood in terms of a relationship with him. Spiritual direction seeks, therefore, to foster a personal knowing of and response to God. It seeks to help individuals find their ground in God and to live their lives out of that ground.

Since prayer is such an integral part of the Christian experience of God, it usually also forms an integral part of spiritual direction. The spiritual director is interested in understanding and facilitating the person's experience of prayer. Does prayer involve a personal engagement with God? Does it involve listening as well as speaking? Can it begin to involve the simple but profoundly transforming enjoyment of being in God's presence—a contemplative gazing upon him and communing with him that goes beyond words? Can prayer, in other words, move from the head to the heart?

Spiritual direction holds a unique place in the spectrum of Christian soul care activities. Unlike pastoral counseling, its focus is not problems but growth. Unlike Christian counseling, its concern is not so much with behavior as with the inner life. And unlike Christian psychotherapy, the focus on the inner life is not primarily psychopathology but the experience of God. In contrast to pastoral counseling and psychotherapy, spiritual guidance is meant to be a way of life not a resource for problems. Furthermore, while pastoral counseling and psychotherapy both give a central role to the place of understanding or insight, spiritual guidance is more oriented to deepening faith, increasing awareness of the presence of God, and furtherance of spiritual growth.

Advocates for spiritual guidance argue that every Christian should have a spiritual guide. Spiritual direction provides a safeguard against the dangers of spiritual individualism by establishing a relationship of accountability. Emphasizing the need for spiritual direction, Thomas Merton warned of the hazards of solitary spirituality:

> The most dangerous man in the world is the contemplative who is guided by nobody. He trusts his own visions. He obeys the attractions of an inner voice but will not listen to other men. He identifies the will of God with anything that makes him feel . . . a big warm interior glow. The sweeter and the warmer the feeling is the more he is convinced of his own infallibility. . . . The world is covered with scars that have been left in its flesh by visionaries like these.[2]

All Christians, not just contemplatives, need spiritual direction. This is not the more general relationship of parishioner to pastor, although one's spiritual guide could very well be one's pastor. Nor is it the more common but often somewhat benign relationship of generalized Christian fellowship. Rather, this is a more intentional, personal, and individualized relationship. Such relationships seldom just happen; they must be established with intentionality as well as with much care and prayer.

Options for structuring relationships of spiritual direction allow considerable room for individual preferences. In addition to the traditional model of one spiritually less mature person relating to another judged to be more mature, alternate arrangements include mutual guidance (wherein two people take turns serving as guide for the other) and even group guidance. Small Bible study and fellowship groups, increasingly common in many Christian circles, may share aspects of such group guidance. Groups formed for the purpose of Christian accountability also share some similarity. However, the most central aspect of spiritual guidance is not fellowship, study, or accountability; rather, it is discernment of the leading of the Holy Spirit and nurture in Christian growth and spirituality.

Spiritual direction is a seriously underdeveloped component of the spectrum of contemporary Christian soul care options. Many Christians have no understanding of what it involves, and of those who do, most would have little idea of how to find a qualified spiritual director.[3] More Christians seeking to prepare themselves for work in soul care need to consider spiritual direction as a possibility for their calling, and more seeking soul care should consider it as a potential means of that care. Spiritual direction is particularly helpful for people receiving counseling or psychotherapy that does not explicitly explore the spiritual implications of such work from a Christian perspective. It is also particularly helpful for those who seek to provide the other forms of Christian soul care.

Christian Psychotherapy

Whereas the term *counseling* generally refers to activities that are short-term and either problem or solution focused, *psychotherapy* refers to those that are longer-term and more oriented toward an uncovering and resolution of the roots of the issues under exploration. Furthermore, while counseling is usually understood to be primarily oriented toward problem amelioration, the goals of psychotherapy are considerably broader, involving an expansion of the individual's capacity for emotional freedom and an enhancement of his or her mental health. Christian psychotherapy can be thought of as psychotherapy that is offered by a Christian, shaped by a Christian understanding of persons, guided by the Holy Spirit, and carried out with the intent of increasing the psychospiritual well-being and maturity of the one seeking help.

Christian psychotherapy has great potential as soul care and cure, perhaps particularly as cure. Unfortunately, this potential is once again not always realized. Too often Christian psychotherapists work from a dualistic view of the world and of the nature of the inner life of persons. While they may have some realization that psychological and spiritual matters interrelate, they often focus on the psychological aspects of persons to the virtual exclusion of spiritual ones. Consequently, the soul cure they offer is seriously one-sided. Too often they settle for making their work Christian by simply trying to be Christians themselves, believing that there is little more that can be done to Christianize their psychotherapy without reducing it to Christian counseling or advice giving. In doing so, however, they fail to recognize the nature of the implicit spirituality they inevitably shape through the intensive work of psychotherapy.

Psychotherapy is much too powerful and the relationship it involves too significant to ever allow it to be spiritually neutral. With the exception of the rare technical and very focused intervention, such as the behavioral treatment of a tic, psychotherapy inevitably deals with a broad enough slice of personality that spiritual considerations are involved. We are always either growing spiritually, that is, becoming more sensitive and responsive to the spiritual call in our life, or we are becoming more spiritually dead. At times of crisis or transition in our lives, the opportunity for spiritual movement in one direction or another is particularly great. This is even more so the case when we face these times with the assistance of a psychotherapist and begin to listen to messages from our inner selves. Psychotherapy is, therefore, inevitably a spiritual process. The only question is whether or not the spirituality it shapes is Christian.

To suggest that psychotherapy is a spiritual process is not to reduce it to religious instruction or to equate it to spiritual direction. Psychotherapy focuses on matters of the inner life from a psychological perspective. Christian psychotherapy does the same, differing, however, in its recognition of the spiritual significance of these matters and approaching them from a Christian perspective. Even if explicitly spiritual or religious matters are raised in psychotherapy, they are treated in a manner different from that in pastoral counseling or spiritual direction; the focus remains the person's experience. If, for example, the topic of discussion is God, the Christian psychotherapist should continue to focus on the person's experience of God. How is God understood? What are the images of God, and how do these relate to the internal representations of parents and significant others from childhood? Because persons are unified psychospiritual beings, relationships with God, self, and others are all mediated by the same internal psychological processes. It is these processes that psychotherapy most appropriately addresses. It is this, therefore, with which psychotherapists, Christian or non-Christian, should occupy themselves.

Understanding the differences between psychotherapy and other soul care approaches must also include the awareness of the limitations of psychotherapy. Psychotherapy may lead persons into a place of readiness for spiritual growth and may even help them take significant steps toward God. However, the Christian gospel proclaims that the mechanism of the new birth is trust in the redemptive work of Christ, not insight or increased emotional health. One Christian psychotherapist makes this point as follows:

> While the need for ultimacy may emerge in the process of psychotherapy, . . . justification certainly is not implicit there. The journey through the depths does not guarantee salvation. While it does often have the paradoxical effect of leading the person to awareness of transcendence and ultimacy . . . it does not identify the person's ultimate need as a relationship with God nor confront the person with the need for confession or the acceptance of Christ's redemptive work.[4]

At its best, Christian psychotherapy combines the spiritual resources of the Christian life with the psychological resources of depth psychology to effect radical and deep repair of psycho-spiritually damaged souls. Such damage principally manifests itself in a lack of freedom, that is, in emotional, volitional, cognitive, or behavioral bondage of some sort. One sign of such a lack of freedom is repeatedly doing what we wish we would not do, or being unable to do what we wish to do. Other evidence includes being incapable of deep love or intimacy, chronically angry or mistrustful, overly controlling of self or others, incapable of deep and enduring commitments, or bound by irrational needs to please others and be loved by them. These are the sorts of bondages of the spirit that psychotherapy is uniquely able to address.

Intensive Soul Care

In an earlier book, I argued that Christian psychotherapy and spiritual direction differ significantly enough in role demands and focus that they could not be combined.[5] The fact that so few people are capable of offering both also seemed to support this conclusion.

Since that time I have encountered people who are effectively combining these two forms of soul care and have myself been offering a combination of them. As a result of these experiences, I have changed my mind on the question of whether psychotherapy and spiritual direction differ in some intrinsic manner or whether it is simply that we lack models for and experience in combining them. I am now convinced that the latter is the case. At least two models exist, a well-developed one described by Bernard Tyrrell as *Christotherapy*[6] and a less well-formulated one that I have been offering and describing as an *intensive soul care retreat.*

Intensive soul care assumes that the separation of the tasks of care and cure of souls is both arbitrary and unnecessary if sufficient time, intensity, and intentionality can be brought to the effort. It also suggests that there is no need to choose between the psychological focus of Christian psychotherapy and the spiritual focus of spiritual direction. Each fits naturally with the other in an approach that integrates spiritual exercises and resources with psychotherapeutic insights and techniques. The goal of such intensive soul care is the remediation of core psychospiritual problems that impair a vital engagement with others and God and the nurture of Christian spirituality.

The overall framework for Tyrrell's Christotherapy is the Ignatian Spiritual Exercises. Following the four stages or weeks of these exercises, Tyrrell identifies four basic stages of Christotherapy:

1. *Reforming* involves an unmasking of the person's psychospiritual deformation that results from sin and facilitating the awareness of the need for Christ's redemptive grace. According to Tyrrell, an awareness of who we are before God and the reality of our rebellion against him should lead to repentance, and this is the beginning of all true psychospiritual growth.
2. *Conforming* is the active turning toward Christ that must follow after the turning away from sin. Here the goal is conforming the self to the mind of Christ, bringing about a new disposition of heart and mind that will allow a person to grow in love of God.
3. *Confirming* refers to the affirmation of our death to sin and life as a new creation in Christ. Here the initial turning from sin is confirmed by understanding ourselves to be baptized in Christ's death and thereby raised to life in him.
4. *Transforming* refers to our movement from identification with Christ in his death to contemplation of him in his glory. Through this the Holy Spirit empowers us to turn more fully toward Christ and thereby be transformed into his image.

Within this overall framework of spiritual growth, Tyrrell employs a variety of psychotherapeutic techniques and spiritual exercises to facilitate the growth of the one seeking soul care.

The intensive soul care retreat I have been developing also draws on the resources and approach of the classic spiritual retreat and incorporates select techniques from psychotherapeutic work. It also borrows elements from the model of intensive existential psychotherapy developed by John Finch and briefly discussed in chapter 4.

The overall framework within which the intensive soul care retreat is offered is the model of Christian spirituality described in chapter 5. The components that receive the most intense work are:

- the deep knowing of Jesus and, through him, the Father and Holy Spirit;
- the deep knowing of self, including the identification of the false selves that interfere with our response to God and maintain our egocentricity;
- the discovery and actualization of one's true self in Christ.

Depending on the length of the retreat and the psychospiritual health of the individual, more or less progress on each of these goals can be achieved. However, in each retreat, work on all three major goals structures the experience.

Retreats are normally conducted on an individualized basis, although group retreats can often accomplish many of the same goals. In either format, they can be for as short a time as a weekend or as long as three weeks. Two or three weeks is ideal, although this sometimes must be done in a series of shorter retreats. The first retreat is preceded by at least a month of guided work on an autobiographical essay, regular journal writing, dream reporting, and the completion of a number of psychological tests. These materials are all submitted and processed prior to the commencement of the retreat, which begins with an identification of the important spiritual and psychological issues for the individual and the development of a tentative plan for the use of the time.

The retreat is conducted within a context of abstinence from such things as drugs and alcohol, sex, the stimulation of television, and social interaction or conversation with anyone other than the retreat director. It also eliminates the distractions of work, travel, phone calls, and other responsibilities of daily life. Beyond the Bible and other devotional resources, reading is restricted to material that supports the soul work being undertaken. Suggested readings are individualized, drawn from Christian psychological and devotional literature, and offered at appropriate times during the course of the retreat. Suggestions for meditation and structured Bible studies are also a routine part of the retreat. Between one and two hours a day are spent in dialogue with the retreat director. Exercise, eating, and sleep provide the only breaks from the meditation, prayer, reflection, and journal writing that fill the rest of each day. In multiweek retreats, weekends are free for the individual to do whatever is desired.

Not surprisingly, this format affords a unique opportunity for psychospiritual healing and growth. Freedom from distractions allows people to deal with issues in a manner that is impossible when they are addressed within the context of the routines and pressures of regular daily life. Problems that have proven intractable to previous psychotherapeutic work are often profitably dealt with in this context. Also, the deep engagement with both the self and God that occurs offers rich possibilities for significant movement toward wholeness.[7]

Intensive soul care retreats are not a magic solution to all problems, nor do they produce guaranteed psychospiritual health or maturity. Typically at the end of the retreat the time is judged to have been insufficient and the issues remaining far greater than those resolved. However, such retreats do offer the possibility of integrated soul work that gives equal attention to the spiritual and psychological aspects of functioning. Along with the efforts of an increasing number of others who seek to combine Christian psychotherapy and spiritual direction, they represent an important form of Christian soul care.

The Spectrum of Christian Soul Care

Contemporary Christian soul care is in a fragmented state. Those associated with its various expressions seldom talk to each other and generally never consider the possibilities of working together. Although referrals between groups of practitioners sometimes occur, almost always they are referrals up the hierarchy. Thus, psychotherapists are accustomed to receiving referrals from clergy but seldom make referrals to them. This is quite lamentable. It seems to be based on an incorrect assumption that some forms of care are inherently superior to others, the inferior ones being made redundant by the presence of the superior.

Each of the expressions of Christian soul care has distinctives, advantages, and limitations. While some relationships (particularly counseling and psychotherapy) are primarily oriented toward the cure of damaged souls, others (pastoral care and spiritual direction) are oriented toward the care and nurture of anyone who seeks spiritual growth. Only intensive soul care regularly attempts to combine these objectives, but its practitioners are still quite limited in number. While Christian psychotherapists are relatively abundant, they typically charge rates that make them inaccessible to many people. Spiritual directors seldom charge for their services but are relatively few in number and often difficult to find. Christian counselors (both clergy and nonclergy) are quite abundant and form the backbone of most of the professional Christian soul care that is delivered. Pastoral care is available to even larger numbers of people, but because of its limited intensity, it tends to be more a relationship of support than transformation. Mutual and family care are unquestionably the most available forms of soul care; however, the needs that are presented to soul friends in these relationships often exceed the abilities of those friends.

The various forms of Christian soul care complement each other. None can do the whole job, and none is superior to another. Cooperation should replace competition. Each should be embraced and redeemed as the church seeks to restore soul care to a place of centrality in its life and mission.

10

Challenges of Christian Soul Care

There is no higher calling than that associated with the care of souls. What could be more important than for parents to make the nurture of the inner life of their children part of their calling in life, working to help them become strong, robust, and vital persons? Or what could be more important than friends, teachers, health care professionals, and clergy making the care of the inner lives of those within their sphere of personal and professional relationships part of their vocation?

Henrik Ibsen reveals his understanding of the immense importance of the vocation of soul care when he speaks through Solness, the central character of his play *The Master Builder.* In act 2, Solness is discussing his vocation as a builder with Hilda, a young acquaintance. He refers to his wife Aline, whom Hilda and the audience had not to this point perceived as having either a vocation or a life directed by any sense of calling.

Solness: Aline, you know, she had a talent for building too.

Hilda: She! For building?

Solness: Not houses and towers and spires—the kind I do.

Hilda: What, then?

Solness: For building up the small souls of children, Hilda. Building those souls up to stand on their own, poised, in beautiful, noble forms, till they'd grown into the upright human spirit. That's what Aline had a talent for.[1]

Aline was a builder of souls. While her husband understood his calling in terms of making things, she understood hers in terms of shaping souls. Unfortunately, many more people seem to share Solness's vocation than Aline's. It is so much easier to build things than people. It is easier to see progress and to know what works and what doesn't when we deal with the tangible tasks of making things. Things don't resist our helping interventions in the way in which people so often do. Unquestionably, dealing with souls is more demanding than dealing with things.

How do souls and things compare in importance? Listen to the familiar words of Jesus: "What is a man profited if he gains the whole world, and loses his own soul?" (Matt. 16:26 NKJV). In God's economy, people are worth more than things—infinitely more. In God's kingdom there can be no higher calling than that of the care and nurture of people whose worth is forever secured by having been created in his image and redeemed by the death of his only Son.

Qualifications for Christian Soul Care

Who is qualified for such a calling? Who is capable of caring not only for his or her own soul but also for the souls of others? Properly understood, nothing qualifies anyone to receive God's call except the fact of that call. God calls whom he chooses and equips those whom he calls. God looks on the heart, not externals, and therefore, his call will often be surprising. Sometimes it will be absolutely shocking. No one expected Samuel to select David as God's anointed king, least of all David's family, who had completely overlooked him as a possibility. So too it is with the calling to soul care.

Nonetheless, we can still offer some generalizations about the sort of person who should consider whether soul care is God's call for him or her. The following seven characteristics are ideals for those who seek to serve God through the care of souls.

1. *Those who care for souls should possess a deep and genuine love for people.* How terrifying to think that a person might choose to care for the souls of others for reasons other than a deep love of people. But it is obviously true that some who have little care for people choose care of people as a job.

Caring for people means caring for ordinary people. A soul guide should be one who delights in the ordinary people of the world not simply in those who are intelligent or interesting or who have something special to commend them as objects of investment of self. Thomas Oden notes, "Neither analytical skill nor theoretical knowledge can have positive effect if there is no genuine and compassionate care for others."[2]

The nurture of souls is the learning of love. Those who care for the souls of others and those who receive such care both engage in a relationship of love. In his book *Soul Making*, Alan Jones states that soul care is helping people become human and that at the core of this is the learning of love. He goes on to state, "We are more or less human insofar as we are in the school of love."[3] If those who care for souls are to teach in the school of love, they too must be pupils in the same school. The presence of deep love for ordinary people and, more particularly, the presence of a desire to even further develop such love, marks the first ideal of the soul guide.

Caring for people also means caring for them as they are. One's love for another is not real when it is love for them as they could be. This is conditional love. The love required for Christian soul care is a love that both longs for nothing short of the best and fullest possible life for the other and at the same time accepts and cares for them unconditionally, just as they are, even if they never change in the smallest way. Anything else, even if it appears as love, is simply manipulation. Christian soul care disavows itself of all such manipulation through conditional love.

2. *Those who care for souls should be people who are trustworthy and who are capable of trusting others.* Soul care dialogue cannot occur apart from a deep sharing of self, and this is only possible within a climate of trust. Soul guides are people who are recognized by others as being trustworthy. They are also recognized to be a safe and dependable container for the trust of the gift of self. Without such trust, soul care is impossible.

Christians who offer soul care must exercise trust in both God and in those for whom they care. Trust in God is essential because all growth and healing comes from him. God's Spirit is the supreme source of support and guide toward truth. In the absence of a deep trust in God, the soul guide is prone to place that trust in self. This is a posture of arrogance and an antecedent to burnout. The soul guide must also trust the person seeking help. This person must be trusted as being genuine in his or her seeking and trusted as a partner on the journey about to be undertaken.

Finally, those who care for the souls of others must also be trustworthy themselves. This means, among other things, guarding confidences, resisting temptations to use the relationship for self-gratification or ends other than the other person's good, and disavowing any use of manipulation or coercion to obtain those ends.

3. *Those who care for souls should be spiritually and psychologically mature.* Christians who care for the souls of others should be people who possess a high degree of psychospiritual maturity. This includes:

- being relatively unafraid of strong emotions and tolerant of painful experiences in themselves and others
- possessing a well-developed capacity for empathy that never confuses the experience of the other with that of oneself
- having a reasonable base of self-confidence
- being relatively free of a need for the love (or even liking) of those they seek to help

- being able to learn from their own experience as well as the experience of others

They should also be characterized by a deep and ever deepening knowledge of both God and self, personal holiness, a desire for service that springs from love of God, a capacity for productive use of solitude, well-developed habits of prayer, an abiding sense of the presence of God, and a growing knowledge of the Bible and orientation toward it as the authoritative rule of life and conduct.

Maturity such as this does not come quickly; it emerges only from the rich soil of life experience. Mature people have experienced good times and bad, success and failure, ease and struggle, sin and forgiveness, hope and despair. Having encountered all these things, those characterized by psychospiritual maturity are relatively at ease with themselves and with life. They are also relatively unafraid of life, which is accepted with all its darkness, mystery, ambiguity, and uncontrollability.

Soul guides cannot lead others to places of greater psychospiritual maturity than those they themselves experience. If personal health and maturity are lacking, soul care resembles one with a beam in his or her eye trying to help someone else remove a sliver from his or hers. Those who would attempt to do so should recall the sobering words of Jesus who warned that when the blind lead the blind, both run the risk of falling into the ditch (Matt. 15:14). Soul guides can only lead others to places they themselves regularly inhabit.

4. *Those who care for souls should be characterized by genuineness, honesty, interpersonal accessibility, internal congruence, and candor.* They should be capable of giving themselves in ways that are unaffected and natural and should possess an ability to relate to others with ease and friendliness. This means that others experience them as accessible and present to them. They have what has been called a "vibrant sense of personal availability."[4] They bring their self to interpersonal encounters and are ready to share it in ways that are honest and immediate and that invite engagement and dialogue. Others experience them as authentic—what they see is what they get.

Soul guides must be capable of approaching others as real people, not as actors hiding behind a role or technicians hiding behind their tools. This means they bring themselves to the engagement with those for whom they care, not simply their ideas, wisdom, listening skills, or desire to help. They realize the most important thing they have to give is their own self. If they either do not have a self to share or are unwilling or unable to share it, they have nothing to give. Those best equipped for the work of soul care regularly offer their self to others in a way that is engaging, direct, and honest. This is why they are experienced by others as authentic and accessible.

5. *Those who care for souls should have a deep experiential knowing of God's grace.* Apart from a deep knowing of God's grace, those who offer care for the souls of others will be bound to do so out of a framework of self-justification and works-righteousness. They will also tend to have unrealistic expectations of others, be unforgiving, and be overly rigid. A firm grasp of the centrality of grace in the Christian religion is the only hope for freedom from these things. Unless soul guides personally know this as experiential truth, they will inevitably inculcate their own graceless spirituality in others.

Christians who care for the souls of others must be people who know deeply the God who loves sinners, redeems failures, and delights in second chances and fresh starts. This is the God who never tires of pursuing lost sheep, of waiting for prodigal children, or rescuing those damaged by the world and left on the side of its paths. Those who seek to follow this God by caring for his children must acquire his heart and offer his care through his Spirit.

6. *Those who care for souls should be characterized by deep faith that light will overcome darkness.* The faith of soul guides is ultimately, of course, in God. One important aspect of such faith for the work of soul care is, however, the assurance that light will ultimately overcome darkness. This means that as people who have lived through their own dark nights of the soul, Christian soul guides have a quiet but steady trust that God will see others through their dark nights. Having experienced their own fears, anxieties, darkness,

and demons as well as God's deliverance from them, they have the assurance that God will do the same for others. As a result of this, they are "less afraid of real people and of the darker sides of real people because they have experienced a God who loves and saves real people like themselves, warts and moles, and all."[5]

This faith that light will ultimately overcome darkness gives the soul guide the ability to enter the pain, distress, or anxieties of others without a need to fix things. Such people are prepared to be tolerant of darkness and ambiguity, believing that the greatest good is only born out of struggles in the midst of uncertainty and confusion. They are, therefore, content to be with the other in these situations, not to have to effect a change in either the person or the situation. This is, of course, precisely what is most needed—the presence of someone who will be with them in the midst of whatever they face, thereby mediating the grace of God who is also with them.

7. *Those who care for souls should be characterized by wisdom and humility.* Soul guides should be both wise and humble. Their wisdom will be reflected in their adaptability, flexibility, sensitivity, and ability to speak words that fit the need and occasion. They must be prepared to offer advice but will do so "sparingly, chiefly on invitation and with full respect for the conscience and self-directive resources of the other person."[6] They will be tolerant of silence and characterized by listening more than speaking. But when they speak, their words will reflect good judgment and wisdom.

The soul guide's humility will be reflected in his or her reticence to tell others how to live their lives or to assume that the things that have worked for themselves will work for others. It will also be reflected in an absence of dogmatism about their ideas and in an absence of guilt-inducing strategies if the other chooses to ignore advice or live life according to a different plan.

Who is capable of being and doing all these things? The answer is, "No one, at least not on their own." Thomas Oden reminds us, "It is only in the companionship of grace, drawing on resources beyond one's own, that wisdom will be found for this task."[7] It is only by a practiced dependence on the Holy Spirit, the true and only qualified soul guide, that anyone can hope to respond to the call of God to take up the vocation of the care of souls.

These ideals do not mean that soul guides are perfect. Like anyone else, they have blind spots, are at times guilty of self-deception and ulterior motives, know themselves imperfectly, and occasionally allow self-interests to blind them to the needs of others. This means they are human. But they are growing, and they have been making a habit of such growth for some time. It is this, more than anything else, that suggests readiness for soul care responsibilities.

Demands of Christian Soul Care

Few vocations are as demanding as the care of souls. Yet seldom, if ever, is this understood when people first accept such responsibilities. Motivated by the potential satisfactions associated with deep engagement with others around the important issues of their lives, awareness of the immense demands of such work is often limited to such matters as the difficulty of listening. In actuality, the demands of soul care extend well beyond this, having much more to do with being than doing.

1. *Soul care demands truthfulness.* Superficially understood, this appears to be a simple requirement to not tell lies. But speaking the truth is only one manifestation of a deeper commitment to seeking and living the truth, and this is required of the soul guide. Understanding the penetrating wisdom of Jesus' words that it is the truth that sets us free, Christian soul guides seek to live life centered and grounded in truth. This means, among other things, that they disavow deception of either themselves or others. Realizing the immense ease with which people can slip into living the lies of their own rationalizations, they commit themselves to living in truth.

No one who fails to take seriously the immense creativity of human rationalizations and the seemingly limitless nature of our capacity for self-deception can take anything but the first faltering steps toward this goal of living in truth. But this commitment to living the truth is foundational to the work of caring for the souls of others, and unless one lives in truth, he or she cannot meaningfully lead others to a life of truth. Ultimately, of course, Christians understand such truth to be found only in Jesus Christ, who is truth incarnate. Sadly but obviously, however, not all followers of Christ are characterized by seeking and living truth.

Part of this demand of living the truth is the demand of being and not just pretending. Understanding the ideals of soul care, soul guides may be tempted to "fake it until they make it," that is, content themselves with the external appearances of deep love, empathy, psychospiritual maturity, faith, and humility. But the demands of living the truth outweigh all the other ideals. If love is limited—even if liking is totally absent—truthful living demands that one demonstrate only what is genuinely part of one's own experience. Any gap between the inner reality and outward appearances of the soul guide will impose a corresponding limitation on the usefulness of the care provided.

2. *Soul guides must continue to grow.* Commitment to living the truth is a commitment to growth and development. Psychospiritual health is such that we cannot simply maintain our ground; we are always either progressing or regressing. Growth, unlike aging, is not an automatic consequence of the passage of time. If anything, the passage of time is more likely to lead to a loss than a gain of psychospiritual health and well-being. Past gains are only maintained at a great personal cost. The price is a commitment to living the truth, to deeply know oneself, and to relate to others with genuineness and honesty.

While moments of growth may be quite attractive, particularly when they are behind us, it is very easy to tire of continuing to live in a place of growth. It is understandable, therefore, why soul guides may begin to resent the demands of continued growth—demands that do not seem to be placed on anyone else to the same degree. Accountants, surgeons, lawyers, scientists, and teachers must all continue to hone technical skills, but none of them face the relentless, ever present demands to continue to grow personally, not just professionally. Only soul guides face this demand.

3. *Soul care also demands that its practitioners not seek gratification of their personal needs within soul care relationships.* Needs that are quite legitimate and benign in other relationships cannot be gratified within soul care without contaminating the relationship. If, for example, the soul guide needs to be liked, respected, or even seen to be helpful, it is his or her needs that are directing the relationship rather than the needs of the one receiving care. Even more malignant are voyeuristic and exhibitionistic needs, a need for control, a need to be seen as omnipotent, and even a need to be needed. The use of the soul care relationship for the gratification of sexual needs is obviously always inappropriate, as is its use for the gratification of needs for intimacy.

Christian soul care is a gift of self-sacrificial love. This is why soul guides must set aside the gratification of their own needs when in a relationship of soul care. It is also the reason we must be prepared to be used, and sometimes even abused, by those for whom we care. While other helpers routinely enter their relationships of service watchful of not having their rights or needs violated, Christian soul guides take Christ as their example and approach the care of the souls of others prepared for such care to be often personally costly for them. Just as Jesus sensed strength being sapped from him when someone touched the hem of his garment, so too, Christian soul guides enter their relationships of care ready to be used up, drawn upon, expended, and depleted. While one's own needs and the integrity of one's own person set some outer limits on how far this can go, personal needs can be set aside much further than we would ever guess by looking at most professional helpers.

Ultimately, we do not serve others well if we allow them to continuously mistreat or abuse us, or if the demands of their needs destroy our own selves or our significant personal relationships. However, there is a great deal of distance between that extreme and a posture of not being willing to be used or abused in any way. Christian soul guides follow their Lord down a path of self-sacrifice that will inevitably be personally costly.

Offering oneself in ways that support the growth of the inner life of others makes immense demands on the soul guide. Beyond those already identified, other demands of the soul care relationship include the challenges of limit setting, of maintaining confidentiality, of genuine dialogue, and of allowing people to grow beyond and away from us. Awareness of the immensity of the challenge of soul care can either immobilize or lead to a place of dependence on God. The confidence of those who respond to God's call to take up the work of the care of the souls of his people should come from the knowledge that those whom he calls he always equips and supports.

Challenges of Christian Soul Care

The challenge of offering distinctively Christian soul care at the doorstep of a new millennium is considerable. The church has been marginalized in a society that is rapidly moving beyond secularization to re-sacralization. The life of the soul has acquired great importance to large numbers of people who, reacting to the bankruptcy of materialism, seek meaning and purpose within the context of a recovery of the sacred and the spiritual. Unfortunately, their search is often defined in terms that leave them open to any spirituality but Christian. Ironically, while interest in the soul has reached best-seller proportions, openness to the Christian answer to the soul's deepest needs is rapidly disappearing. Judged to have been responsible for the evils of modernity, Christianity and its approach to the care of souls is often viewed by postmodern individuals with mistrust and resentment.

The challenge of offering distinctively Christian soul care to those who have retained an identification with the church is also great. Socialized within the therapeutic culture of the West, church members have been conditioned to view soul care through a clinical lens. Such a perspective positions soul care as a therapeutic offered by someone with technical and professional competence to someone with problems. Care offered by nonprofessionals is, in such a view, often judged to be substandard, and care that seeks to be distinctively Christian is easily dismissed as naively spiritual.

Care offered by professionals is expected to adopt the norms and form of the clinical psychotherapies.

Yet, for all these challenges, there is both a hunger and great need for soul care that is offered in an authentically Christian manner, grounded in the historic Christian understandings of the spiritual needs and resources and informed by the vision of psychospiritual dynamics associated with the best insights of depth psychology. Such soul care has the potential to revitalize the church's ministry to spiritual seekers both within and beyond its walls.

Seven challenges must be confronted by Christians who seek to care for the souls of others in such a manner. They must:

1. guard against the erosion of the personal in such care
2. develop an integrated inner core
3. continuously renew their own inner psychospiritual resources
4. not allow professionalism to dilute a sense of Christian vocation
5. rediscover the formative and transforming power of story
6. recover the uniquely Christian resources of soul care
7. avoid sacrificing *being* on the altar of *doing*

1. *Guarding against the erosion of the personal.* We have noted that soul care involves a relationship between two or more people who engage with each other in the manner Martin Buber described as an I-Thou encounter. This deeply personal engagement is the foundation of all true dialogue. It is also the dynamic engine of the soul care relationship.

In spite of this obviously fundamental role of the personal in soul care, however, forces exist that continuously threaten to replace the personal with the impersonal. One such force that we have already noted is professionalism. While an adoption of a professional attitude may bring with it commendable standards of service, it also emphasizes doing over being and technical competence over the giving of self. A professional attitude also predisposes the one offering soul care to view the relationship as fundamentally asymmetrical. In such a view, one party is designated as the giver of care and the other as the receiver. When mutual care is ruled out *a priori*, however, so too is genuine dialogue. While not all soul care relationships must be totally balanced in their mutuality, the adoption of a posture of professionalism tends to result in the self that is brought to the relationship being less personal. In fact, professionalism is such a powerful depersonalizing force that the self of the professional is often totally eliminated from the relationship—the individual hiding behind a role rather than extending his or her self.

The clinical emphasis of therapeutic soul care also threatens to erode the personal. An emphasis on diagnosis, pathology (either spiritual or psychological), or even theory can lead to an encounter with constructs, not persons. When held tentatively, theoretical models of psychospiritual dynamics can be very helpful road maps of the terrain. The challenge, however, is never to lose sight of just how crude the maps really are.

The challenge is also to resist the temptation to reduce soul care to the skillful application of techniques. When techniques are understood as disciplined ways of offering one's self, they can greatly enhance the care that is provided. But when they become ways in which the soul guide avoids engagement as a genuine self, their effect is to depersonalize the engagement and render it an I-It encounter.

2. *Developing an integrated inner core.* Those who care for the souls of others must be integrated in the depths of their being. This is part of what it means to describe the character ideal of integrity. But integrity involves more than moral soundness; it also involves being integral or whole, and integrality involves a wholeness that is based on a psychospiritual integration and maturity.

Soul guides should be people who are both psychologically and spiritually mature and in whom that integrated core of psychospiritual health represents the foundation of an ever increasing integration of the totality of their experience and being. An integrated inner core means the presence of a minimal number of isolated pockets of experience that are split off from the total fabric of personality. This means that such people do not have a compartment for spiritual experiences related to God and another for psychological experiences with other people. Their experience with God touches and transforms the totality of their being and becomes the core around which everything else is integrated and is given its meaning and direction.

People with an integrated inner core are growing both psychologically and spiritually. Their commitment to living a life of integrity and authenticity demands that they seek to live life with a pure heart, such purity being, in the words of Kierkegaard, to love one thing. Such singleness of heart comes only from an inner core that is integrated around a single master affection. For the Christian, this is the love of God.

3. *Continuously renewing inner psychospiritual resources.* Christians who engage in the work of soul care must be in relationships with others in which their own needs are being continuously and dependably met. This is the only way in which they can set those same needs aside in relationships of soul care.

The renewal of personal psychospiritual resources requires that soul guides be in continuous close relationship with both God and other people. The development and maintenance of psychospiritual health and maturity demands that they learn to live with intimacy and authenticity in these relationships. If they are to have something to give to others, these relationships must also be places where they are able to present themselves as they are and be accepted and affirmed. In other words, soul guides must live within a network of significant relationships of grace if they are to be in a position to share that grace with others.

The alternative to being in relationships in which inner needs are being met and resources renewed is either to give nothing of self or to become increasingly depleted at the core of one's being. Such inner depletion forces one to live out of the periphery of self, not from one's depths. While such living is not uncommon, it cannot provide a foundation for the sort of deep encounter and dialogue that are essential in genuinely Christian soul care. It is only when life emanates from one's depths that one can help others move toward the abundant life we are promised in Christ. But living from one's depths demands that one's own deepest needs be continuously met and one's resources renewed.

4. *Not allowing professionalism to dilute a sense of Christian vocation.* Throughout its long history, soul care has been primarily understood as a religious calling. This meant both that it was understood as religious work and that this work was taken up in response to a call of God to service. This is the core of the Christian understanding of vocation.

Professionalism began to erode this sense of religious calling and Christian vocation when, in the eighteenth century, specialized training for soul care began to replace the historic emphasis on spiritual maturity. This development, seen in embryonic form in the eighteenth and nineteenth centuries, came into ascendancy in the twentieth century with the rise of therapeutic soul care. The professionalization of soul care meant that rather than having to passively wait for a call from God, one could actively prepare for such work by pursuing the prerequisite training and credentials. Clergy can pursue advanced clinical pastoral education, while counselors and psychotherapists acquire therapeutic skills. Even spiritual directors can now prepare for their work with specialized training and credentialing.

Such preparation is not incompatible with an understanding of soul care as a vocation, but it easily obscures such an understanding. Professionalism easily leads to a de-emphasis on the all-important foundation of any Christian vocation, that is, the call of God to kingdom service and servanthood. Without this call, soul care is nothing more than a job. Unfortunately, this appears to be the case for many soul guides. When soul guides can interpret their work as a response to a call of God, however, their service can flow from a heart of love, and servanthood can be central to their identity and relationships. This is what is needed in soul care.

The church needs to recover a strong sense of vocation—not simply God's call to religious vocations but his call to whatever it is we are to do with our lives. Soul care is not the only important Christian vocation. But it is an important sphere of service, so important, in fact, that it should only be undertaken as a response to God's call, never simply a choice of a job.

5. *Rediscovering the formative and transforming power of story.* Having previously noted that dialogue is the dynamic core of the soul

care relationship, it is important to also observe the place of story in such dialogue. Christianity makes an important place for the telling of stories. This is rooted in Judaism, where the past is kept alive and its lessons remembered by retelling its stories. Jesus did the same. In fact, the telling of stories is perhaps the primary characteristic of his soul care relationships.

Narrative psychologists note that the creation of stories is the fundamental way in which humans make sense of their experience. They also argue that the telling of these stories is essential in both the formation of identity and the healing of emotional wounds.[8] Humans seem to need to give their experiences some sort of coherence. We achieve this by making up stories about the things that happen to us. These stories become the way in which we define ourselves and order our lives.

Because our self-narratives are so fundamental to our identity and are the way in which we make sense of our experience, the sharing of our stories with others is crucial for our growth and healing. Soul care involves allowing someone to share his or her story and then helping that person to consider the implications of the way in which he or she has put that story together.

Learning to listen to, interact with, and tell stories involves skills. But it is more than a skill; it is a posture. It stands in contrast to the usual clinical posture of an expert who seeks to offer specialized therapeutic help as much as it is in contrast to the frequent religious posture of listening long enough to be polite before preaching. It fits perfectly, however, with a relationship structured to maximize dialogue. In such a relationship, the soul guide should seek to avoid both the trap of clinical efficiency as well as that of religious indoctrination or proselytization. Stories cannot be rushed, and they must be taken seriously. Those who care for souls must enter the reality of the other person's world through their story. As noted by Alistair Campbell, a creative and participative listening changes a jumbled presentation of details into a living drama in which hope may be found, growth facilitated, and healing secured.[9] This is the challenge of Christian soul care as dialogue.

6. *Recovering the uniquely Christian resources of soul care.* These resources, which nourished and supported soul care for centuries,

have fallen into disuse and ill repute during the last century. Much has been sacrificed by positioning soul care as a clinical therapeutic, and much must be recovered.

Such a recovery might begin with theological language. It is remarkable how absent such language is from the contemporary literature of pastoral care and counseling and spiritual direction. The concept of sin has been largely replaced with pathology, forgiveness with insight, grace with unconditional acceptance, sanctification with growth, and holiness with wholeness. While there has been value in making these and other psycholinguistic translations, there is a richness in the theological concepts that is lost in their supposed psychological equivalents. Christian soul care does not need to eliminate psychological language and concepts; it merely needs to rediscover and utilize the traditional theological concepts that gave Christian soul care its direction for so long.

Of even more importance is the recovery of religious acts that long had an important place in relationships of Christian soul care. Prayer, meditation, the use of the sacraments, laying on of hands, anointing with oil, the reading and study of Scriptures, and the use of religious or devotional literature all have an important role to play in authentically Christian soul care. It is obviously important that they be used with care and never employed in a manner that blocks dialogue. The Christian soul guide can hide behind religious actions and use them as a way of avoiding deep and personal encounter. Religious resources are also misused when they are employed in a mechanical, legalistic, or magical manner. The essence of these resources is the dynamic connection they can provide between God and the one receiving care. Used with sensitivity, they can uniquely help that person come into direct contact with the caring, healing, and sustaining presence of a personal God. If they enhance this personal contact with God, they make an indispensable contribution to Christian soul care.

A final, uniquely Christian resource that should be recovered for soul care is Christian community. Under the influence of therapeutic culture, soul care came to be seen as the care offered by one individual to another. Even Christian counseling has typically retained this individualistic character. But properly understood, Christian soul care is never an activity of an individual

Christian; it is a ministry of the church. Individuals may offer soul care, but the intent of Christian soul care is that they do so as an agent or representative of the church. If soul care is to be a Christian vocation, it must be kingdom service. It should also be understood to be a process taking place within a community of caring Christians and utilizing the resources of that community.

7. *Avoiding the sacrifice of being on the altar of doing.* Christian soul guides must exercise great diligence to ensure that they do not do clever things to people but instead give themselves in such a way that those receiving care come into closer contact with Christ. As such, Christian soul guides can be thought of as midwives of grace.[10] Divine grace, not human guidance, is the active ingredient in soul care, and any psychospiritual growth and healing that occurs is a direct result of that grace. The soul guide is, therefore, the midwife of that grace.

This is the reason that *being* is more important than *doing* in the life of those who seek to offer Christian soul care. Compulsive activism is the enemy of psychospiritual depth and substance. Soul guides must learn how to embrace solitude, but more importantly, they must develop a solitude of the heart. Or put another way, those who seek to care for the souls of others must have a still, quiet, inner space if they are to be capable of providing a place of refuge and stillness for another. Someone has captured this wonderfully, noting that "we can make our lives so like still water that beings gather about us that they may see, it may be, their own images, and so live for a moment with a clearer, perhaps even with a fiercer life, because of our quiet."[11] Without such a place of inner stillness, no one has much to offer another. With it, particularly when it is shaped by and filled with the Spirit of Christ, simply being with another is a gift of grace. This is the goal of Christian soul care.

11

Receiving Soul Care

To this point our principal focus has been on the giving of soul care. In this final chapter we turn to the matter of receiving care. Who needs soul care? How does one choose among the various forms of care and find the right provider? How should one prepare to receive soul care? These are some of the practical matters that we will consider as we focus on receiving Christian soul care.

Who Needs Soul Care?

The short answer to the question of who needs soul care is everyone. Humans are social creatures. This means we need others in order to live our lives, and more importantly, we need others if we are to live our lives out of our depths. Any identity, purpose, meaning, or spirituality that is discovered apart from relationships should be viewed with suspicion. The discovery of these inner compasses and the ongoing task of allowing our lives to be guided by them is tremendously enhanced by dialogue with others.

No one should attempt to travel the spiritual road alone. But while any fellow traveler on the way can provide support and encouragement, their help is usually limited to that if they are no further along than we are on the pilgrimage. What we really need are companions who have more experience than we do in the Christian spiritual journey. Such persons can help us recognize false paths, anticipate hazards, and discern the directions provided for us by the Master Soul Guide. Ideally, everyone should have such soul companions to accompany them at various points on life's journey.

Some people are blessed with soul companions who accompany them through most of their adult years of journeying. When marriages achieve the ideal of soul friendships, the mutual care they provide affords the possibility of a constancy of soul care that is seldom possible in other human relationships. However, even when this occurs, other significant friendships must supplement the relationship with one's spouse. To fail to do so is to overload the circuits of the marriage and to ask of it more than can be delivered. Significant nonmarital friendships also provide deep and constant soul companionship. Once again, however, even when one is blessed by such a friendship, other relationships of soul care are also periodically necessary.

Friendships (both marital and nonmarital) hold great promise as contexts for mutual soul care. As noted earlier, this is the foundation of all other soul care. All people need relationships of mutual care, but at some point in their lives most people also need one of the more specialized forms of soul care. Four groups of people in particular should recognize their need for such care:

1. those who seek to provide soul care themselves
2. those who seek freedom from inner bondage
3. those who seek greater depths of psychospiritual maturity and vitality
4. those who seek assistance in developing a moral perspective on their life.

1. *Those who seek to provide soul care for others.* It is essential to receive soul care yourself before offering such care to others. This

includes all clergy who preach or counsel, all counselors and psychotherapists, all spiritual directors, all teachers and leaders, all who influence or have responsibility for others, and all parents who seek to nurture the inner life of their children. These people, all seeking to lead others to places of wholeness and well-being, must themselves be growing in their inner persons. Such growth is uniquely facilitated by being on the receiving end of a relationship of soul care.

2. *Those who seek freedom from inner bondage.* Anything that impairs one's capacity to be fully free and alive to the present, whether this involves bondage to the past or an anxious preoccupation with the future, is an appropriate focus of soul care work. These sources of inner bondage may involve such things as unresolved emotional wounds, addictions or patterns of compulsive behavior, an inability to experience the love or gracious presence of God, self-preoccupation or other impediments to love or empathy, or an inability to give or receive forgiveness. The more intensive forms of soul care all offer unique opportunities to gain freedom from such sources of inner bondage, and those who experience an absence of freedom in their lives should seriously consider one of the therapeutic forms of soul care.

3. *Those who seek greater depths of psychospiritual maturity and vitality.* Some people who are free from significant impediments to a deeper and more vital life have simply not taken the necessary steps to walk through the doorway to such life. Such people may be blessed by an absence of serious problems and, to all appearances, their lives may be satisfying and fulfilling. They may also be seen by others to be models of psychological and spiritual health and maturity, but they sense an inner call to something further. They may feel a degree of spiritual deadness, a loss of clarity about their calling, a desire to experience God's presence more deeply, a desire to be more whole or holy, or a longing to know themselves more fully. These are but a few of the manifestations of the spiritual quest—the call of Spirit to spirit inviting them to a deeper, fuller, and more abundant life. All who seek greater depths of psy-

225

chospiritual maturity and vitality can also benefit from a relationship of soul care.

4. *Those who seek assistance in developing a moral perspective on their life.* Some may face circumstances that suggest the need for ethical reflection or moral reorientation. They may have drifted into ethically questionable behavior and wonder how their moral compass became so flawed as to allow them to get there. Others may have violated one of their most deeply held moral principles and feel a need to review their personal moral philosophy. Yet others may simply feel the need for moral stocktaking or an opportunity to reflect on their stewardship of life. What better context for reflection could such people find than a relationship of soul care?

At one time or another in their life, most people experience themselves in at least one of these groups. The majority of us frequently find ourselves in more than one. For this reason, all of us need ongoing mutual soul care, and most of us periodically need more specialized forms of care. Mutual soul care forms the sustaining base of our psychospiritual growth, but from time to time, this must be supplemented by more intensive forms of care. At such times, how does one choose the best form of care?

Choosing the Best Form of Soul Care

The best form of care is obviously determined by the needs and circumstances of the one seeking care, but some general principles can provide a framework that may help in making the choice:

1. *Those who provide soul care should themselves have an experience of receiving the form of care they provide.* How can one presume to lead others on a journey one has not previously taken oneself? Yet this is precisely what too many soul guides seek to do. Thus, for example, psychotherapists should receive psychotherapy, spiritual directors should receive spiritual direction, and pastoral and

other Christian counselors should receive the form of counseling they provide.

2. *Those who provide soul care themselves should also experience a form of care that complements the primary focus of that which they provide.* Thus, Christian counselors and psychotherapists should have an experience of spiritual direction, while pastoral counselors and spiritual directors should have an experience of Christian counseling or psychotherapy. If available, members of each of these groups should also consider an intensive soul care experience that combines a spiritual and psychological focus.

3. *The greater the sphere of one's influence over others, the greater the need for a form and intensity of soul care that ensures deep and genuine knowing of both self and God.* If all clergy, leaders, and teachers had experiences of spiritual direction and Christian psychotherapy, they would have a depth of psychospiritual health and maturity that would greatly enhance their kingdom service. They would also have a knowledge of self that would decrease the probability of the disastrous abuses of responsibility that periodically occur.

4. *The presence of significant distress indicates a need to select a form of soul care with a therapeutic focus.* Some form of counseling or psychotherapy is ideal when one faces problems that limit freedom or involve emotional pain.

5. *A desire for spiritual growth suggests that one consider a relationship of spiritual direction.* Longings to know God more deeply, discern and live his will more fully, or be attuned to his presence more completely all ideally fit the shape of this form of soul care. Spiritual direction is for anyone who seeks to pay attention to God's call and respond with a life of prayer, obedience, holiness, service, and love.

6. *Prior experiences with one form of soul care should suggest consideration of another form when the need next arises.* Each form of care complements the others, having distinctive emphases and foci.

For this reason, one should consider experience with several of them as the felt need for care emerges at the various stages of life.

7. *As a general rule, one should not simultaneously engage in multiple therapeutic soul care relationships.* Thus, one should not see two counselors or psychotherapists or a counselor and a psychotherapist at the same time. However, both counseling and psychotherapy are well complemented by simultaneous spiritual direction. This is particularly useful when the counselor or psychotherapist is not a Christian or when one may have questions about the spiritual implications of the therapeutic work being done. Spiritual direction also complements pastoral counseling if the latter has a more therapeutic, problem-solving focus.

Choosing a Soul Guide

The choice of the person who will provide the soul care is at least as important as the choice of the form of that care. Overlap between the various forms of care and the large common core shared by all of them sometimes makes the choice as to form somewhat incidental. But the person who actually provides the care will always do more to effect the shape of that care than any other single factor.

Finding the right soul guide is frequently quite challenging. Sometimes the choices are limited, perhaps to one's pastor and a Christian counselor in one's church or community. While working with someone who is known may reduce some of the uncertainty about the experience, seeing that person in other contexts may introduce awkwardness into these other contacts. The choice of whom to work with is also sometimes made more difficult by an absence of clarity about what one is seeking, either from the experience or the other person. It is often easier to know what one does not want than it is to know what one wants.

The search for a soul guide often begins with a recommendation of a friend who names someone he or she has found helpful. This is a good start. However, it does not mean the recommended person will be right for you. To know this, you will have to talk to him or her, ideally in person, although sometimes out of necessity, on the phone. In arranging this, be clear about the fact that what you initially seek is simply information that will help you decide from whom to get help. Be prepared to pay for this consultation if the person you approach normally offers his or her services for a fee and if you meet face-to-face. Don't be discouraged by any who refuse to meet with you on these terms, asking instead that you be prepared to take them on faith and start work together directly. By such a reaction, unsuitable soul guides disqualify themselves, making your work easier.

In this preliminary discussion with a potential soul guide, you should try to obtain an understanding of his or her approach to soul care and a sense of who he or she is as a person. What you are attempting to determine is whether you wish to trust your care to this person. This has something to do with the potential soul guide's ideas about that care but should have at least as much to do with how you experience him or her as a person.

In response to your question about the nature of the care they offer, some people will be readily able to identify a theoretical orientation that guides them or to articulate a personal philosophy of care; others will be much more vague and inarticulate. Having been professionally socialized to view questions about their approach as resistance to therapeutic engagement, some psychotherapists may even be reluctant to answer more than the most basic questions about their approach. While this obviously makes it difficult to know much about either their work or them as persons, it should raise a note of caution in that it clearly indicates an unwillingness to bring one's self to the relationship of care. Whatever else such a relationship may be or provide, it will not likely involve the sort of deep, personal, dialogical engagement described in chapter 7.

Most commonly, an inquiry about the nature of the help the person provides will yield a forthright answer that should be of assistance in determining the suitability of what he or she offers you at the present time. As you listen to this description of what the potential soul guide offers, make particular effort to ensure that you understand how he or she envisages his or her role and yours. Does their description make sense to you? If it doesn't, don't hesitate to ask questions. Does the description of what the potential soul guide has to offer inspire your confidence and make you want to begin work with him or her? Also note the effort he or she demonstrates to listen and respond to your questions. Are you engaged as an active participant in the process or treated as a passive object of benevolence? If your questions are treated with respect, so are you. If, on the other hand, they are treated with condescension, so are you.

As part of this discussion, you might want to ask the potential soul guide about his or her qualifications and experience. These matters are particularly important as one moves up the hierarchy of soul cure described in chapter 9. Counselors and psychotherapists should be trained in accredited institutions and programs and hold current credentials in relevant professional associations. Since training programs in spiritual direction are relatively new, those offering this form of soul care may not always have formal training in it. Nonetheless, they should still be able to describe their informal preparation, which should usually include personal experience in spiritual direction as well as a program of reading or workshops. A question about how the potential soul guide supports his or her own continued personal growth and development is also often helpful. Does he or she engage in periodic relationship of soul care? Does he or she show any evidence of an awareness of the limitations of giving care that is not accompanied by ongoing personal replenishment?

After the encounter, ask yourself if you like and respect the person with whom you spoke. Both are important ingredients in successful soul care. It is hard to work in a soul care relationship with someone you simply do not like, and it would be senseless to do so with someone you do not respect. Assume that the course of the work you will do together will result in you becoming like this person. To one degree or another this will always be true, particularly if you both judge that work to have been successful. You have, therefore, a very visible indication of the potential outcome of your work. Do you like what you see?

People who are anxious, rigid, dogmatic, or humorless will have trouble helping you move to places of greater freedom and health than they experience. But those who strike you as authentic, empathic, vital, and integral will be in a position to help you take steps toward the same ends. What you see is what you get. So be observant, inquisitive, and discerning.

Regardless of whom you select, view the decision to undertake such work as open to ongoing review. This does not mean you should terminate the relationship the moment you are unhappy with something about the soul guide or the process. But it does mean that if you are not getting the help you desire, you should clearly communicate this fact to the person with whom you are working. Don't terminate an unsatisfactory soul care relationship without discussing your dissatisfactions with the care giver. Be prepared for struggle, dark nights of the soul, and regress that will inevitably accompany progress, but if you continue to feel you are not getting the help you need and desire, don't be afraid to discontinue the relationship and seek help from someone else.

Preparing for Soul Care

Christian soul care involves a deep engagement with oneself, with God, and with another person. Preparation for this engagement should, therefore, take the form of reflection on each of these relational spheres.

Self-reflection is aided by a number of disciplines. The first and most important of these is the discipline of solitude. Taking time prior to the commencement of a relationship of soul care for inner stillness will pay great dividends in the usefulness of that care. The practice of contemplative prayer—learning to quietly sit in God's presence, gazing upon him, and allowing him, not our worded response, to fill our consciousness—is a transforming discipline for Christians more accustomed to prayer of the head than prayer of the heart. To become people whose lives are not merely full but whose selves are whole, we must be prepared to be still within ourselves and quiet before our God. Such prayerful solitude is the womb of psychospiritual growth. The space it creates allows for the birth of a transformed self. It also teaches a discipline that will not only aid subsequent soul care work but will sustain the inner life thereafter.

The discipline of journal writing also uniquely aids preparation for the receipt of soul care. Such writing also supports the discipline of prayerful reflection on one's life, including one's actions and reactions, moods, and thoughts. It is also the ideal place for reflection on one's dreams. Dream work done prior to beginning any significant soul journey is often quite rewarding, particularly when accompanied by prayer and the request that God use the dreams to help one see things that should be considered for one's growth.

The discipline of writing an autobiography is also extremely helpful in focusing oneself prior to receiving soul care. Such an articulation of one's story should focus on the issues in the inner life that one hopes to address. For example, if one's concern is with regard to discerning the presence of God, the story should be built around one's experience of God—experiences of both his presence and his absence. Or if one's concern is with anger, it should be focused on experiences of entitlement, resentment in the face of frustration, and success or failure in then letting go of this resentment or rage. Similarly, if one's primary concern relates to matters of integrity, the historical review should principally focus on the integration of the inner self and the correspondence of this internal reality to external behavior. These features will never be the totality of the autobiography, but they should provide the framework for its preparation.

The soul care autobiography should differ from an autobiography written for public consumption in that it is not written for others but for oneself. In writing it, there is no reason to be anything less than ruthlessly honest. It should be undertaken with prayer for God's help in seeing one's story and oneself clearly. False humility and flattery should be equally avoided; remember, the audience is simply yourself. The result should be a better understanding of your response to God's call to know him and find your true self in loving surrender to him. Reflection on your progress on the spiritual journey should identify issues for further work. This is the purpose of the soul care autobiography.

Writing such an autobiography is usually a deeply rewarding experience. After first doing so, many people commit themselves to regular updatings of these autobiographies, often undertaking this as part of an annual soul review. A soul care autobiography is a way to put life into perspective. It is also a way to learn one's story. After telling this story to oneself, it is usually easier to both tell it and live it with others.

Another potentially fruitful focus of prayerful reflection is on characteristic patterns of self-deception. If a person is to experience any significant growth, the deceitfulness of the heart must be known not simply as a theological proposition but as experiential truth. Knowledge of the specific ways in which we bend the truth and attempt to reshape reality is crucially important if we are to truly know ourselves. By means of rationalizations (plausible but not actual reasons for our behavior), denial (a simple refusal to accept unpleasant reality), and projection (a refusal to accept something about ourselves that we subsequently attribute to others), to one degree or another we all refuse to live in the truth and choose instead to live a lie. Identifying our preferred patterns of self-deception prior to commencing a soul care relationship with someone else will greatly facilitate the work done in that relationship.

So too will reflection on our symptoms. Obsessions, addictions, anxieties, depression, and anger are the voice of the soul telling us that all is not well in the inner world. Such symptoms can often be therapeutically eliminated, but they are much too important to simply silence. Their message must be discerned and the underlying psychospiritual malady corrected. Frequently, however, we cannot do this until the force of the symptom is reduced. The grace of God is manifest in the availability of pharmacological and psychological treatments that provide a quieting of these symptoms. But once subdued, it is still important to attend to them as the voice of the soul.

Reflection on fears and anxieties provide particularly useful preparation for soul care work. Our anxieties tell us important things about how we perceive ourselves and what we feel we need to be whole. We may, for example, discover that behind a fear of failure lies a more basic fear of being discovered to be a fraud. The implication, of course, is that we feel we are a fraud. This suggests very profitable material for further reflection. Similarly, fears of a loss of respect, of pain or suffering, or of financial disaster tell us about what we think we need and the importance we attach to those needs. Both matters warrant reflection.

Some people will have little conscious sense of anxiety. They should instead focus on the things they do to avoid anxiety. Lurking behind our compulsions, obsessions, and overreactions are strategies for anxiety management that are designed to help us avoid the unpleasant distress of anxiety. These strategies can also often be found in our tactics of avoiding solitude and managing threatening aspects of intimacy. Anxiety is an inevitable part of human existence. Among other things, its presence tells us we are alive. Its total absence tells us we are living a life that is overly invested in anxiety prevention and elimination. Understanding the ways in which we achieve this will always be instructive for our growth.

Preparation for Christian soul care should also involve reflection on one's spiritual life. In fact, both before and during the receipt of such care, one should take care to balance a focus on self with a focus on God. One potential framework for spiritual reflection is the model of Christian spirituality described in chapter 5. Using this framework, one can assess one's spiritual health and note areas of relative weakness, deficiency, or pathology. One might, for example, discern a notable faintness to the call of Spirit to spirit and profitably explore what one is doing to deaden spiritual sensitivity. Or one may note a lack of commitment to the means of grace and subsequent spiritual growth or a relative imbalance in deep knowing of both God and self. Or one might observe that one's spirituality is being lived out too privately, independent of Christian community and apart from appropriate engagement with kingdom tasks in the world.

The same sort of spiritual assessment can also be undertaken by examining the New Testament descriptions of the fruit of the Spirit (Gal. 5:22–23) or love (1 Corinthians 13) and considering how one measures up. An important caution to such an undertaking, however, is that one must do this with a firm grasp of God's grace. Apart from this, the standards of Christian spirituality will function as a source of oppression rather than as a source of motivation and direction.

Beyond this, reflection on one's spiritual life should also include reflection on one's experience of God. How do my ideas about God fit my direct experience of him? How do I experience his love? How well do I know his will for me? Was I more clear about either of these things at some previous point in my life, and if so, why? How confident am I that God hears my prayer? What do I learn from my pattern and habits of prayer? These and related questions provide rich opportunities for spiritual stocktaking that is always excellent preparation for Christian soul care.

Finally, preparation for soul care should also include reflection on one's relationships. What do I learn about myself from how I relate to those closest to me? To what am I most attracted in others? With what do I become most easily irritated? Of what am I most afraid? How free am I to be my true and deepest self in relationships? When I am not this true self, what false selves do I create to assuage my anxiety? In what ways do I attempt to control others, and under what circumstances am I most likely to do this? How do I manage conflict, sexuality, intimacy, anger or resentment, and disappointment in my relationships? These are a few of the questions that can serve as points of departure in reflection on one's relationships.

Reflection on the different faces of self we show in various relationships also provides us with an opportunity to come to know and embrace our various part-selves. Each of us is much more than a single unified self. Some unintegrated parts of self are within our awareness, while others operate outside such awareness, but there is great value in naming and owning these parts of self that manifest themselves in our relationships. For example, in one relationship we may discover that we present a playful self while in another a cautious, exhibitionistic, competitive, or fearful self. These are not necessarily false selves, which are the willful, egocentric constructions we create in order to live our life apart from the will of God and outside our true self as discovered in Christ. Often they are simply fragments of our true self that need to be reclaimed.

Powerful childhood conditioning to only acknowledge the most acceptable parts of self teaches most people to deny the presence of these fragments. Unfortunately, this blocks us from experiencing Christ's transforming friendship in our depths. Psychospiritual health comes from acknowledging our part-selves and exposing them to God's love. Commenting on Christ's comparison of the kingdom of God to a banquet (Luke 14:16–24), Trevor Hudson suggests the way in which the kingdom within us relates to God's process of internal conversion:

> The divine host presides over the banquet at the deep center of our beings. . . . [He] invites us to search out the poor, crippled, blind, and lame aspects of our own inner lives and bring them into the banqueting chamber. Here the living Christ receives them with open arms and begins to include them in the new person that he is patiently forming.[1]

A review of the history of one's significant relationships, including attachments and losses, is also almost always a profitable part of such reflection. Some of this may have been done in the autobiographical work. If not, one should take time to name and reflect on one's most significant relationships and consider what can be learned from them. Are people more important to you now than was the case at previous points in your life? Have you been loyal to your friends, even when they would never have opportunity to know? How would your friends assess the depth and quality of your love, and what would they suggest as the major impediments to that love?

This brings us to a final discipline in the preparation for soul care, namely, talking with one's closest friends about issues to which you should attend. Although this takes a great deal of courage, such vulnerability also holds immense potential for growth. Spouses, children, roommates, and close friends all see faces of your self that no one else sees. They are, therefore, usually in a position to give feedback about issues that are important for one's psychospiritual growth and well-being. All it takes is an invitation.

The Experience of Soul Care

Finding the right person to provide soul care and preparing for the receipt of that care are only, of course, the beginning of the process. Then comes the challenge of maintaining the honesty, courage, vulnerability, and commitment to truth and growth that are necessary in order to make the dialogue rewarding and the experience successful.

How much one benefits from a soul care relationship with another has something to do with the one who provides the care, but it has at least as much to do with the one receiving the care. Central to these personal qualities that determine benefit are motivation and honesty. Those who come to relationships of care desperate to know themselves and God more deeply and unswervingly committed to live their lives in truth never fail to experience significant growth as a result of the care they receive. An unrelenting degree of honesty and a burning desire to more deeply live out of one's truest self will not be thwarted by even the most inept provider of soul care. When such a person engages with a caring Christian who has some knowledge of psychospiritual dynamics and significant personal experience on the Christian journey, the possibilities of growth are limitless.

An experience in a relationship of soul care has the potential to be life transforming. It holds the promise of stimulating one's mind, nourishing one's spirit, and restoring one's soul. Sometimes this occurs as a result of even a brief encounter. More often, however, the gains will be slow and incremental, and, as noted earlier, regress will usually accompany progress.

Rather than approaching an experience of soul care hoping or expecting it to be a once-in-a-lifetime matter, instead expect to periodically return for further care of one form or another. Take from the experience what you need and can use at the moment, and return later when you need or can use more. On commencing a therapeutic relationship of care, people are particularly inclined to want to fix the problem and be cured, thereby eliminating the need for further help. Usually this is not realistic, and even less commonly is it the wisest way to approach the experience. Soul care should be undertaken as need and interest arises and should be viewed as a part of the ongoing psychospiritual journey.

The experience of receiving soul care should make us more capable of caring for both our own souls as well as the souls of others. The interaction between the giving and receiving of care to self and others is rich and multidirectional. In giving care, we receive it, and in receiving it, we are often able to give something in return. In caring for our own souls, we are better able to care for those of others, and in caring for others, we learn to better care for ourselves. Soul care forms a central plank in the process of Christian formation. By giving and receiving it, we become more whole and are blessed by being able to participate in the growth of others.

Notes

Introduction: The Rediscovery of Soul and the Recovery of Its Care

1. See Jeffrey Boyd, *Reclaiming the Soul: The Search for Meaning in a Self-Centered Culture* (Cleveland: Pilgrim Press, 1996), for a helpful discussion of the contribution of theologians to the loss of the soul. This fascinating and important book, which only came to my attention after the present manuscript was completed, argues for the recovery of the traditional Christian view of the soul and suggests important ways in which such a recovery could provide a much needed paradigm shift for those who offer soul care.

2. Robert Woodworth summed up these sentiments in his *Psychology: A Study of Mental Life* (London: Methuen, 1923) when he stated "psychology does not like to call itself the science of the soul for that has a theological tang and suggests problems that have so far not seemed accessible to scientific investigation" (p. 1).

3. Thomas Moore, *Care of the Soul: A Guide for Cultivating Depth and Sacredness in Everyday Life* (New York: HarperCollins, 1992).

Chapter 1: What Is Soul Care?

1. George Eldon Ladd, *A Theology of the New Testament* (Grand Rapids: Eerdmans, 1974), 457. Such an understanding is supported by Hugh McDonald, *The Christian View of Man* (Westchester, Il.: Good News, 1981), and G. C. Berkouwer, *Man: The Image of God* (Grand Rapids: Eerdmans, 1962).

2. It should also be noted that viewing humans as unified and whole does not require the acceptance of the philosophical doctrine of monism. This is made clear by John Cooper, *Body, Soul, and Life Everlasting: Biblical Anthropology and the Monism-Dualism Debate* (Grand Rapids: Eerdmans, 1989), who argues for what he calls a "holistic dualism."

3. Thomas Oden, *Pastoral Theology* (San Francisco: Harper & Row, 1983), 187. An almost identical definition was offered in the fourth century by Gregory of Nyssa, *Pastoral Care* (Westminster, Md.: Newman, 1950), 13: 210.

4. Pedro Lain Entralgo, *The Therapy of the Word in Classical Antiquity* (New York: Basic Books, 1970).

5. Plato, "Apology," in *Great Books of the Western World*, ed. Robert Maynard Hutchings (Chicago: Encyclopedia Britannica, 1952), 7: 206.

6. John McNeill, *A History of the Cure of Souls* (New York: Harper & Row, 1951), vii.

7. This discussion of Jewish soul care draws primarily on John McNeill's *A History of the Cure of Souls*. An excellent discussion of the implications of Jewish soul care for that offered by Christians is found in Don Browning, *The Moral Context of Pastoral Care* (Philadelphia: Westminster Press, 1976).

8. McNeill, *Cure of Souls*, 7.

9. Ibid., 77.

10. Martin Luther, *Three Treatises* (Philadelphia: Fortress Press, 1960), 210.

11. Kenneth Leech, *Soul Friend* (San Francisco: Harper & Row, 1977), 44.

12. For a further discussion of this theme of the incarnational quality of Christian soul care, see David G. Benner, "The Incarnation as a Metaphor for Psychotherapy," *Journal of Psychology and Theology* 11 (1983): 287–94.

13. T. Tapert, ed. and trans., *Luther: Letters of Spiritual Counsel* (Philadelphia: Westminster Press, 1955).

14. Tilden Edwards, *Spiritual Friend* (New York: Paulist, 1980). (See note 11 for Leech.)

15. William Clebsch and Charles Jaekle, *Pastoral Care in Historical Perspective* (New York: Aronson, 1964).

16. Stephen Pattison, *A Critique of Pastoral Care* (London: SCM, 1988), 13.

17. Browning, *Pastoral Care*, 59.

Chapter 2: The Rise of Therapeutic Soul Care

1. McNeill, *Cure of Souls*, 178.

2. Leech, *Soul Friend*, 77.

3. E. Brooks Holifield, *A History of Pastoral Care in America* (Nashville: Abingdon Press, 1983), 201.

4. Ibid., 356.

5. Jan Ehrenwald, *Psychotherapy: Myth and Method* (New York: Grune & Stratton, 1966), 10.

6. Ibid., 16.

7. Jacob Needleman, *A Sense of the Cosmos* (Garden City, N.Y.: Doubleday, 1975), 107.

8. Commenting on the absence of the term *soul* in the vocabulary of contemporary psychotherapists, Jeffrey Boyd notes that while clinical mental health professionals may not use the word, they cannot avoid talking about, and dealing with, the reality. He argues, "Psychotherapists have more names for the soul than Eskimos have names for snow: I, you, myself, yourself, self, psyche, whole person, mind, heart, consciousness, personality, psychic energy, libido, subjective experience, subjectivity, identity, essence, feelings, emotions, cognitive process, thoughts, inner self, human nature, being, inner being, who I am, who you are—all these are names for the soul. And there are dozens more" (*Reclaiming the Soul*, 53).

9. Thomas Oden, *Care of Souls in the Classic Tradition* (Philadelphia: Fortress Press, 1984), 33.

10. Thomas Szasz, *The Myth of Psychotherapy* (Garden City, N.Y.: Anchor, 1978), 188.

11. Ibid., 27–28.

12. Thomas Oden, *The Intensive Group Experience: The New Pietism* (Philadelphia: Westminster Press, 1972).

13. Paul Vitz, *Psychology as Religion* (Grand Rapids: Eerdmans, 1977).

14. Lucy Bregman, *The Rediscovery of Inner Experience* (Chicago: Nelson-Hall, 1985), 1.

15. E. Mansell Pattison, "Psychosocial Interpretations of Exorcism," *Journal of Operational Psychiatry* 8 (1977): 18.

16. Ehrenwald, *Psychotherapy*, 10.

17. Vitz, *Psychology as Religion*.

18. Phillip Rieff, *The Triumph of the Therapeutic* (New York: Harper & Row, 1966).

19. Perry London, *The Modes and Morals of Psychotherapy*, 2d ed. (Washington, D.C.: Hemisphere, 1986). See also Stanton Jones, "A Constructive Relationship for Religion with the Science and Profession of Psychology," *American Psychologist* 49 (1994): 184–99.

20. Carl Jung, *Modern Man in Search of a Soul* (New York: Harcourt, Brace & Co., 1933), 238.

21. Don Browning, *Religious Thought and the Modern Psychologies* (Philadelphia: Fortress Press, 1987).

22. Brock Kilbourne and James Richardson, "Psychotherapy and New Religions in a Pluralistic Society," *American Psychologist* 39 (1984): 237–51.

23. Rieff, *Triumph of the Therapeutic*.

24. Browning, *Religious Thought*, 120.

25. Ibid. See particularly the author's discussion of the implicit ethics of the humanistic psychologies in chapter 4, pp. 61–93.

Chapter 3: The Boundaries of the Soul

1. Glen Whitlock, "The Structure of Personality in Hebrew Psychology," *Interpretations* (January 1960): 10–11.

2. Berkouwer, *Man*, 200.

3. Laidlaw, *Doctrine of Man*, 55.

4. Leech, *Soul Friend*, 106.

5. Arnold DeGraaff, *Views of Man and Psychology in Christian Perspective* (Toronto: Association for the Advancement of Christian Scholarship, 1977), 164.

6. John Watson, *Introduction to Behaviorism* (Chicago: University of Chicago Press, 1930), v.

7. Calvin Hall and Gardner Lindzey, *Theories of Personality*, 3d ed. (New York: Wiley, 1978), 270–71.

8. For a succinct and helpful discussion of Freud's view of religion, see Edwin Wallace, "Freud and Religion: A History and Reappraisal," in *The Psychoanalytic Study of Society*, vol. 10, ed. L. Bryce Boyer, Werner Muensterberger, and Simon Grolnick (Hillsdale, N.J.: Erlbaum, 1983).

9. Carl Jung, "Modern Man in Search of a Soul," in *The Collected Works of C. G. Jung*, vol. 11, ed. Herbert Read and Michael Fordham (New York: Harcourt, Brace & Co. 1933), 164.

10. Moore, *Care of the Soul*, particularly chapters 10 and 11.

11. See, for example, David G. Benner and C. Stephen Evans, "Unity and Multiplicity in Hypnosis, Commissurotomy, and Multiple Personality," *The Journal of Mind and Behavior* 5 (1984): 423–32.

12. Robert Ader, ed., *Psychoneuroimmunology* (New York: Academic Press, 1981).

13. As daunting as the term *psychoneuroimmunology* may be, some researchers are calling for inclusion of the endocrine system in the field of PNI investigations. When this is included, the new term for the field that results is *psychoneuroendocrinoimmunology*, usually abbreviated to PNEI.

14. Good nontechnical overviews of PNI research can be found in Kenneth Pelletier, *Mind as Healer, Mind as Slayer* (New York: Dell Publishing, 1992); Steven Locke and Douglas Colligan, *The Healer Within* (New York: Dutton, 1986); Joan Borysenko, *Mending the Mind, Minding the Body* (Reading, Mass.: Addison-Wesley, 1987); and Bernie Siegel, *Love, Medicine and Miracles* (New York: Harper, 1986). Additional material for this section was also drawn from Ulrich Kropiunigg, "Basics in Psychoneuroimmunology," *Annals of Medicine* 25 (February, 1993): 473–78.

15. Siegel, *Love, Medicine and Miracles*, 148.

16. C. B. Thomas et al., "Cancer in Families of Former Medical Students Followed to Mid-Life," *Johns Hopkins Medicine* 151 (1982): 193–202.

17. Siegel, *Love, Medicine and Miracles*, 178.

Chapter 4: Psychology and Spirituality

1. Paul Tillich, *Systematic Theology* (Chicago: University of Chicago Press, 1951).

2. Robert Doran, "Jungian Psychology and Christian Spirituality: III," *Review for Religious* 38 (1979): 857–66.

3. Sigmund Freud, "Totem and Taboo," in *The Standard Edition of the Complete Psychological Works of Sigmund Freud*, vol. 13, trans. and ed. James Strachey (London: Hogarth Press, 1913), 157.

4. Sigmund Freud, "The Future of an Illusion," in *Complete Psychological Works*, vol. 21, trans. and ed. Strachey, 31.

5. Verda Heisler, "The Transpersonal in Jungian Theory and Therapy," *Journal of Religion and Health* 12 (1973): 337–38.

6. Michael Fordham and Herbert Read, eds., *The Collected Works of C. G. Jung*, vol. 11 (Princeton, N.J.: Princeton University Press, 1985).

7. Browning, *Religious Thought*, 168.

8. Doran, "Jungian Psychology," 861.

9. John Sanford, ed., *Fritz Kunkel: Selected Writings* (New York: Paulist Press, 1984), 54–55.

10. Ibid., 140, 149.

11. Ibid., 154.

12. Søren Kierkegaard, *Fear and Trembling and the Sickness unto Death* (Princeton, N.J.: Princeton University Press, 1954), 146.

13. Kresten Nordentoft, *Kierkegaard's Psychology* (Pittsburgh: Dusquesne University Press, 1972), 89–90.

14. Kierkegaard, *Fear and Trembling*, 211.

15. H. Newton Malony, ed., *A Christian Existential Psychology: The Contributions of John G. Finch* (Washington, D.C.: University Press of America, 1980), 207.

16. Ibid., 377.

17. Ibid., 183.

18. Adrian van Kaam, *On Being Yourself: Reflections on Spirituality and Originality* (Denville, N.J.: Dimension Books, 1972).

19. Ibid., 7.

20. Ibid., 54.

21. Gerald May, *Will and Spirit: A Contemplative Psychology* (San Francisco: Harper & Row, 1982), 30.

22. Ibid., 6.

23. Ibid., 32–33.

24. Ibid., 30.

25. Ibid.

26. William McNamara, "Psychology and the Christian Mystical Tradition," in *Transpersonal Psychologies*, ed. Charles Tart (New York: Harper & Row, 1975), 405.

Chapter 5: Christian Spirituality

1. May, *Will and Spirit*, 33.

2. Ibid.

3. Urban Holmes, *A History of Christian Spirituality* (New York: Seabury, 1980), 4.

4. Wayne Oates, ed. and trans., *Basic Writings of Saint Augustine* (Grand Rapids: Baker, 1980), 1:3.

5. John Calvin, *Institutes of the Christian Religion*, ed. John T. McNeill (Philadelphia: Westminster Press, 1960).

6. James Finley, *Merton's Palace of Nowhere: A Search for God through Awareness of the True Self* (Notre Dame, Ind.: Ave Marie Press, 1978), 31.

7. Thomas Merton, *New Seeds of Contemplation* (New York: New Directions, 1961), 32.

8. van Kaam, *On Being Yourself*, 8.

9. Dag Hammarskjöld, *Markings* (New York: Knopf, 1969), 19.

10. Christopher Levan, *The Dancing Steward: Exploring Christian Stewardship Lifestyles* (Toronto: United Church Publishing House, 1993), 129.

11. Alistair Campbell, *Paid to Care* (London: SPCK, 1985), 20.

12. Dallas Willard, *The Spirit of the Disciplines* (San Francisco: Harper & Row, 1988), 31.

Chapter 6: The Psychospiritual Focus of Soul Care

1. Victor Frankl, *Man's Search for Meaning: An Introduction to Logotherapy* (New York: Simon & Schuster, 1962).

2. Dorothy Sayers, *The Mind of the Maker* (San Francisco: Harper & Row, 1941).

3. Abraham Maslow, *Motivation and Personality* (New York: Harper & Row, 1970).

4. Henri Nouwen, *Reaching Out* (Garden City, N.Y.: Doubleday, 1966), 26.

5. Rudolf Otto, *The Idea of the Holy* (London: Oxford University Press, 1923).

6. Ibid., 8–9.

7. For further discussion of the dynamics of psychospiritual health, see David G. Benner, *Free at Last* (Belleville, Ontario: Essence Publishing, 1998).

8. Howard Clinebell, *Mental Health Through Christian Community* (Nashville: Abingdon Press, 1965), 20.

Chapter 7: Dialogue in Soul Care

1. David Bohm, *Unfolding Meaning* (Loveland, Col.: Foundation House, 1985).

2. This point was drawn to my attention by Peter Senge, promoter of the use of dialogue in organizational discourse. The distinction between dialogue and discussion that follows reflects a number of his ideas, as found in Peter Senge, *The Fifth Discipline: The Art and Practice of the Learning Organization* (New York: Doubleday, 1994).

3. Martin Buber, *The Knowledge of Man* (London: George Allen & Unwin, 1965).

4. Ibid.

5. Sigmund Freud, "Fragment of an Analysis of a Case of Hysteria," in *Complete Psychological Works*, vol. 7, trans. and ed. Strachey, 77.

6. Sigmund Freud, "Recommendations to Physicians Practicing Psycho-analysis," in *Complete Psychological Works*, vol. 11, trans. and ed. Strachey, 111.

7. Carl Rogers, "A Theory of Therapy, Personality, and Interpersonal Relationships, as Developed in the Client-Centered Framework," in *Psychology: A Study of a Science*, vol. 3, ed. S. Koch (New York: McGraw-Hill, 1959), 184–256.

8. Harry Stack Sullivan, *The Psychiatric Interview* (New York: Norton, 1954).

9. Theodore Reik, *Listening with the Third Ear: The Inner Experience of a Psychoanalyst* (New York: Noonday Press, 1983).

10. Maurice Friedman, *Dialogue and the Human Image: Beyond Humanistic Psychology* (Newbury Park, Calif.: Sage Publications, 1992), 60, 4.

11. François Fénelon, *Spiritual Letters to Women* (New Canaan, Conn.: Keats, 1980), 24.

12. Dietrich Bonhoeffer, *Life Together* (New York: Harper, 1959), 97–98.

13. C. S. Lewis, *Mere Christianity* (New York: Macmillan, 1943).

14. Browning, *Pastoral Care*, 77–79.

15. James Mundackal, *Man in Dialogue* (Alwaye, India: Pontifical Institute Publications, 1977), 106.

Chapter 8: Dreams, the Unconscious, and the Language of the Soul

1. John Sanford, *Dreams and Healing: A Succinct and Lively Interpretation of Dreams* (New York: Paulist Press, 1978), 12.

2. Ibid., 101.

3. Ibid., 109.

4. Books on the theory of dream interpretation include: Sigmund Freud, *The Interpretation of Dreams* (New York: Basic Books, 1955); James Hilman, *The Dream and the Underworld* (New York: Harper & Row, 1979); Carl G. Jung, *Dreams* (Princeton: Princeton University Press, 1974). Books on techniques of dream interpretation include: Mary Mattoon, *Applied Dream Analysis: A Jungian Approach* (Washington, D.C.: Wiley, 1978); Jeremy Taylor, *Dream Work: Techniques for Discovering the Creative Power in Dreams* (Ramsey, N.Y.: Paulist Press, 1983); Strephon Williams, *Jungian-Senoi Dreamwork Manual* (Berkeley: Journey Press, 1980).

5. Morton Kelsey, *Dreams: A Way to Listen to God* (New York: Paulist Press, 1978); Louis Savary, Patricia Berne, and Strephon Williams, *Dreams and Spiritual Growth: A Judeo-Christian Way of Dreamwork* (New York: Paulist Press, 1984); Sanford, *Dreams and Healing*.

6. John Sanford, *Dreams and Healing* (New York: Paulist Press, 1978), 21.

7. Cited in Kelsey, *Dreams*, 11–12.

8. See, for example, W. R. D. Fairbairn, *An Object Relations Theory of Personality* (New York: Basic Books, 1952); Otto Kernberg, *Object Relations Theory and Clinical Psychoanalysis* (New York: Aronson, 1976).

9. The following material draws principally on Savary, Berne, and Williams, *Dreams and Spiritual Growth*. This book offers helpful discussion of thirty-seven techniques of dream work that are suitable for Christian soul care.

10. Ibid., 23.

11. Ibid., 60.

Chapter 9: Forms of Christian Soul Care

1. David G. Benner, *Strategic Pastoral Counseling* (Grand Rapids: Baker, 1992), 199.

2. Merton, *New Seeds of Contemplation*, 194–95.

3. Most spiritual directors are associated with retreat centers although some are attached to churches or centers for pastoral counseling. As it is the Roman Catholics who have best kept the flame of spiritual direction alive, the majority of the retreat centers across North America are Catholic. Several Protestant training programs in spiritual direction have been developed in recent years, and these are beginning to produce graduates. This, in turn, is beginning to support the development of transdenominational spiritual retreat centers.

4. Hendrika Vande Kemp, "Spirit and Soul in No-Man's Land: Reflections on Haule's 'Care of Souls,'" *Journal of Psychology and Theology* 11 (1983): 119.

5. David G. Benner, *Psychotherapy and the Spiritual Quest* (Grand Rapids: Baker, 1988).

6. Bernard Tyrrell, *Christotherapy II* (New York: Paulist Press, 1982).

7. Further information about intensive soul care retreats can be obtained by consulting the web site of the Institute for Psychospiritual Health at www.redeemer.on.ca/~iph or by contacting the author by E-mail at iph@redeemer.on.ca or in care of the publisher.

Chapter 10: Challenges of Christian Soul Care

1. *Henrik Ibsen: Four Major Plays* (New York: Penguin Books, 1965), 1:351.

2. Thomas Oden, *Pastoral Theology* (New York: Harper & Row, 1983), 189.

3. Alan Jones, *Soul Making: The Desert Way of Spirituality* (San Francisco: Harper & Row, 1985), 1.

4. Ibid., 189.

5. William Barry and William Connolly, *The Practice of Spiritual Direction* (San Francisco: Harper & Row, 1982), 125.

6. Oden, *Pastoral Theology*, 189.

7. Ibid., 195.

8. See, for example, Theodore Sarbin, ed., *Narrative Psychology: The Storied Nature of Human Conduct* (New York: Praeger, 1986) for a good introduction to this fertile and increasingly important new perspective. For a Christian perspective, focusing particularly on the role of stories in counseling, see Paul Vitz, "Narratives and Counseling, Part 1: From Analysis of the Past to Stories about It," *Journal of Psychology and Theology* 20 (1992): 11–19, and Paul Vitz, "Narratives and Counselling, Part 2: From Stories of the Past to Stories for the Future," *Journal of Psychology and Theology* 20 (1992): 20–27.

9. Campbell, *Paid to Care*, 68.

10. This notion of the soul guide as midwife of grace comes from E. Glenn Hinson, "Recovering the Pastor's Role as Spiritual Guide" in *Spiritual Dimensions of Pastoral Care*, ed. G. Borchert and A. Lester (Philadelphia: Westminster Press, 1985), 27–41.

11. This quote has been attributed to William Butler Yeats. However, I am unable to find it in his published works.

Chapter 11: Receiving Soul Care

1. Trevor Hudson, *Christ-Following: Ten Signposts to Spirituality* (Grand Rapids: Revell, 1996), 81.

Index

Italicized page numbers refer to tables and figures.

Dr. David G. Benner is a clinical and consulting psychologist. His educational background includes an honors B.A. in psychology (McMaster University), an M.A. and Ph.D. in clinical psychology (York University), and postdoctoral studies at the Chicago Institute of Psychoanalysis. He has lectured and offered workshops and retreats throughout North America, Europe, South Africa, and Southeast Asia and has authored or edited fifteen previous books.

Dr. Benner has held numerous clinical and academic appointments in Canada and the United States, including serving as senior psychologist for Child and Adolescent Services at Queen Street Mental Health Centre (Toronto), clinical director for the Institute for Eating Disorders (Carol Stream, Illinois), professor and founding chair of the Department of Graduate Psychological Studies at Wheaton College (Wheaton, Illinois), and adjunct professor of psychology and Christianity at the University of Toronto (St. Michael's College). His current appointments are professor of psychology at Redeemer College (Ancaster) and chief psychologist at Child and Adolescent Services (Hamilton). He is also the founding director of the Institute for Psychospiritual Health, an international network of scholars and practitioners concerned with the understanding and promotion of the well-being of the soul within the context of Christian spirituality. He also maintains a private practice of clinical psychology.

Dr. Benner may be contacted at the Institute for Psychospiritual Health through its web site at www.redeemer.on.ca/~iph, by E-mail at iph@redeemer.on.ca, or in care of the publisher.